Between Ideals and Reality: Charity and the *Letters* of Barsanuphius and John of Gaza

by
Hyung Guen Choi

SCD Press
2020

Between Ideals and Reality:
Charity and the Letters of Barsanuphius and John of Gaza
(Early Christian Studies, 21)
By Hyung Guen Choi
© 2020

SCD Press
PO Box 1882
Macquarie Centre NSW 2113
Australia
scdpress@scd.edu.au

All rights reserved. No part of this book may be reproduced or transmitted in any form or by any means, electronic or mechanical, including photocopying, recording or by any information and storage system without permission in writing from the publishers.

ISBN-13: 978-1-925730-17-3 (paperback)
ISBN-13: 978-1-925730-18-0 (ebook)

Layout and design by: Lankshear Design Pty Ltd
Printed and bound by: Ingram Spark

Between Ideals and Reality: Charity and the *Letters* of Barsanuphius and John of Gaza

by
Hyung Guen Choi

SCD Press
2020

The work resulting in this book was supported by Humanities Korea Plus Project through the Ministry of Education of the Republic of Korea and the National Research Foundation of Korea (NRF-2019S1A6A3A03058791).

Early Christian Studies 21

SCD Press Editorial Board

Professor Diane Speed

Professor James R. Harrison

Associate Professor Peter G. Bolt

Additional Series Editors

Professor Pauline Allen (Australian Catholic University)

Professor Wendy Mayer (Australian Lutheran College)

Professor Bronwen Neil (Macquarie University)

Early Christian Studies

1. Jan Harm Barkhuizen, *Proclus Bishop of Constantinople. Homilies on the Life of Christ* (2001).
2. Robert C. Hill, *Theodoret of Cyrus. Commentary on the Song of Songs* (2001).
3. Johan Ferreira, *The Hymn of the Pearl* (2002).
4. Alistair Stewart-Sykes, *The Life of Polycarp. An anonymous vita from third-century Smyrna* (2002).
5. Daniel Van Slyke, *Quodvultdeus of Carthage. The Apocalyptic Theology of a Roman African in Exile* (2003).
6. Bronwen Neil & Pauline Allen, *The Life of Maximus the Confessor. Recension 3* (2003).
7. George Kalantzis, *Theodore of Mopsuestia. Commentary on the Gospel of John* (2004).
8. Rudolf Brändle, *John Chrysostom. Bishop – Reformer – Martyr* (2004).
9. J. Mark Armitage, *A Twofold Solidarity. Leo the Great's Theology of Redemption* (2005).
10. Alistair Stewart-Sykes, *The Apostolic Church Order. The Greek Text with Introduction, Translation and Annotation* (2006).
11. Geoffrey D. Dunn, *Cyprian and the Bishops of Rome: Questions of Papal Primacy in the Early Church* (2007, 2018).
12. Pauline Allen, Majella Franzmann, & Rick Strelan (eds.), *"I Sowed Fruits into Hearts" (Odes Sol. 17:13). Festschrift for Professor Michael Lattke* (2007).
13. David Luckensmeyer & Pauline Allen (eds.), *Studies of Religion and Politics in the Early Christian Centuries* (2010).
14. Oliver Herbel, *Sarapion of Thmuis: Against the Manicheans and Pastoral Letters* (2011).

15. Raymond Laird, *Mindset, Moral Choice and Sin in the Anthropology of John Chrysostom* (2012, 2017).
16. Alexander L. Abecina, *Time and Sacramentality in Gregory of Nyssa's Contra Eunomium* (2013).
17. Johan Ferreira, *Early Chinese Christianity: The Tang Christian Monument and Other Documents* (2014).
18. Wendy Mayer & Ian J. Elmer (eds.), *Men and Women in the Early Christian Centuries* (2014).
19. Silouan Fotineas, *The Letters of Bishop Basil of Caesarea: Instruments of Communion* (2018).
20. Andrey Romanov, *One God as One God and One Lord. The Lordship of Jesus Christ as a Hermeneutical Key to Paul's Christology in 1 Corinthians (with a special focus on 1 Cor 8:6)* (2020).
21. Hyueng Guen Choi, *Charity and the Letters of Barsanuphius and John of Gaza* (2020).

Contents

List of Abbreviations x
List of tables x
Abstract xi
Acknowledgements xiii

Chapter 1: Introduction 1
1.1 Previous research 3
1.2 Aim and structure 11
1.3 Epistolography as an historical source 14
1.4 Other research issues 27

Chapter 2: The City of Gaza in Late Antiquity 30
2.1 Socio-economic context of late-antique Gaza 30
2.2 Lay Christians in late-antique Gaza 39
2.3 Monks in late-antique Gaza 50
2.4 A bishop in late-antique Gaza 63
2.5 Conclusion 71

Chapter 3: Gazan Monasticism and the Letters 72
3.1 The history of Gazan monasticism before
 the sixth century 72
3.2 Barsanuphius and John of Gaza 84
3.3 The Letters of Barsanuphius and John of Gaza 91
3.4 Conclusion 98

Chapter 4: Giving Gifts in the Letters 100
4.1 Giving gifts in the ancient world 101
4.2 Laypeople and gift giving 108
4.3 Monks and gift giving 126

4.4	Ecclesiastical leaders and gift giving	136
4.5	Conclusion	139

Chapter 5: Entertaining the Stranger in the Letters 141
5.1	Hospitality in the ancient world	143
5.2	Laypeople and entertaining strangers	148
5.3	Monks and entertaining strangers	158
5.4	Conclusion	172

Chapter 6: Caring for the Sick in the Letters 174
6.1	Caring for the sick in the ancient world	175
6.2	Sickness and healing as portrayed in the Letters	184
6.3	Laypeople and caring for the sick in the Letters	190
6.4	Monks and caring for the sick	201
6.5	Conclusion	208

Chapter 7: Concluding Remarks 210

Bibliography 219
Primary sources 219
Secondary sources 223

Abbreviations

CSCO – Corpus Scriptorum Christianorum Orientalium
CTh – *Theodosian Code and Novels and the Sirmondian Constitution*
FC – Fathers of the Church
LCL – Loeb Classical Library
NPNF[1] – *Nicene and Post-Nicene Fathers*, First Series
NPNF[2] – *Nicene and Post-Nicene Fathers*, Second Series
PG – Patrologia Graeca
PL – Patrologia Latina
PO – Patrologia Orientalis
SC – Sources Chrétiennes
NVal – *Novels of Valentinian III*. In *Theodosian Code and Novels and the Sirmondian Constitution*

List of Tables

Table 1. The dates of Christian buildings in Gaza 36
Table 2. The dates of church foundations in Palestine 37

Abstract

This book examines the compiled letters of Barsanuphius and John, each a respected holy man, analyzing both their view of charity (giving gifts, welcoming strangers, and caring for the sick) and investigating the relationship between social inferiors, wealth and benefactors. In order to lay the foundation for the study, we explore the geographical, socioeconomic, intellectual and religious background of the city of Gaza during Late Antiquity. Then a discussion of the history of Gazan monasticism and the correspondence of the Barsanuphius and John is undertaken.

Following this overview, we investigate the spiritual guidance provided by the Gazan holy men in relation to giving gifts to the poor. They primarily advise their lay interlocutors to get involved in gift-giving by appealing to the divine injunctions in the Scriptures and to the spiritual rewards available for donors. However, they impose some limitations on monastic giving. They suggest that only mature monks should participate in giving in order to protect the younger monastic disciples from distractions that might interrupt their ascetic lives. Episcopal leaders are also expected to protect their congregations from outside officials by performing their role as guides and protectors.

With regard to entertaining strangers, the respected Gazan elders place a great deal of emphasis on hospitality within the scope of one's personal ability. Furthermore, they recommend different levels of hospitality in proportion to the status of recipients, as well as charity with discernment. They suggest that their interlocutors do what they can to help the destitute, taking into consideration their physical, material and psychological needs. However, just as with the giving of charity, the main focus of

John and Barsanuphius is not the poor themselves, but rather the care of their own followers.

The last charitable activity examined in this book is caring for sick laymen and monks. In this, both Barsanuphius and John generally advocate different solutions to different groups of disciples (laypeople and monks). The Gazan anchorites encourage their lay patients to seek cures for their illnesses with contemporary medical care and practices. Conversely, they take a somewhat ambivalent attitude towards monastic patients. While they permit some sick monks to use medical facilities and nursing care to cure their illnesses, they also encourage others to endure bodily suffering in order to obtain spiritual profit.

Overall, while on the one hand Barsanuphius and John suggest an ideal guideline regarding charity, on the other hand they simultaneously offer realistic advice to their lay and monastic disciples on the basis of their personal circumstances. In addition, they consider not only the beneficiaries, but also the benefactors. Nevertheless, their spiritual direction is basically concentrated on the latter, especially their spiritual and ascetic wellbeing. This style of spiritual direction is related to their self-understanding as spiritual fathers, meditators and intercessors, as well as defenders of the faith and their disciples.

Acknowledgements

This monograph is a revised version of my doctoral dissertation, which was the fruit of several years of research and work in the Department of Ancient History at Macquarie University, Sydney, Australia. My research towards the dissertation would have been impossible without the direct and indirect support and encouragement of many people. Prof. Wonmo Suh guided my first steps in early Church history and taught me how to read and analayse historical documents when I went to PUTS (Presbyterian University and Theological Seminary) in Seoul. Professor Alanna Nobbs and Professor Paul McKechnie offered invaluable comments and advice, and constant encouragement during my PhD candidature. In addition, Dr Doru Costache, Dr Michael Champion and Dr David Gwynn, who served as external examiners, gave useful suggestions and corrections to improve my dissertation.

The Anyang HK+ team has greatly assisted me in diverse ways during the revision of my PhD dissertation. I especially owe a great debt of gratitude to the Humanities Korea Plus Project team at Anyang University. Finally, these acknowledgements should not complete without giving special thanks to my lovely wife and companion, Park Heayoung and my two sons Seojin and Seowoo, who have encouraged me to complete this research project.

Chapter 1
Introduction

Wealth or property is considered as one of the key elements in elucidating human societies and cultures. It is through material possessions and their uses that we are able to perceive not only the socio-economic structure of a society, but also what happened to actual people in that society. The late Roman Empire is no exception to this. In his book *Through the Eye of a Needle: Wealth, the Fall of Rome, and the Making of Christianity in the West, 350–550 A.D.*, Peter Brown says that "[t]he issues of wealth in general touched on all aspects of the life of the Roman Empire and of the societies that succeeded it. For this reason, the issue of wealth can be a diagnostic tool. To see wealth in this way enables us to enter into the very heart of Roman society".[1] In other words, studying wealth and the use of money is not just exploring wealth itself in late-antique society, but it is also research into the heart of the ancient society in which it circulated.

Since the last part of the twentieth century, thus many scholars have focused attention on poverty, wealth and philanthropy, in order to understand late-antique society and Christianity, from theological, ecclesiastical, socio-economic and comparative

---

[1] Peter Brown, *Through the Eye of a Needle: Wealth, the Fall of Rome, and the Making of Christianity in the West, 350–550 A.D.* (New Jersey: Princeton University Press, 2014), xxvi.

perspectives.² With regard to the eastern Mediterranean world during Late Antiquity in particular, most of them have mainly limited themselves to Egypt and Syria, as well as Judea in Byzantine Palestine. By contrast, curiously, little attention has been paid to Gaza, one of crucial traffic hubs in the Mediterranean world from ancient times, on the southern coast of Palestine (today's Gaza Strip).³ In this respect, the study of wealth and its uses in the region of Gaza appears to be very significant. It involves not just an examination of the diverse charitable activities in sixth-century Gaza. It also probes more fundamental things to understand regarding the city and its areas: for example, the principles or mechanisms relating to charity, contemporary socio-economic structures and religious ethos, the perceptions of benefactors and beneficiaries, and the connection between philanthropy and power. In addition, the study of the

---

2   See Paul Veyne, *Bread and Circuses: Historical Sociology and Political Pluralism*, trans. Brian Pearce (London: Allen Lane, 1990), 19–34; Evelyne Patlagean, "The Poor," in *The Byzantines* ed. Guglielmo Cavallo, trans. Thomas Dunlap, Teresa Lavender Fagan and Charles Lambert (Chicago: The University of Chicago Press, 1997), 15–42; Michael James DeVinne, "The Advocacy of Empty Bellies: Episcopal Representation of the Poor in the Late Roman Empire" (PhD diss., Stanford University, 1995); Peter Brown, *Poverty and Leadership in the Late Roman Empire* (London: University Press of New England, 2002); Peter Brown, *Treasure in Heaven: The Holy Poor in Early Christianity* (Charlottesville: University of Virginia Press, 2016); Richard Finn, *Almsgiving in the Later Roman Empire* (Oxford: Oxford University Press, 2006); Louis W. Countryman, *The Rich Christian in the Church of the Early Empire* (New York: Edwin Mellen Press, 1980), 1–4; Demetrios J. Constantelos, *Byzantine Philanthropy and Social Welfare* (New Brunswick; New Jersey: Rutgers University Press, 1968), 16 n. 89.

3   For the geographical background of Gaza, see Yizhar Hirschfeld, "The Monasticism of Gaza: An Archaeological Review," in Brouria Bitton-Ashkelony and Aryeh Kofsky, eds., *Christian Gaza in Late Antiquity* (Leiden: Brill, 2004), 62–4. For descriptions of the social, economic, philosophical and religious situation in Gaza in Late Antiquity, see Carol A. M. Glucker, *The City of Gaza in the Roman and Byzantine Periods*, BAR International Series 325 (British Archaeological Reports, 1987); Michael W. Champion, *Explaining the Cosmos: Creation and Cultural Interaction in Late-Antique Gaza* (Oxford: Oxford University Press, 2014), 21–42.

Letters of Barsanuphius and John of Gaza[4] offer valuable clues about how Christian documents were circulated, exchanged and adopted in the Mediterranean world of the late antique period. All of these provide crucial information for understanding local communities and Christianity in early sixth-century Gaza. This chapter firstly identifies the lacunae in scholarship on this issue by surveying past studies on charity and wealth in ancient Christianity. It then outlines the aim and structure of this book, discusses the use of epistolography as a historical source, and, last, deals with some other research issues.

1.1 Previous research

In the past two decades, a considerable amount of research on charity and wealth in ancient Christianity has been published.[5] Michael J. DeVinne's unpublished dissertation, "The Advocacy of Empty Bellies: Episcopal Representation of the Poor in the Late Roman Empire", delves into the eloquent rhetoric of Christian bishops on the subject of the destitute from the fourth to the fifth century. According to DeVinne, the Christian leaders transmuted the indigent (previously viewed as pitiful people in the streets) into "athlete-soldier-gladiators", who ran the race of faith and were advocates or prosecutors before God at the Last Judgment. As a result of these rhetorical portraits, the destitute were no longer considered marginalised in their societies. Such a huge change in the perception of the poor then made it easier for ecclesiastical leaders to invite wealthy Christians to support the needy in their local communities. Their

---

4   Barsanuphius and John of Gaza, *Barsanuphe et Jean de Gaza, Barsanuphe et Jean de Gaza: Correspondance*, ed. and trans. François Neyt, Paula de Angelis-Noah, and Lucien Regnault, SC 426-427, 450-451, 468 (Paris: Éditions du Cerf, 1997-2002); Barsanuphius and John of Gaza, *Barsanuphius and John: Questions and Responses*, ed. and trans. John Chryssavgis. 2 vols. (Washington, DC: Catholic University of America Press, 2006-2007).
5   See n. 2.

consequent redistribution of gifts to the poor from the private property of the wealthy, according to DeVinne, made bishops and their assistants able to monopolise almsgiving in the late-antique period.[6] DeVinne's study enabled a better understanding of how the bishops' rhetoric concerning the poor encouraged wealthy Christians to participate in eleemosynary activity, helping the poor in rural and urban areas, and improving the relationship between the poor and the bishops.

But while DeVinne investigated the connection between late-antique bishops, their rhetoric and their charitable works, he failed to offer any insights into how they became prominent figures in late Roman society through their merciful works. In contrast, this area was covered in Richard Finn's *Almsgiving in the Later Roman Empire*. Finn first explored the characteristic forms of Christian almsgiving undertaken by bishops as well as monastics and lay Christians, and then proceeded to investigate the meaning of charitable practices in Christian discourses on almsgiving and the poor. Finn found that some ecclesiastical leaders influenced their congregations' theological and social notions of benefaction more than others because of their homiletic discourse on almsgiving and the poor. He suggested they did this in order to promote care for the socially disadvantaged. However, Finn believed, unlike DeVinne, that clergymen emerged as major benefactors in Christian antiquity, due partly to almsgiving based on their influential discourses, and also due to competition and co-operation with their rivals (monks, lay Christians, pagan and Jewish nobles) in their communities. In this respect, Finn contradicted DeVinne's position, arguing that "there was no 'monopolization of almsgiving' by the bishops in this period, nor as a result of their almsgiving did they emerge as 'the megapatrons of their communities'".[7]

---

6   DeVinne, "The Advocacy of Empty Bellies," iv, 117–18.
7   Finn, *Almsgiving in the Later Roman Empire*, 266.

Finn's study was certainly a helpful tool in understanding not merely the charitable practices of bishops, monks and the laity in the later Roman Empire, but also the dynamic relationship pertaining to eleemosynary works. Building upon Finn's study, this book will compare episcopal almsgiving and alms by monks and laity in the city of Gaza. However, the aim is to take his research one step further, by investigating how the Gazan holy mens' perception of their interlocutors (bishops, monks and the laity) affected their spiritual direction towards those interlocutors.

While DeVinne and Finn concentrated on bishops' homilies and their rhetoric on charity in order to elucidate how Christian bishops established their authority in late Roman society through their merciful works, Peter Brown approached the issue in a different way. In his *Poverty and Leadership in the Later Roman Empire*, Brown argued that there was a transition in the perception of the poor from a Greco-Roman to Christian perspective in Late Antiquity, and that this perception shifted as a result of their sustained efforts to support those in need. In order to demonstrate his point, Brown first and foremost advocated a view of a bishop as *a lover or guardian of the poor*, and traced how bishops cared for the poor and other social inferiors in the transition period. For example, they not only distributed almsgiving to the poor and economically disadvantaged citizens, but also served as their mouthpiece, delivering the demands and needs of the socially disadvantaged.[8] In this process, Christian bishops improved their power in late Roman society. He sums up his position as follows:

> The bishop and his clergy came to be intimately involved with the protection of the *tenuiores*, of the "weaker" classes of the late Roman cities as a whole, as well as with the destitute poor to which their care was officially directed.

---

8   See Brown, *Poverty and Leadership in the Late Roman Empire*, 78–85.

> The care of those who were vulnerable to impoverishment on all levels of urban society, and not only the care of the destitute, was crucial to the consolidation of the power of the bishop as a local leader.[9]

That is, Brown believed that bishops took their place as civic leaders in late Roman society because of their social role as lovers and governors of the poor.

This generous image of Church leaders, discerned in the works of DeVinne, Finn and Brown, was challenged by Pauline Allen, Wendy Mayer and Bronwen Neil in *Preaching Poverty in Late Antiquity*. Probing into poverty and almsgiving in the writings of John Chrysostom, Augustine of Hippo and St. Leo the Great, they argued that the late-antique bishops, when discoursing on poverty and charity, actually did not serve as genuine lovers of the destitute in their civil communities to the degree suggested by DeVinne, Finn and Brown. Because Greco-Roman euergetism still exerted a strong influence upon the Christian Church in the fourth and fifth centuries,[10] the massive shift from pagan perspectives on the poor and charitable giving to the Christian view, according to Allen et al., did not occur in the case of at least three ecclesiastical bishops (Chrysostom, Augustine and Leo). In addition, they thought that, whether intentionally or not, the contemporary Christian leaders made little attempt to change the *status quo* of the poor despite the fact that they encouraged their congregation to practise charity.[11] In particular, Augustine saw charitable giving as "as a means of forgiveness of sin" and "of avoiding further sin", whereas Leo I, according to Neil, depicted it as holy usury or a deposit made for eternal life.[12] For them, almsgiving was thus viewed as a primary means of

---

9 Brown, *Poverty and Leadership in the Late Roman Empire*, 78–79.
10 Allen et al., *Preaching Poverty in Late Antiquity*, 228.
11 Allen et al., *Preaching Poverty in Late Antiquity*, 111, 147, 197, 228.
12 Allen et al., *Preaching Poverty in Late Antiquity*, 131.

obtaining salvation for their donors, rather than having mercy on the poor themselves. However, the shift from a Greco-Roman perspective on euergetism to the Christian perspetive of almsgiving may have occurred, as Neil assumed, sometime in the sixth century.[13]

With regard to the debates on the relation between the helping the poor in homilies of late-antique bishops and the social reality, Brown revisited the issue in *Through the Eye of a Needle: Wealth, the Fall of Rome, and the Making of Christianity in the West, 350–550 A.D.* He surveyed the relationship between wealth and pagan and Christian elites in the western Mediterranean world during Late Antiquity, and scrutinised the attitudes of the fourth to sixth centuries leaders towards the use of wealth, self-renunciation, and caring for the poor, as well as the various roles of almsgiving. Here Brown asserted that the extent and the ways in which the leaders conducted charitable works varied in accordance with the local socio-economic, political and ecclesiastical conditions of the societies in which they lived. In addition, he demonstrated how Christian leaders in the West competed with contemporary pagan benefactors in relation to caring for the poor.

So far, the debates on wealth and philanthropy in late-antique Christianity have been mainly limited to episcopal leaders and their works in the fourth and fifth centuries, although sixth-century leaders were occasionally mentioned, as explored in the works of Peter Brown. Little attention, however, has been paid to the eleemosynary works in late-antique monasticism. Recently, some studies on poverty and wealth have paid attention to monastic charity in the Mediterranean East in Late

---

13 Allen et al., *Preaching Poverty in Late Antiquity*, 228.

Antiquity.[14] Ariel G. López, in his study *Shenoute of Atripe and the Uses of Poverty: Rural Patronage, Religious Conflict, and Monasticism in Late Antique Egypt*, detailed an Egyptian monk's public career through an analysis of his works on poverty and charity. Shenoute, the monk, was described as both a defender of the poor and as an enemy of the rich. In this way López portrayed him as a true and holy patron for the poor. In chapter 2 "A Miraculous Economy" in particular, López outlined Shenoute's charitable works with regard to the abundant wealth offered by lay Christians and the imperial government. Here he asserted that Shenoute extended his care for the poor through the Classical practices of euergetism (as did Theodoret of Cyrrhus), and was driven by a desire to increase his own reputation through his generous benefactions, including lavishing gifts and establishing public buildings.[15] Such an open attitude of the Egyptian monk toward the world he had renounced was similar to that of his contemporaries—for example, Hypatius and Theodoret of Cyrrhus, Alexander the Sleepless and Symeon the

---

14 See Ariel G. López, *Shenoute of Atripe and the Uses of Poverty: Rural Patronage, Religious Conflict, and Monasticism in late antique Egypt* (Berkeley: University of California Press, 2013); Elizabeth L. Platte, "Monks and Matrons: The Economy of Charity in the late antique Mediterranean" (PhD diss., University of Michigan, 2013); Daniel Caner, "Wealth, Stewardship, and Charitable 'Blessings' in Early Byzantine Monasticism," in *Wealth and Poverty in Early Church and Society*, ed. Susan R. Holman (Grand Rapids: Baker Academic, 2008), 221–42; Wonmo Suh, "A Study of 'Poverty Discourses' in the Sixth-Century Gaza," *Korea Journal of Christian Studies* 82 (2012): 203–30 [Korean]; David Brakke, "Care for the Poor, Fear of Poverty, and Love of Money: Evagrius Ponticus on the Monk's Economic Vulnerability," in *Wealth and Poverty in Early Church and Society*, ed. Susan R. Holman (Grand Rapids: Baker Academic, 2008), 76–87; Arthur Vööbus, *History of Asceticism in the Syrian Orient* II CSCO 197: subsidia 17 (Louvain: Peeters, 1960), 361–83; Satoshi Toda, "Pachomian Monasticism and Poverty," in *Prayer and Spirituality in the Early Church*, vol. 5: *Poverty and Riches*, ed. Geoffrey Dunn, David Luckensmeyer and Lawrence Cross (Strathfield: St. Paul's Publications, 2009), 191–200; Roger Bagnall, "Monk and Property: Rhetoric, Law, and Patronage in *the Apophthegmata Patrum* and the Papyri," *Greek, Roman, and Byzantium Studies* 42 (2001): 7–24.
15 López, *Shenoute of Atripe and the Uses of Poverty*, 70–72.

Stylite—in the late-antique world.[16] Charity at times functioned as a key means to make connection between the monastic world and secular society in late antique Egypt and Syria.

The close relationship of monks to the secular world through charity was also examined in a study of Christian charity in sixth-century Gaza.[17] Unlike López, Wonmo Suh explores the ways in which the two Gazan anchorites—Barsanuphius and John of Gaza—provided pastoral care for different groups of questioners (monks, laypeople and ecclesiastical leaders) who asked them about philanthropic activities. On the basis of the pastoral care that they provided for their lay, monastic and sometimes clerical recipients, he argued that the two Gazan anchorites in the early sixth century must have had different views of the poor and charity from those arising out of the model of Classical civil euergetism.[18] In keeping with their understanding of the poor, they urged their questioners to treat the poor as equal to themselves, and even equal to Christ himself. Building on the attitude of these two holy men to the poor and possessions, this book will probe how and why they encouraged their followers to extend eleemosynary works in the light of the contemporary socioeconomic, philosophical, and geographical background of Gazan monasticism.

Elizabeth L. Platte, in contrast to both López and Suh, focused on two women ascetics in late-antique monastic literature, offering a counterbalance to the previous male-focused studies of late-antique Mediterranean monasticism.[19] Outlining late-antique hagiography as a source for her project and exploring ascetic monasticism from contemporary perspectives—social network theory, gender studies, New Institutional Economics

16 López, *Shenoute of Atripe and the Uses of Poverty*, 17–18, 41–42, 149 n. 62.
17 Suh, "A Study of 'Poverty Discourses' in the Sixth-Century Gaza," 203–30.
18 Suh, "A Study of 'Poverty Discourses' in the Sixth-Century Gaza," 225.
19 Elizabeth L. Platte, "Monks and Matrons: The Economy of Charity in the Late Antique Mediterranean" (PhD diss., University of Michigan, 2013).

(NIE) and economic rationality[20]—she expounded the socio-economic motivations and charitable actions of Melania the Elder and her granddaughter Melania the Younger. Here she argued that the charitable gifts enabled the two Melanias to form social connections with ascetics and other aristocratic women. In addition, she also noted that, through generous benefaction, Melania the Younger in particular became the superior of her monastic community and eventually kept her familial property from the threat of invasion by a foreign enemy.

Modern scholars have, so far, devoted a fair amount of attention to diverse issues regarding wealth and charity in late-antique Christianity: the shift from a Greco-Roman perspective on the poor and charity to that of a Christian approach (DeVinne, Finn, Brown [2002], Allen et al., and Suh); the impact of philanthropy on the establishment of Christian leaders' authority (DeVinne, Finn, Brown [2002], López and Platte); the cooperation and competition between Christian charity and Greco-Roman civil euergetism (Finn, Allen et al., López and Brown [2014]); the spiritual and social advantages of charity (Allen et al., López and Platte); the relationship between an ideal charity and its reality (Brown [2002] and Allen et al.); and finally, episcopal rhetorical strategies on charity in poverty and wealth discourses (DeVinne, Finn, Brown [2002 and 2014] and Allen et al.).

Previous works on wealth and charity in the late Roman Empire have primarily focused on the perspectives of the ecclesiastical elites (especially between the fourth and fifth centuries), while little attention has been given to monastic leaders' guidance. This is particularly true when we consider the merciful

---

20 For her methodology, see Platte, "Monks and Matrons," 9–16. For late-antique hagiography as historical sources, see Allen et al., *Preaching Poverty in Late Antiquity*, 53–63. For a more comprehensive study concerning hagiography, see Stephanos Efthymiadis, ed., *The Ashgate Research Companion to Byzantine Hagiography*, 2 vols. (Burlington, VT; Farnham, Surrey, UK: Ashate Publishing Company, 2011, 2014).

activities which these leaders encouraged. In addition, López suggested that Shenoute, the fifth-century monastic leader, extended charity in keeping with the model of Greco-Roman euergetism, although Suh argued in contrast that Barsanuphius and John represented a different perspective to that of Classical euergetism. Thus, the shift from the classical civic model to the model of Christianity in late-antique Egyptian-Gazan monasticism still needs to be investigated.

Furthermore, because modern scholarship on late-antique monasticism and charity has primarily limited its attention to Egyptian and Syrian monasteries, the Gazan monasteries have received far less notice, even though Gaza was one of the more important monastic centers in the eastern Mediterranean world during the late-antique period. This book, therefore, focuses on the relationship between wealth, diverse donors and monasteries in Gaza and in its neighbouring areas in light of their connection to monastic movements in Egypt as well as Antioch and Minor Asia during Late Antiquity.

1.2 Aim and structure

The compiled *Letters* Barsanuphius and John of Gaza include a considerable amount of correspondence from laypeople, monks and clergymen regarding giving alms to the poor, entertaining strangers and caring for the sick. The intention of this study is not to provide a systematic and comprehensive understanding of the poor and charity represented in the *Letters*. Instead, the study concentrates on the perception of charity and its relationship to wealth and benefactors in the *Letters*, focusing on the context of the spiritual advice (or pastoral care) that the Gazan holy men offered to their diverse disciples in the Mediterranean East. With regard to the various merciful works touching on poverty and the wealth discourses in these sixth-century letters, there are three significant questions that need to be answered:

1. How do the two Gazan hermits provide spiritual direction for their clerical, monastic and lay followers who ask questions related to wealth and philanthropic activities?
2. In what ways, and to what extent, do they use similar or different advice towards the individual questioners?
3. What reasons lay behind their spiritual advice regarding charity?

Answering these questions is likely to yield convincing evidence regarding their attitudes towards charity and the poor, as well as their opinions of diverse donors (church and civil authorities, monks and the laity). The evidence shows that although both of these hermits, as spiritual fathers and defenders, suggested biblical ideas relating charity, they simultaneously recommended that their disciples help the poor, sensing their physical, material and psychological needs. In addition, they also emphasised a donor-centered charity that sought to care for their interlocutors and protect them from any internal or external dangers which could happen to benefactors. This examination leads us to a more holistic picture of the issue of charity in late-antique Gaza.

To begin the examination, chapter two explores the geographical position of Gaza as an important centre for traffic, education, and monasticism in the sixth-century. This helps to reconstruct the socio-economic status and ethos of the people, including that of Barsanuphius and John of Gaza. It is also essential to establish the relationship between charity, wealth and pastoral care in eastern Mediterranean monasticism and particularly in late-antique Gaza. Chapter three is divided into two parts. The first half explores a history of Gazan monasticism before the sixth century, paying particular attention to the lives of St. Hilarion, Abba Isaiah of Scetis and Peter the Iberian, and to their perspectives on wealth and charity. The second part delves into the identity and roles of both Barsanuphius and John of Gaza—the Great Old Men—and offers a further window into their compiled letters.

After these two foundational chapters, the main issues of this book—almsgiving, entertaining outsiders and caring for the sick—will be considered in the next three chapters. Chapter four investigates how Barsanuphius and John of Gaza responded to their lay, monastic and episcopal questioners, answering questions about diverse facets of almsgiving. By focusing on the extension of gifts to the poor in the Greco-Roman tradition and in early Jewish and Christian practice, this chapter will investigate the customs of almsgiving by lay Christians, showing how the holy men, in their *Letters*, were able to persuade ordinary lay Christians to give alms in an indirect way rather than in person, and to provide realistic and moderate advice for their followers. Then it deals with the advice given to prospective monks regarding renunciation of their possessions, as well as the advice given to people regarding offerings made on their deathbed and the reminder of the spiritual rewards given to donors through almsgiving. In contrast, the two Old Men advise not all monks to engage in philanthropic activity, differentiating between a mature monk and a beginner, and encouraging the former only to distribute monastic alms to those in need by their warning against the dangers inherent in philanthropic work. Finally, the *Letters* demonstrate a perception of bishops as protectors of the poor and urges them to care for social inferiors in their communities by distributing alms to the poor and protecting them.

Chapter five analyzes the spiritual directions given by Barsanuphius and John of Gaza on the subject of entertaining strangers, including beggars, poor travelers and traveling monks. After examining the practice of hospitality in the ancient world, this chapter looks at guesthouses, as well as lay and monastic hospitality, as demonstrated in the *Letters*. The Gazan mentors, who are the subject of this book, stress differing forms of welcome depending on the audience. They recommend moderate and sensitive welcoming, by suggesting different levels of welcome in proportion to the socio-religious status of individual guests. This is tied to their limited material resources and intention to keep their interlocutors from outside dangers. They also suggest that their lay and monastic disciples extend hospitality within their ability and resources. In the last part of this chapter, the discussion centers on entertaining mendicant monks, who are considered as a potential threat to the monastic and secular communities.

The final chapter deals with caring for the sick in the coenobium of Seridos and its neighbouring areas. It consists of three sections. The first section provides an overview of what illness and healing meant in Greco-Roman antiquity and early Christianity respectively. The second section explores the Gazan anchorites' understanding of sickness and healing, and their portrayal of Christ the Physician (*Christus medicus*) in the *Letters*. Finally, this chapter deals with the holy men's direct advice with regard to sick laymen and monks. They suggest different levels of advice to different lay questioners, while appearing somewhat reluctant to allow their sick ascetics to seek medical help themselves. Their advice in encouraging care for the sick seems primarily directed towards what could be profitable to the patient in a spiritual and psychological sense, rather than resulting from an understanding of the suffering itself.

1.3 Epistolography as an historical source

However, before we take a closer look at charity in the letters of Barsanuphius and John of Gaza, it is necessary to understand the nature of epistolography. This is the genre to which the main source of this project belongs in the late-antique context.[21] The epistolary genre appears to have been widely employed in the Hellenistic Roman and late-antique world.[22]

21   For ancient Graeco-Roman letters, see Abraham J. Malherbe, *Ancient Epistolary Theorists*, Society of Biblical Literature, Sources for Biblical Study 19 (Atlanta: Scholars Press, 1988); Stanley Stowers, *Letter Writing in Graeco-Roman Antiquity* (Philadelphia: Westminster John Knox Press, 1986); Ruth Morello and A. D. Morrison, eds., *Ancient Letters: Classical and late antique Epistolography* (Oxford: Oxford University Press, 2007); Michael Trapp, ed., *Greek and Latin Letters: An Anthology with Translation* (Cambridge: Cambridge University Press, 2003). Andrew Gillett, "Communication in Late Antiquity: Use and Reuse," in *Oxford Handbook of Late Antiquity*, ed. Scott Fitzgerald Johnson (Oxford: Oxford University Press, 2012), 815–47, doi: 10.1093/oxfordhb/9780195336931.013.0025. For episcopal letters in Late Antiquity, see Allen et al., *Preaching Poverty in Late Antiquity*, 44–53; Pauline Allen and Bronwen Neil, *Crisis Management in Late Antiquity (410–590CE): A Survey of the Evidence from Episcopal Letters* (Leiden; Boston: Brill, 2013), 11–35; Pauline Allen, "It's in the Post: Techniques and Difficulties of Letter-Writing in Antiquity with Regard to Augustine of Hippo," Australian Academy of the Humanities, A. D. Trendall Annual Memorial Lecture, September 2005, *The Australian Academy of the Humanities Proceedings 2005* (Canberra: The Australian Academy of the Humanities 2006). For monastic letters in Late Antiquity, see Malcolm Choat, "Monastic Letter Collections in Late Antique Egypt: Structure, Purpose, and Transmission," in *Cultures in Contact: Transfer of Knowledge in the Mediterranean Context*, ed. Sofía Torallas Tovar and Juan Pedro Monferrer-Sala (Cordoba: CNERU (Cordoba Near Eastern Research Unit) – Beirut: CEDRAC (Centre de Documentation et de Recherches Arabes Chrétiennes) – Oriens Academic, 2013), 73–90; Malcolm Choat, "Epistolary Formulae in Early Coptic Letters," *Orientalia Lovaniensia analecta* 163 (2007): 667–77; Bernadette McNary-Zak, *Letters and Asceticism in Fourth-Century Egypt* (Lanham: University Press of America, 2000); Samuel Rubenson, *The Letters of St. Antony: Monasticism and the Making of a Saint* (Minneapolis: Fortress Press, 1995); James E. Goehring, *The Letter of Ammon and Pachomian Monasticism* (Berlin; New York: De Gruyter, 1985).

22   For evidence of letters in the ancient world, see Trapp, *Greek and Latin Letters*, 6–11; Raffaele Luiselli, "Greek Letters on Papyrus: First to Eighth Centuries: A Survey," in *Documentary Letters from the Middle East: the Evidence in Greek, Coptic, South Arabian, Pehlevi, and Arabic (1st–15th c CE)*, ed. Andreas Kaplony and Eva Mira Grob (Bern: Peter Lang, 2008), 679–81. Costa argues that epistolography was popular in the Graeco-Roman world, and suggests four reasons for this: contemporary educational and scholastic backgrounds; a culture of letter writing; the perception of letters as a crucial method as communication; and the attractiveness of letters themselves. See C. D. N. Costa, ed., *Greek Fictional Letters* (Oxford: Oxford University Press, 2001), xi–xii. For further discussion of the significance of letters in the early church, see Stowers, *Letter Writing in Graeco-Roman Antiquity*, 44.

A considerable number of letters composed by Christians in the Roman Empire have been found, identified and studied. Michael Trapp, for example, notes that over 9,000 letters have survived from the early Church.[23] Allen and Neil mention over 1,000 letters by Greek-speaking bishops and at least 630 by Latin bishops from the fifth and sixth centuries,[24] and May O'Brien offers some 2,000 letters composed by 52 Latin Christian writers in the same period.[25] In addition to episcopal correspondence, many monastic letters from Late Antiquity have also survived.[26] Written on papyrus or ostraca they are known from several studies on Greek papyrus letters from late-antique Egypt.[27]

There are diverse limitations with regard to any investigation of the genre of late-antique letters. Allen suggests that since matters relating to form, function, audience and the rationale

---

23   Trapp, *Greek and Latin Letters*, 18.
24   Allen and Neil, *Crisis Management in Late Antiquity*, 26, 28.
25   Mary O'Brien, *Title of Address in Christian Latin Epistolography to 543 A.D.* (Washington, DC: Catholic University of America, 1930), 161.
26   See McNary-Zak, *Letters and Asceticism in Fourth-Century Egypt*; Rubenson, *The Letters of St. Antony: Monasticism and the Making of a Saint*; Goehring, *The Letter of Ammon and Pachomian Monasticism*.
27   Lincoln Blumell, *Lettered Christians: Christians, Letters and late antique Oxyrhynchus* (Leiden: Brill, 2012); Erica Mathieson, *Christian Women in the Greek Papyri of Egypt to 400 CE* (Belgium: Brepols, 2014); Roger S. Bagnall and Raffaella Cribiore, *Women's Letters From Ancient Egypt: 300BC–AD 800* (Ann Arbor: University of Michigan Press, 2006); Alanna Nobbs, "Formulas of Belief in Greek Papyrus Letters of the Third and Fourth Centuries," in *Ancient History in a Modern University: Early Christianity, Late Antiquity, and Beyond*, ed. Tom Hillard et al. (Grand Rapids: William B. Eerdmans, 1988), 2:233–37.

of compilation are all problematic,[28] ancient letters must be approached with great caution and be open to reconsideration due to the genre of letter writing as a whole, although they are a wonderful source for insight into the ancient world.

1.3.1 Definition of a letter

There have been a variety of definitions for what constitutes a letter from the ancient world. Ancient theorists called a letter: "one half of a dialogue" (Cicero), "speak[ing] to an absent friend as though he was present" (Cicero, Seneca, Pseudo Libanius and Julius Victor) or alternatively, a "speech in the written medium" (Cicero and Seneca).[29] The fourth-century bishop Ambrose of Milan also regarded the letter as "talking with those who are absent".[30] Although the ancients defined the genre with a wide

---

28 In *Preaching Poverty in Late Antiquity* (52-3), Allen comments that:

   [Chrysostom and Augustine] chose the letter-form for moral disquisitions which on the one hand resemble a homily, and on the other a tractate, conforming the fact that however much the epistolographical genre was manipulated, the letter remained an act of "public intimacy".

   Furthermore, she also notes in *Crisis Management in Late Antiquity* (15) that

   [t]he form and function of the epistolographical genre in late antiquity presents its own problematic, with its many hybrid forms that do not fit the strict Classical definition of a letter. We then turn to the public/private nature of letters, i.e. the question of their audiences. We shall address the question of how far we can trust the relatively small number of letters which have survived to us for an accurate picture of crisis management in late-antique society. The rationale behind letter compilations, when more than accidental, also impinges on their usefulness as a historical source for episcopal crisis management.

   She once again summarises weaknesses form, length, limited survival of ancient letters and the potential reasons behind the compilation of letter-collections—in the epistolary genre. See Pauline Allen, "Challenges in Approaching Patristic Texts from the Perspective of Contemporary Catholic Social Teaching," in *Reading Patristic Texts on Social Ethics: Issues and Challenges for Twenty-First-Century Christian Social Thought*, ed. John Leemans, Brian J. Matz and Johan Verstraeten (Washington, DC: Catholic University of America Press, 2011), 30-42.

29 Malherbe, *Ancient Epistolary Theorists*, 12.

30 I take this expression from Pauline Allen, "It's in the Post," 113. For the original text, see Ambrose, *Epistola* 66 (PL 16:1225): "Epistolarum genus propterea repertum, ut quidam nobis cum absentibus sermo sit, in dubium non venit".

range of expressions, they are all linked to the functional aspect of the letter as a form of communication, specifically, one half of a conversation in written form. This interpretation of the letter is also echoed by some modern scholars including Constable and Allen.[31]

William Doty, however, provides a slightly different definition: "a letter is a *literary* product, intended for a *private or public* reader/s, originally or only formally in epistolary form".[32] Unlike other scholars, Doty lays primary emphasis on structural aspects of the epistolary genre—the sender and the private or public addressee—as well as epistolary components and formulae. Taking this definition further, Trapp defines a letter as

> A written message from one person (or set of people) to another, requiring to be set down in a tangible medium, which itself is to be physically conveyed from sender(s) to recipient(s). Formally, it is a piece of writing that is overtly addressed from sender(s) to recipient(s), by the use at beginning and end of one of a limited set of conventional formulae or salutation (or some allusive variation on them) which specify both parties to the transaction.[33]

In his definition, he combines the two components—one half of communication in written mode and epistolary formulae. Nevertheless, although he tries to provide a thorough definition that seeks to embrace all types of letter, including those from the

---

31 For the term "half a conversation or dialogue" see Giles Constable, *Letters and Letter-Collections*, Typologie des Sources du Moyen Âge Occidental, fasc. 17, (Turnhout: Brepols Publishers, 1976), 13; Allen, "It's in the Post," 113.
32 William G. Doty, "The Classification of Epistolary Literature," *The Catholic Biblical Quarterly* 31.2 (1969): 193. For more detail on epistolary formulae and format in Greek and Coptic letters, see Luiselli, "Greek Letters on Papyrus: First to Eighth Centuries: A Survey," 677–737; Tonio Sebastian Richter, "Coptic Letters," in *Documentary Letters from the Middle East: The Evidence in Greek, Coptic, South Arabian, Pehlevi, and Arabic (1st–15th c CE)*, ed. Andreas Kaplony and Eva Mira Grob (Bern: Peter Lang, 2008), 739–70.
33 Trapp, *Greek and Latin Letters*, 1.

Classical and late-antique periods, his definition cannot cover all the different substyles found within the genre. For example, both *Epistula* 140 and *Epistula* 157 of Augustine and the *De Officiis* of Cicero are all long treatises in epistolary form without epistolary formulae.[34] As a result of the difficulties involved in finding a definition that covers all the different subgenres of letter-writing, some modern scholars have sought to provide alternative approaches to definition. Rather than trying to find a definition that embraces all letters, they have instead sought a broader and more flexible definition that takes account of the differences as much as the similarities. Classicists Roy Gibson and Andrew Morrison employ the concept of the *family resemblances* (as described by Ludwig Wittgenstein) to define the epistolary genre. Just as family members may share some similar characteristics, different texts may also share at least one or more features, so that they bear a slight resemblance to each other.[35] Gibson and Morrison apply this theory to epistolography and note that

> texts usually considered firmly within the category of letter can be seen to share core characteristics with marginal examples of the genre or even ... with quite different genres—and yet without doing damage to the idea of the letter as a useful category of literature.[36]

34 For *De Officiis* of Cicero, see Gibson and Morrison, "Introduction: What is a Letter?" in *Ancient Letters: Classical and Late Antique Epistolography*, ed. Ruth Morello and A. D. Morrison (Oxford: Oxford University Press, 2007), 10–12. For *Epistula* 140 and 157 of Augustine, see Allen et al., *Preaching Poverty in Late Antiquity*, 51–53. For further information on hybrid forms in epistolography, see Allen and Neil, *Crisis Management in Late Antiquity*, 21–23.
35 Gibson and Morrison, "Introduction: What is a Letter?,"13–15. For Wittgensteins' theory of family resemblances, see Ludwig Wittgenstein, *Philosophical Investigations*, trans. G. E. M. Anscombe, P. M. S. Hacker and Joachim Schulte, 4th ed. (Malden, MA: Willy Blackwell, 2009), 67–77. For family resemblance theory as applied to arts and literature, see Alastair Fowler, *Kinds of Literature: An Introduction to the Theory of Genres and Models* (Oxford: Clarendon Press, 1982), 41–42.
36 Gibson and Morrison, "Introduction: What is a Letter?," 13.

The genre theory of Wittgenstein has recently been challenged by Carol Newsom. She points out the contradictions inherent in applying this definition, stating that while some texts within a genre may share one or more features with each other, other texts share no characteristics in common at all.[37] Instead, as a result of her study on the Apocalypse genre she suggests the *prototype theory*. This is a sort of graded classification, based on the degree to which a particular style represents the prototype of a category. Some texts which appear very similar to the prototype of a category are considered "central members", while others bearing no resemblance to it are viewed as "peripheral members".[38] This approach is helpful in grouping letters with wide variation into the epistolary genre. However, it is undeniable that the boundary between "central" and "marginal texts" is still blurred.

Since it seems impossible to pursue a watertight and categorical definition of the letter genre as a whole, this book will not try to include all forms of letters from antiquity, but instead focus on the basic components of the letter form: a one-way conversation; a written message; the nature of a sender and a receiver. Using these elements leads to a broad definition as *one half of a conversation in written form on a tangible medium, which an addresser sends to an addressee.*

---

37   Newsom says that

> [f]or example, text in group A might exhibit features a, b, c, group B might exhibit features b, c, d, and group C might exhibit features c, d, e, and so forth. One is left with the uncomfortable conclusion that the family resemblance model could produce a genre in which two exemplars in fact shared no traits in common!

See Carol Newsom, "Spying Out the Land: A Report from Genology," in *Bakhtin and Genre Theory in Biblical Studies*, ed. Roland Boer (Atlanta: Society Biblical Literature, 2007), 23.

38   For prototype theory and its limitations, see Newsom, "Spying Out the Land: A Report from Genology," 24–26.

1.3.2 Authors

Epistolary correspondence in antiquity was employed by people from all levels of society, from the top political leaders to the lowest class of people. In terms of the former, Hellenistic and Roman imperial authorities composed letters both directly and indirectly. Particularly in the case of personal letters and written petitions sent from governmental officials and prominent figures, they often wrote letters with their own hands. In contrast, when it came to official correspondence regarding political, legal, administrative, diplomatic and religious issues, this may have been dictated to royal scribes.[39] With regard to Hellenistic and Roman imperial correspondence, although royal correspondence was written in epistolary form, in many cases such a text (in letter form) actually functioned as a royal decree.[40]

In addition, the practice of letter writing was widely adopted by Christian leaders in the late Roman world because it acted as an useful medium not only to bridge a geographical gap with their addressees including other church officials and their friends, but also to maintain their network of

---

39 For comprehensive Hellenistic royal correspondence, see Charles Bradford Wells, *Royal Correspondence in the Hellenistic Period: A Study in Greek Epigraphy* (New Haven: Yale University Press, 1934; reprint, Roma: L'Erma di Bretschneider, 1966); Karen Radner, ed., *State Correspondence in the Ancient World: From New Kingdom Egypt to the Roman Empire* (Oxford: Oxford University Press, 2014); Hans-Josef Klauck, *Ancient Letters and the New Testament: A Guide to Context and Exegesis* (Waco: Baylor University Press, 2006), 77–100; Hennie Stander, "Chrysostom on Letters and Letter-Writing," in *Patrologia Pacifica: Selected Papers Presented to the Asia Pacific Early Christian Studies Society*, ed. Vladimir Baranov, Kazuhiko Demura and Basil Lourié (Piscataway, NJ: Gorgias Press), 52–54. For an example of a reply by a Roman emperor to a written petition sent from Roman officials and persons. This was called "subscriptions". See Fergus Millar, *The Emperor in the Roman World: 31BC–AD 337* (London: Duckworth, 1977), 240–52.
40 See Stander, "Chrysostom on Letters and Letter-Writing," 53; Simon Cororan, "State Correspondence in the Roman empire from Augustus to Justinian," in *State Correspondence in the Ancient World*, ed. Karen Radner (Oxford: Oxford University Press, 2014), 173.

influence.[41] Particularly, Allen and Neil's study on episcopal letters clearly indicates how epistolography functioned as a primary means for fifth and sixth-century bishops to manage socioeconomic, political, religious and natural crises that they faced.[42]

In Late Antiquity, some ascetics also sent letters to their interlocutors instead of meeting face-to-face. Spiritual fathers in Egypt and Palestine consulted with their monastic and lay disciples on spiritual and religious concerns as well as practical matters by letters.[43] For monastics in particular, letter writing was seen as a vital method to wield monastic authority because it helped them not only to maintain their social networks, but also to keep their ascetic practices such as separating themselves from the world and keeping their vow of silence.[44]

Unlike the many examples of letter writing by imperial administrators and religious elites, relatively few letters written by ordinary people have survived. However, a closer look at these letters shows that they also dealt with diverse topics: from spiritual or religious matters to everyday issues including cloth and weaving.[45] Some wrote their own letters, while others, who

---

41   Pauline Allen, "How to Study Episcopal Letter-Writing in Late Antiquity: An Overview of Published Work on the Fifth and Sixth Centuries," in *Patrologia Pacifica: Selected Papers Presented to the Asia Pacific Early Christian Studies Society*, ed. Vladimir Baranov, Kazuhiko Demura and Basil Lourié (Piscataway, NJ: Gorgias Press), 130–42; Stander, "Chrysostom on Letters and Letter-Writing," 51–52.

42   Allen and Neil, *Crisis Management in Late Antiquity*. See John R. C. Martyn, "Introduction" to vol. 1 of *The Letters of Gregory of the Great*, trans. and ed. John R. C. Martyn, (Ontario: Pontifical Institute of Mediaeval Studies, 2004), 72–98.

43   For examples of letters in Egyptian from the Gazan fathers, Jennifer L. Hevelone-Harper, *Disciples of the Desert: Monks, Laity and Spiritual Authority in Sixth-Century Gaza* (Baltimore: John Hopkins University Press), 18–23. On the role of epistolography in late-antique monasticism, see Malcolm Choat, "The Epistolary Culture of Monasticism between Literature and Papyri," *Cistercian Studies Quarterly* 48.2 (2013): 234; McNary-Zak, *Letters and Asceticism in Fourth-Century Egypt*, 8–9.

44   Choat, "The Epistolary Culture of Monasticism between Literature and Papyri," 234; McNary-Zak, *Letters and Asceticism in Fourth-Century Egypt*, 9.

45   Bagnall and Cribiore, *Women's Letters from Ancient Egypt*, xi–xii.

were most probably illiterate, sent letters composed by scribes on their behalf.[46]

1.3.3 Length and subject of letters

Both pre-Christian and late Roman Christian authors principally accept that correspondence should be restricted in subject and length.[47] Gregory of Nazianzus, in his *Epistula* 51 to Nicobulus, provides a comprehensive account of the appropriate length and subject of letters.

> Among people who write letters (since you have also inquired about this subject) there are some who write at greater length than is fitting, and others who are much too brief. They both completely miss achieving the mean, just as archers either undershoot or overshoot when they try to hit the target they miss equally, though for opposite reasons. [2] What determines the length of letters is the need they aim to meet. One should not write on and on when the subject matter is limited, nor be stingy with words when there is much to say.[48]

The first half of *Epistula* 51 deals with the ideal length of a letter. The second half of the text above indicates a close connection between the length of an epistle and subject matter. This link is also found in *Epistolary Styles* written by pseudo Libanius.[49]

---

46 See Hevelone-Harper, *Disciples of the Desert*, 80; Lincoln H. Blumell, "The Message and the Medium: Some Observations on Epistolary Communication in Late Antiquity," *Journal of Graeco-Roman Christianity and Judaism* 10 (2014): 36.
47 Both Demetrius and Julius Victor note that a letter should be kept within limited length, while Sidonius strictly say a correspondence has only one topic. See Demetrius, *De Elocutione*, 228, in Malherbe, *Ancient Epistolary Theorists*, 19. Julius Victor, *Are Rhetorica* 27 in Malherbe, *Ancient Epistolary Theorists*, 63. Sidonius, *Letters: Books 3–9*, VII, 18, 4, trans. W. B. Anderson, LCL 420 (Harvard University Press, 1965), 399. On brevity and subject in letters of Middle Ages, see Constable, *Letters and Letter-Collections*, 18–20.
48 Gregory of Nazianzus, *Epistula* 51 in Malherbe, *Ancient Epistolary Theorists*, 59.
49 Pseudo Libanius, Ἐπιστολιμαῖοι χαρακτῆρες, 50 in Malherbe, *Ancient Epistolary Theorists*, 73.

If we compare the criteria set out above by the fourth-century bishop with the available primary sources, it is clear that many letters do not accord with his suggestions regarding length and subject. In particular, flexible length and subject matter are both often found in so called "hybrid form letters" that "are letters in the technical sense but in terms of their nature content and function have in fact crossed over into the realm of homilies or treatises".[50] For example, the *Quod nemo laeditur* of John Chrysostom, which preaches about a proper Christian's attitude to riches and money, is made up of a 40-page letter. Likewise, Augustine's two long letters, *Epistulae* 140 and 157, deal with questions about scriptural passages and refutation of Pelagian teachings.[51] It is clear that this form of hybrid correspondence often exceeds the theoretical length and topics of the defined letter form.

1.3.4 Scribes

Another issue is the role of the scribe in letter writing. Scribes are, as Lincoln Blumell says, classified into three types depending on the degree of influence exerted in letter composition:
1. a scribe as *a transcriber* who writes down the letters exactly as his author dictates;
2. a scribe as *an editor* who takes note of the author's dictation, but makes some corrections or changes in content and/or form if necessary; and
3. a scribe as *a composer* who actually composes letter on behalf of his employer according to his (the employer's) purposes.[52]

---

50 Allen and Neil, Crisis Management in Late Antiquity, 21. For further information on "hybrid form letters", see Allen and Neil, Crisis Management in Late Antiquity, 21–23.
51 For more information of these letters, see Allen et al., Preaching Poverty in Late Antiquity, 51–53.
52 Lincoln H. Blumell, "The Message and the Medium," 40–43. Richards also divides scribes into similar categories: the scribe as a transcriber, as a contributor and as a composer. See Ernest Randolph Richards, Paul and First-Century Letter Writing: Secretaries, Composition and Collection (Downer Grove, IL: InterVarsity Press, 2004), 64–80.

This taxonomy alerts us to several things involved in the practice of letter-writing. First and foremost, it indicates that there were varied degrees of participation among ancient scribes in terms of writing correspondence. Secondly, it suggests that letters written by scribes or secretaries led, to a greater or lesser degree, to editorial changes because of intentional or unintentional causes. Such causes may include author requests, mishearing and even errors on the part of the scribes.[53] Finally, some ancient scribes can also be seen as composers of letters. When this happens, the works are potentially more likely to be influenced and amended by scribes than by their original authors. These works may therefore be considered as the work of scribes, although we can assume they consulted an authors' rough draft or instructions during composition.

Of the three things discussed above, the last two relate specifically to the authenticity of letters and their reliability as a source. Given imperial practice regarding official letter-writing, a final draft of an official letter is likely to have been rechecked and proofread by administrative staff.[54] However, although ancient private correspondence also appears to have undergone a proofreading process, it is not easy to determine the extent to which senders checked and modified the final draft of their personal correspondence because there is little concrete evidence indicating direct correction and editing of final drafts in this context.[55]

While some ancient authors carelessly overlooked mistakes in their letters before sealing them,[56] most tried to minimise any unintended slips made by scribes when copying or composing letters. There was a variety of methods that could be used to identify and correct errors. For example, although an exceptional case,

---

53 Allen, "It's in the Post," 115; Richards, *Paul and First-Century Letter Writing*, 75.
54 Blumell, "The Message and the Medium," 41–42.
55 Ernest Randolph Richards, *The Secretary in the Letters of Paul*, WUNT 2.42 (Tübingen: Mohr Siebeck, 1991), 55.
56 Richards, *The Secretary in the Letters of Paul*, 55.

Origen, the third-century theologian employed many shorthand-writers and copyists in writing biblical commentaries (thanks to his patron Ambrose) in an effort to avoid errors and omissions.

> Starting from that time also Origen's commentaries on the divine Scriptures had their beginning, at the instigation of Ambrose, who not only plied him with innumerable verbal exhortations and encouragements, but also provided him unstintingly with what was necessary. For as he dictated there were ready at hand more than seven shorthand-writers, who relieved each other at fixed times, and as many copyists, as well as girls skilled in penmanship; for all of whom Ambrose supplied without stint the necessary means.[57]

1.3.5 Compilations of collected letters

One further issue relating to epistolography is that of compilations of collected letters. Carol Poster and Raffaele Luiselli suggest that ancient and late-antique letters, depending on whether or not they were compiled for posterity, generally belong to one of three categories: "documentary", "literary" and "fictitious" letters.[58] Documentary letters include handwritten letters which have not been subsequently recopied for publication. Particularly, Poster suggests two important benefits of the documentary letter form: it provides not only glimpses into "how epistolary instruction was applied across broad social and temporal spans", but also practical help in counterbalancing the current tendency to focus on the letters of elite writers—Plato, Isocrates, Cicero, Augustine

---

57 Eusebius, *Ecclesiastical History*, VI. XXIII, trans. J. E. L. Oulton. LCL 265 (Cambridge, MA: Harvard University Press, 1932).
58 Carol Poster, "A Conversation Halved: Epistolary Theory in Graeco-Roman Antiquity," in *Letter-Writing Manuals and Instruction from Antiquity to the Present: Historical and Bibliographic Studies*, ed. Linda Mitchell (Columbia: University of South Carolina Press, 2007), 37–41; Luiselli, "Greek Letters on Papyrus: First to Eighth Centuries," 678. For documentary and literary letters in Egyptian monasticism, see Choat, "The Epistolary Culture of Monasticism between Literature and Papyri," 227–37.

and so on—in the ancient world.[59] In contrast, unlike documentary texts, literary and fictional letters are usually created as part of a letter-collection for publication. The term "literary letters" in particular refers to letters which were, according to the purpose or intention of the compiler(s), selected and edited from genuine letters between sender and addressee, whereas "fictional letters" are predominantly written to form part of a collection of invented correspondence for future generations to consume.[60]

Two main difficulties are encountered when studying letters in edited collections from Late Antiquity.[61] The first is that not all letters written by original authors have been passed down. Because some have survived but some others have not, these sources offer a limited understanding of the writer's thought in the context of their time. Secondly, compiled letters are likely to be collected on the basis of the intentions and interests of compilers rather than original authors or their agents. Thus, the compilers' perspectives, and even the purpose behind any redactions, naturally exert a profound influence on any collection of correspondence. As a result, it is essential not only to recognize that, although limited, the original author's thought still exists in documentary and literary letters in particular, but also to distinguish between the thought of the original letter-writer and that of the compiler, when using letters as a primary source.

1.4 Other research issues

1.4.1 Definition of charity

This book is about charity in the context of the correspondence of Barsanuphius and John of Gaza. The term "charity" is, in gen-

---

59 Poster, "A Conversation Halved," 40.
60 Poster, "A Conversation Halved," 39; Luiselli, "Greek Letters on Papyrus: First to Eighth Centuries," 678.
61 For more detailed analysis of difficulties which compiled letters have, see Allen et al., *Preaching Poverty in Late Antiquity*, 47–49.

eral, understood to relate to giving money and other necessities to poor people and beggars. However, in this study, it will be used in the broader sense indicated by the Greek word ἐλεημοσύνη, which means not only "almsgiving", but also "mercy".[62] The term "charity" will therefore to denote a general concept of showing mercy to the poor and social inferiors, by giving gifts to them, entertaining them, and caring for them with medical treatment.

1.4.2 Manuscripts and editions

According to some modern scholars, the oldest manuscripts of the compiled letters of Barsanuphius and John of Gaza are *Sinai 34* and *35*. Dating from tenth century, these manuscripts are Georgian translations of 79 letters.[63] Other manuscripts containing extracts from the two Gazan anchorites' writings survive from the eleventh century, including: *Sinai* 410 and 411; *Vatopedi* 2 and 355; *Bodleian Cromwell* 18; *Coislin* 124 and 128; *Paris Grec* 873; *Koutloumousiou* 3; *Iviron* 1307; *Panteleimon* 192; *Dionysiou* 717; *Xenophontos* 9; and *Athènes* 541.[64] Among these, the *Iviron 1307* and *Panteleimon 192* contain almost all of the letters of the Gazan monks, and so are regarded as "the most important texts".[65]

There have been several attempts to publish printed editions of the correspondence, starting in 1569 with J. Grinaeus' publica-

---

62 W. H. Lampe, *A Patristic Greek Lexicon* (Oxford: The Clarendon Press, 1961), s.v. ἐλεημοσύνη, 447–48.
63 John Chryssavgis, introduction to *Barsanuphius and John: Questions and Responses*, by Barsanuphius and John of Gaza, trans. John Chryssavgis. 2 vols. (Washington, DC: Catholic University of America Press, 2006–2007), 15; Neyt, Angelis-Noah, and Regnault, introduction to *Barsanuphe et Jean de Gaza: Correspondance*, by Barsanuphe et Jean de Gaza, ed. and trans. François Neyt, Paula de Angelis-Noah, and Lucien Regnault, SC 426-427, 450-451, 468 (Paris: Éditions du Cerf, 1997–2002), vol.1, t.1, 131.
64 David Mezynski, "The Effects of the Origenist Controversy on the Pastoral Theology of Barsanupius and John" (PhD diss., Fordham University, 2012), 10–11; François Neyt, Paula de Angelis-Noah, and Lucien Regnault, introduction to *Barsanuphe et Jean de Gaza*, 132.
65 Mezynski, "The Effects of the Origenist Controversy on the Pastoral Theology of Barsanupius and John," 10.

tion of some letters of John of Gaza with the works of Abba Dorotheos.⁶⁶ In 1816, the *Biblos Barsanouphiou kai Ioannou*, edited by Nikodemus Hagiorita, was published in Venice including almost all the letters.⁶⁷ This was followed by the work of J-P. Migne (1857–1866) whose *Patrologia Graeca* published the letters relating to Origenism and Dorotheos of Gaza.⁶⁸ A century and a half later, in 1960, the text of Nikodemus Hagiorita was reprinted by Soterios Schoinas in Volos, with partial corrections.⁶⁹ Six years later, Derwas Chitty published a critical edition of 124 letters, comparing *Coislin* 124, *Vatopedi* 2, *Sinai* 411 and Nikodemus.⁷⁰ Since 1997, François Neyt, Lucien Regnault and Paula de Angelis-Noah have produced a new edition of the Greek text with French translation.⁷¹ This edition is regarded as one of the major sources for recent studies on Barsanuphius and John of Gaza.⁷² Finally, in 2006–2007, John Chryssavgis published an English translation of the *Letters*. This text is based not only on the critical edition of Neyt, Angelis-Noah and Regnault, but also on other sources including *Vatopedi* 2, *Bodleian Cromwell* 18, Derwas Chitty's work.⁷³

---

66 Chryssavgis, introduction to *Barsanuphius and John: Questions and Responses*, 15–16.
67 Barsanuphius and John of Gaza, *Barsanuphius and John of Gaza, Biblos Barsanouphiou kai Ioannou*, ed. Nikodemos Hagiorita (Venice: 1816); Jennifer Hevelone-Harper, "Disciples of the Desert: Monks, Laity, and Spiritual Authority in Sixth-Century Gaza" (PhD diss., Princeton University, 2000), 3.
68 Chryssavgis, introduction to *Barsanuphius and John: Questions and Responses*, 16. See PG 86.892–901 and PG 88.1812–1820B.
69 Barsanuphius and John of Gaza, *Biblos Psychophelestate*, ed. Soterios Schoinas (Volos: 1960); Chryssavgis, introduction to *Barsanuphius and John: Questions and Responses*, 16.
70 Barsanuphius and John of Gaza, *Barsanuphius and John: Questions and Answers*, ed. and trans. Derwas James Chitty, Patrologia Orientalis 31.3 (Paris, 1966)
71 See footnote 2 above.
72 See Hevelone-Harper, "Disciples of the Desert: Monks, Laity, and Spiritual Authority in Sixth-Century Gaza," 5 n. 1; Chryssavgis, introduction to *Barsanuphius and John: Questions and Responses*, 16; David Mezynski, "The Effects of the Origenist Controversy on the Pastoral Theology of Barsanuphius and John," 11.
73 Chryssavgis, introduction to *Barsanuphius and John: Questions and Responses*, 16.

Chapter 2
The City of Gaza in Late Antiquity

In this chapter, we attempt to lay the general foundation to understand the city by first offering an analysis of the geographical and socio-economic aspect of late-antique Gaza, and then focusing attention on its inhabitants—laypeople, monks and the clergy—in order to identify the sociocultural ethos of this seaport in early Byzantine Palestine.

2.1 Socio-economic context of late-antique Gaza

2.1.1 Gaza as a trade, traffic and intellectual center

The city of Gaza on the southern coast of Palestine functioned not only as the gateway to the Negev and Egypt for traders or travelers from Phoenicia and Syria, but also as the bridge between the Mediterranean and the traders and goods from southern Arabia and the East of the Jordan River (the Decapolis).[1] Although its origin is obscure, the city emerged in ancient times as one of major commercial hubs in the Mediterranean world because of its geographical position as an important traffic center. It is in the Hellenistic period in particular that Gazans were deeply involved in trade and in transportation pertaining to spice and luxury goods from South Arabia and its neighbors.[2] Such trade was replaced in the early Byzantine period by agricultural

---

1   Hirschfeld, "The Monasticism of Gaza: An Archaeological Review," 61–63.
2   Glucker, *The City of Gaza in the Roman and Byzantine Periods*, 86–93; Aryeh Kasher, "Gaza During the Graeco-Roman Era," in *The Jerusalem Cathedra 2*, ed. Lee I. Levine (Detroit: Wayne State University Press, 1982), 69.

products including wine, wheat, dried fruits and olive oil.³

In terms of the wine trade, in his study on wine presses in Negev, Philip Mayerson focuses on nine large-scale wine presses discovered in Elusa, Sobata and Eboda. These respectively included one or two vats containing between 2230 to 7570 litres. He assumes that surplus wine from the Negev was sold to Syrian or Egyptian wine merchants in Gaza.⁴ Furthermore, Palestinian wine amphorae have been discovered in major cities in Egypt and Asia Minor as well as in the western Mediterranean coast dating from the fourth to seventh centuries.⁵ Although it is not known how many liters of wine were carried through the seaport in Palestine, it is obvious that wine from the Holy Land was "consumed widely within and beyond the borders of the empire in Late Antiquity".⁶ The Palestinian trade, which led to population growth in Byzantine Palestine in the fifth and sixth century,⁷ was linked to the political stability and economic prosperity of major cities in the Mediterranean world.⁸

Moreover, late-antique Gaza was a gateway for travelers or pilgrims from the western provinces who came by land and sea,

---

3   Sean A. Kingsley, "The Economic Impact of the Palestinian Wine Trade in Late Antiquity," in *Economy and Exchange in the East Mediterranean during Late Antiquity*, ed. Sean A. Kingsley and Michael Decker (Oxford: Oxbow Books, 2001), 45; Hevelone-Harper, *Disciples of the Desert*, 3; Glucker, *The City of Gaza in the Roman and Byzantine Periods*, 94–96.
4   Philip Mayerson, "The Wine and Vineyards of Gaza in the Byzantine Period," *Bulletin of the American Schools of Oriental Research*, 257 (1985): 75–80.
5   Kingsley, "The Economic Impact of the Palestinian Wine Trade in Late Antiquity," 51–55.
6   Kingsley, "The Economic Impact of the Palestinian Wine Trade in Late Antiquity," 53.
7   Kingsley, "The Economic Impact of the Palestinian Wine Trade in Late Antiquity," 54; Champion, *Explaining the Cosmos*, 23.
8   Angeliki Laiou and Cécile Morrisson, *The Byzantine Economy* (Cambridge; New York: Cambridge University Press, 2007), 23. For discussion of the early Byzantine economy, see Cécile Morrisson and Jean-Pierre Sodini, "The Sixth-Century Economy," in *The Economic History of Byzantium: From the Seventh through the Fifteenth Century*, ed. Angeliki Laiou (Washington, DC: Dumbarton Oaks Research Library and Collection, 2002), 1:171–220.

making their way to Jerusalem or to other places in Palestine.⁹ Although it is impossible to determine how many pilgrims or travelers from the West came to the Holy Land via Gaza in Late Antiquity, it is evident that the flow of westerners to the Holy City and its monasteries gradually increased from the second half of the fourth century. This increase in pilgrimage may have also contributed, to some extent, to the contemporary economic growth in Byzantine Palestine.[10] According to Leah Di Segni and Yoram Tsafrir, it is during the late-antique period that "pilgrims from all over the West came to Jerusalem, some being members of the aristocracy and connected the emperor's court, while others were ordinary folk", and contemporary "itineraries written by the pilgrims and road maps" prove "how widespread was pilgrimage, and how great the number of pilgrims".[11] In addition to Jerusalem, the presence of the Latin-speaking westerners is noted in the monasteries of the Judean desert between the fifth and seventh centuries: the monasteries of Theoctistus, St. Sabas, St. Theodosius and Choziba, and a monastery on Mount Sinai.[12]

The coastal city of Palestine may have been less attractive to Christian pilgrims when compared to Jerusalem and the Judean desert, although it was a significant traffic center becoming a gateway to Byzantine Palestine for pilgrims. As Mayerson points out, some of the pilgrims to the Holy Land might have visited Gaza to see the city and its neighbouring sites, such as the venue for Samson's

---

9   John Wilkinson, introduction to *Jerusalem Pilgrims Before the Crusades*, 2nd ed. (Warminster, England: Aris & Phillips, 2002), 41; Edward D. Hunt, *Holy Land Pilgrimage in the Later Roman Empire AD 312–460* (Oxford: Clarendon Press, 1982), 72.

10 Avi-Yohan, "The Economics of Byzantine Palestine," *Israel Exploration Journal* 8.1 (1958), 45; Leah Di Segni and Yoram Tsafrir, "The Ethnic Composition of Jerusalem's Population in the Byzantine Period (312–638 CE)," *Liber Annuus* 62 (2012): 413–14.

11 Di Segni and Tsafrir, "The Ethnic Composition of Jerusalem's Population in the Byzantine Period," 413.

12 Di Segni and Tsafrir, "The Ethnic Composition of Jerusalem's Population in the Byzantine Period," 418 n. 49.

last victory, as well as the tombs of Hilarion and some martyrs.[13]

Not only did late-antique Gaza serve as a commercial and traffic hub of the Mediterranean East, during the early Byzantine period it was also as a key intellectual center. The city already seems to have had a school of rhetoric as early as the fourth century,[14] and it was to gradually emerge as an important center for rhetorical study from the fifth century onwards on account of distinguished rhetoricians, philosophers and scholars from Gaza: Zosimus of Gaza, Aeneas of Gaza, Procopius of Gaza and his successor Choricius, the poet and grammarian John of Gaza (who is not the John of Gaza also called "John the Prophet" in the *Letters*) and Procopius of Caesarea.[15] According to Champion, another reason for the development of Gaza as an intellectual hub in the eastern world was closely tied to its geographical networks with other intellectual centers and especially Alexandria. He asserts that the city's intellectual and geographical connection to Alexandria would "make Gaza an attractive option for students who could not gain access to teachers in Alexandria itself".[16] While the seaside city was one of the major centers for rhetoric and philosophy, it was not of the same stature and importance as core centers of Neoplatonic intellectual activity such as Alexandria and Athens within the Mediterranean world.[17] Nevertheless, its academic reputation and the presence of several distinguished rhetoricians and scholars prompted many students and teachers from other places to flock into the rhetorical school in Gaza.

13   Mayerson, "The Wine and Vineyards of Gaza in the Byzantine Period," 79 n. 3.
14   Downey, "The Christian Schools of Palestine," 303, 308.
15   Glucker, *The City of Gaza in the Roman and Byzantine Periods*, 51–57; Downey, "The Christian Schools of Palestine," 307–15. For a detailed study on Gazan rhetorical schools in Late Antiquity, see Champion, *Explaining the Cosmos*, 29–38.
16   Champion, *Explaining the Cosmos*, 33; I. P. Sheldon-William, "The Reaction against Proclus," in *Cambridge History of Later Greek and Early Medieval Philosophy*, ed. A. Armstrong (Cambridge: Cambridge University Press, 1968), 484 notes that "[t]he school of Gaza was an offshoot of Alexandria as Alexandria had been an offshoot of Athens".
17   Champion, *Explaining the Cosmos*, 34.

This school was closely related to local monasteries and churches in Gaza. It is well known that Aeneas of Gaza, a fifth-century philosopher and rhetor, consulted with Abba Isaiah on issues related to Neoplatonic philosophy.[18] Moreover, the *Letters* of Barsanuphius and John demonstrate that there were some lay and monastic Christians who wrote to the Gazan holy men on matters related to philosophical and theological issues such as Origenism (letter 600) and the relationship between the free will of human beings and Divine Providence (letter 763). Such proximity to religious institutions in fifth and early sixth-century Gaza can likewise be observed in the case of the head master of the rhetorical school who was also a bishop of Gaza. Bishop Marcian succeeded Procopius to the headship of the rhetorical school, and it is likely that the bishop encouraged the academy to cooperate with the church in supporting the school administration.[19] This is however challenged by Fotios Litsas, a translator of the works of Choricius. He warns that, on the basis of the address to Marcian, it is not certain whether the church of Gaza "was supporting the school of Gaza financially or Marcian was simply active with its administration" because there is no evidence to explain his economic and administrative help.[20] Notwithstanding, we do not have direct evidence, it is reasonable to assume that Marcian operated the school, given his diverse roles and activities as both an ecclesiastical and civil leader in Gaza.[21]

---

18 Zachariah Rhetor, *Vita Isaiae Monachi*, ed. and trans. E. W. Brook, *Vitae virorum apud Monophysitas celeberrimorum*, 2 vols, CSCO 7–8 (Paris: E typographeo reipublicae, 1907; repr., Peeters, 1960), 12.
19 Choricius, *Funeral Oration to Procopius*, 50 says that "the present deceased (Procopius) left his own [boat, the school] ashore in a secure and great harbor, the bishop [Marcian]". See Yakov Ashkenazi, "Sophists and Priests in Late Antique Gaza: According to Choricius the Rhector," in *Christian Gaza in Late Antiquity*, ed. Bitton-Ashkelony and Kofsky (Leiden; Boston: Brill, 2004), 200–1.
20 Fotios Litsas, "Choricius of Gaza: An Approach to His work," (PhD diss., University of Chicago, 1980), 308 n. 66.
21 For activities of Marcian as civil and religious patronage, see 2.4.1.

2.1.2 Christianity in late-antique Gaza

Several sources reveal diverse Christian communities in late-antique Gaza. According to Jerome, St. Hilarion (291/2–371) returned to his home town of Gaza after a period of study in Alexandria and Egypt, and founded a small ascetic community with his fellows during the reign of Emperor Constantius II (337–361). He then became a head of the coenobium.[22] Although its authenticity is doubtful,[23] the *Life of Porphyry* of Mark the Deacon also provides useful information about Christianity in the end of fourth-century Gaza. When arriving at Gaza as a bishop of Gaza, Porphyry met several Christians already living in the city.[24] Not long after, he then sent his disciple Mark to appeal to the Emperor Arcadius (395–408)[25] on account of threats and violence against him and his fellow Christians from Gazan pagans.[26] Mark came back with both an imperial "decree that the temples of the idols in the city of the Gazaeans should be shut and no longer give oracles" and a directive that Hilarius, a government official, should enforce the decree.[27] Despite the imperial edict, with the Christian population increasing, pagans continued to act harshly towards Christians. Thus, Porphyry and John, Archbishop of Caesarea, themselves went to Constantinople to appeal to the Emperor. They returned with a new decree ordering the destruction of pagan temples and bringing with them a great deal of money for the purpose of building a guest-house linked to the holy church in Gaza.[28] These imperially-funded possessions, as Champion points

---

22 Jerome, *Life of Hilarion*, in Carolinne White, trans. and ed., *Early Christian Lives* (London: Penguin Books, 1998), 14; Hirschfeld, "The Monasticism of Gaza: An Archaeological Review," 67–68.
23 See Champion, *Explaining the Cosmos*, 22 n. 6.
24 Mark the Deacon, *The Life of Porphyry, Bishop of Gaza* (Oxford: Clarendon Press, 1913), 19.
25 Mark the Deacon, *The Life of Porphyry, Bishop of Gaza*, 26.
26 Mark the Deacon, *The Life of Porphyry, Bishop of Gaza*, 20–25.
27 Mark the Deacon, *The Life of Porphyry, Bishop of Gaza*, 26–27.
28 Mark the Deacon, *The Life of Porphyry, Bishop of Gaza*, 32–54.

out, seem to have had an impact on "the growth of the Christian community in Gaza during the fifth century".[29]

Despite Porphyry's efforts as a bishop, Christian believers still appear to have suffered some difficulties in Gaza, mostly as a result of the considerable influence of the pagans in Gaza. The council (βουλή)[30] of Gaza in the early fifth century was, according to Champion, generally governed by pagan members. Because of pagan control of the council, Gazan Christians appeared not to receive material aid for the poor, so that they "apparently did not have sufficient wealth or status to provide such support".[31]

However, things began to change from sometime in the fifth century. Yizhar Hirschfeld's archaeological survey indicates acceleration in the building of monasteries and churches in late-antique Gaza and its environs:

Century	Numbers	Names
4th century	3	The monastery of Hilarion, the monastery of Bethelea and the monastery of Silvanus
5th century	3	The monastery of Zeno, the monastery of Abba Isaiah and the monastery of Peter the Iberian
5th–6th century	4	Tel Sera' (church or monastery), the Church of St. Kyrikos, the monastery of St. Peter in Tel 'Ira and coenobium of Horvat So'a
6th century	7	The monastery of Severus, the monastery of Seridos, the monastery of Dorotheos, the monastery of St. Elias, the monastery of Khirbet Jemameh, Shella (church) and the monastery of Mizpe Shivta
6th–7th century	1	The coenobium of Tel Masos
Unidentified	1	'Ein 'Avdat
Total	19	

Table 1. The dates of Christian buildings in Gaza[32]

29 Champion, *Explaining the Cosmos*, 26–7. The quotation is from 27.
30 For the *boule* (βουλή) in the late Roman Empire, see A. H. M. Jones, *The Later Roman Empire 284–602* (1964; repr., Baltimore: The Johns Hopkins University Press, 1986), 724–25.
31 Champion, *Explaining the Cosmos*, 27.
32 Hirschfeld, "The Monasticism of Gaza," 67–87.

This table demonstrates that the monastic movement in Gaza started to grow rapidly during the fifth century. The monastic growth appears to be linked to events occurring in Egyptian monastic communities in the second half of the fourth century and the first half of the fifth century: the Origenist controversy and the invasion of Scetis by the Mazices.[33] These tragic incidents pushed Egyptian hermits and monks to move up into the Gaza area to take refuge. As a result, Egyptian monasticism was then able to exert some influence on the monastic centers in Gaza.[34]

The table above also indicates that the high number of monastic foundations created in the sixth century is in parallel with the growth of Christianity in early Byzantine Palestine, as Asher Ovidah indicates:

4th cen.	4–5th cen.	5th cen.	5–6th cen.	6th cen.	7th c en.	8th cen.	Unident.	Total
9	3	45	14	56	15	3	52	197

Table 2. The dates of church foundations in Palestine[35]

In sum, Christianity finally emerged as a major religion in Gaza in the sixth century, although some pagans and Jews still remained.[36]

---

33 Bitton-Ashkelony and Kofsky, *The Monastic School of Gaza*, 6–7.
34 See Samuel Rubenson, "The Egyptian Relation of Early Palestine Monastic," in *The Christian Heritage in the Holy Land*, ed. Anthony O'Mahony, Goran Gunner and Kevork Hintlian (London: Scorpion Cavendish, 1995), 35–46. For the connection between *Apophthegmata Patrum* and Gaza monasticism, see G. Gould, *The Desert Fathers on Monastic Community* (Oxford: Clarendon Press, 1993), 1–25; Brouria Bitton-Ashkelony and Aryeh Kofsky, "Gazan Monasticism in the Fourth-Sixth Centuries: From Anchoritic to Cenobitic," *Proche-Orient Chrétien* 50:1–2 (2000): 17 n. 12.
35 Asher Ovidah, *Corpus of the Byzantine Churches in the Holy Land* (Bonn: Hanstein, 1970), 193.
36 See Hevelone-Harper, *Disciples of the Desert*, 12–13.

2.1.3 Population

Like other major cities in the Mediterranean East, Gaza was flourishing at least by the first half of the sixth century. This was as a result of its geographical advantage, as well as its economic and intellectual prosperity. The seaside city was an attractive place for outsiders including traders, students and tourists.[37] An anonymous author from Piacenza provides a vivid description of sixth-century Gaza in the Holy Land: the city "is a lovely and renowned city, with noble people distinguished by every kind of liberal accomplishment. They are welcoming to strangers".[38]

Angeliki Laiou, Cécile Morrisson and Jean-Pierre Sodini offer some estimates for the populations of major cities of the eastern Mediterranean world.[39] According to them, Constantinople, the imperial city of the Byzantine Empire, numbered at least 400,000 inhabitants, while Antioch would have had approximately 200,000 and Alexandria 100,000. In terms of cities in Palestine in particular, they estimate Caesarea and Jerusalem had around between 50,000 and 100,000 inhabitants,[40] while Nicopolis and Scythopolis might have numbered from 30,000 to 40,000 people.

However, Magen Broshi calculates the population of Palestinian cities in the sixth century by means of a different calculation. He estimates Palestine's population on the basis of following three elements:

1. numbers of inhabitants per hectare (i.e. 400 people);
2. the total area of a city; and

---

37 Champion, *Explaining the Cosmos*, 22–23.
38 Piacenza Pilgrim, *Travels* 33 in *Jerusalem Pilgrims Before the Crusades*, ed. and trans. John Wilkinson (Warminster, England: Aris & Phillips, 2002), 144.
39 Laiou and Morrisson, *The Byzantine Economy*, 26; Morrisson and Sodini, "The Sixth-Century Economy," 174–75.
40 Di Segni and Tsafrir also estimate "over 50,000 inhabitants" in Jerusalem and its neighbours in the seventh century. See Di Segni and Tsafrir, "The Ethnic Composition of Jerusalem's Population in the Byzantine Period," 411–12.

3. the area which belonged to public spaces in the city (i.e. average 25% of total area).[41]

According to Broshi's calculations, the population of Jerusalem (120 hectares) is likely to have reached around 36,000 (400 x 120 x ¾ = 36,000), Caesarea (95 hectares) around 28,500 (400 x 95 x ¾ = 28,500), Scythopolis (110 hectares) around 33,000, Nicopolis (40 hectares) 12,000, Gaza (90 hectares) around 27,000 (400 x 90 x ¾ = 27,000), and Maiuma about 9,000 (400 x 30 x ¾ = 9,000).[42] According to these estimates, the combined population of Gaza and its port city Maiuma in the Byzantine period stands at about 36,000, which is the same as that of Jerusalem. Although the accuracy of these calculations to the reality of late-antique Palestine is not known, it is evident that late-antique Gaza was one of the larger cities in Palestine, although not as large as the main cities of the Roman Empire such as Constantinople, Antioch or Alexandra.

2.2 Lay Christians in late-antique Gaza

The compiler of the *Letters* generally uses the terms φιλόχριστος, φιλόχριστος λαϊκός, or sometimes κοσμικός and its varieties to designate lay Christians, and he defines them as people who are

---

41 Magen Broshi, "The Population of Western Palestine in the Roman-Byzantine Period," *Bulletin of the American Schools of Oriental Research*, 236 (1979): 5. As for "numbers of inhabitants per hectare," Broshi notes that "400–500 persons per hectare" is a maximum for populations in ancient cities. See Broshi, "The Population of Western Palestine in the Roman-Byzantine Period," 1.
42 Broshi, "The Population of Western Palestine in the Roman-Byzantine Period," 5.

neither monks nor clerics.⁴³ This section will explore who they were in terms of the city of Gaza, paying close attention to their education, social networks and piety.

2.2.1 Laypeople and education

The southern coastal city of Palestine, as has already been noted above, functioned not only as an important trading and monastic hub in the East during the late-antique period, but also as a major teaching location in the sixth century along with Constantinople, Athens and Alexandria in the Mediterranean East.⁴⁴ In the school of Gaza, rhetoric (including Neoplatonism) was the main focus of education, while law and medicine might be excluded.⁴⁵

However, access to the rhetoric school in Gaza was restricted to those who could pay its relatively expensive tuition fees. According to A.H.M. Jones, tuition for higher education including rhetoric was usually "four or five times as high as" that of a primary school.⁴⁶ He goes on to suggest that because schools of rhetoric were primarily situated in big cities, those students in towns and small cities were forced to relocate, thereby increasing

---

43 For the terms φιλόχριστος (Christ-loving) and its varieties, see letters 37, 382, 399, 454, 463, 570c, 571, 574, 617, 620, 629, 643, 637, 645, 647, 653, 662, 663, 664, 667, 679, 681, 683, 686, 690, 691, 692, 693, 723, 725, 745, 761, 763, 775, 778a, 779, 783, 784, 785, 786, 794, 819, 834, 836, 840, 843 and 845. In particular, see also the Prologue of the *Letters* where the compiler uses φιλόχριστος λαϊκός. For the term κοσμικός and its varieties, see letters 37, 308, 348, 584, 712, 716, 717, 719, 771 and 819. Letter 770 uses κοσμικὸν ἄνθρωπον. See also Lorenzo Perrone, "'Trembling at the Thought of Shipwreck': The Anxious Self in the Letters of Barsanuphius and John of Gaza," in *Between Personal and Institutional Religion: Self, Doctrine, and Practice in Late Antique Eastern Christianity*, ed. Brouria Bitton-Ashkelony, Lorenzo Perrone (Turnhout: Brepols, 2013), 12 n. 8.
44 See Averil Cameron, *The Mediterranean World in Late Antiquity: AD 395–700*, 2nd ed. (London; New York: Routledge, 2012), 130.
45 Glucker, *The City of Gaza*, 51; Bas Ter Haar Romeny, "Procopius of Gaza and His Library," in *From Rome to Constantinople: Studies in Honour of Averil Cameron*, ed. Hagit Amirav and Bas Ter Haar Romeny (Leuven; Paris; Dudley: Peeters, 2007), 190; Champion, *Explaining the Cosmos*, 35–38.
46 Jones, *The Later Roman Empire*, 997.

their costs.[47] The pursuit of higher education also took a long time: students had to spend two or three years, sometimes far longer, in order to study subjects such as law and rhetoric.[48]

It is therefore reasonable to suggest that those who accessed the education offered by the school of rhetoric at Gaza must have had some form of income, either earning a significant living themselves or being financially supported by their family members or other wealthy sponsors. This may indicate that some of the monks and laypersons who appear in the *Letters* as highly educated persons were in fact members of the middle or upper classes, or were supported by such people: for example, Dorotheos, who studied rhetoric and medicine before becoming a monk;[49] a monk ordained as a priest in the church of Jerusalem as a result of his academic career and title (letter 813); a pious philosopher with sick sons (letters 778a–778d); and an ordinary man who seems to have been able to afford a philosophical and theological education (letter 763).

Interestingly, in addition to higher education, the city of Gaza offered to its citizens primary education (reading and writing as well as arithmetic) "as part of the municipal services", just like several other cities in the late Roman Empire.[50] While schooling was theoretically open to anyone who held citizenship, in reality it was really only available to those who could afford the tuition fees. Nevertheless, the overall impression of a scholarly atmosphere in Gaza suggests that those laypeople who enjoyed some level of economic prosperity in late-antique Gaza, did in fact receive at least a basic education including reading and writ-

---

47 A. M. H. Jones, *The Decline of the Ancient World* (1966; repr., New York: Routledge, 2014), 286.
48 Jones, *The Later Roman Empire*, 998–99.
49 Letter 313 and 327 allude to Dorotheos as a physician. For Dorotheos' education, see Hevelone-Harper, *Disciples of the Desert*, 62–63.
50 Ashkenazi, "Sophists and Priests in Late Antique Gaza: According to Choricius the Rhector," 199. On municipal schools in the late Roman Empire, see Jones, *The Later Roman Empire*, 999.

ing. For those with more money to spend there were the rhetorical and philosophical pathways to study.

2.2.2 Lay Christians and their neighbors

Lay Christians in the ancient world, as they do today, interacted with their neighbors in several different places including local churches and monasteries, their homes and marketplaces. The correspondence of the two Gazan ascetics indicates that the laity encountered a wide range of neighbors, including the following: lay and monastic Christians and clergymen as well as pagans, Jews, and heretics. This section will focus on the relationships between lay believers, pagans and Jews as indicated by the *Letters*.[51]

Through the *Letters* we hear of encounters between lay Christians and contemporary Jews and pagans. For example, a Christ-loving person (φιλόχριστος) is said to have asked John cautiously whether or not he would be permitted to press a Jewish neighbour's grapes in his winepress. In answer to this question, John (here referred to as the Other Old Man) advises that he is able to do this, noting that the heavenly Father has mercy on the just as well as on the unjust (letter 686). This view of the relationship between Christians and Jewish people supports Aryeh Kofsky's argument, formed on the basis of literary and archaeological evidence from the fifth to the seventh centuries, that ordinary Christians in late-antique Palestine lived in close proximity to Jewish communities and may have even coexisted with them.[52]

---

51 The relationship of laypeople to heretics is touched on in the secion 2.2.3 while the relationship to monks is mentioned in section 2.3.3.
52 Aryeh Kofsky, "Observation on Christian-Jewish coexistence in Late Antiquity Palestine (Fifth to Seventh Centuries)," *Annali: di storia dell' esegesi* 23:2 (2006): 433–39. On the issues of archaeological evidence, see Gunter Stemberger, *Juden und Christen im 'Heiligen Land'* (München: C. H. Beck Verlag, 1987). For the interaction between Jewish, Christian and pagan neighbours in the Late Roman Empire, see Leonard Victor Rutgers, "Archaeological Evidence for the Interaction of Jews and Non-Jews in Late Antiquity," *American Journal of Archaeology* 96.1 (1992): 101–18.

Nevertheless, other advice contained in the *Letters* indicates that Christians were not always encouraged to develop connections with Jewish people in certain spheres of life. Barsanuphius tells a certain layperson not to accept any invitations or gifts which his Jewish or pagan acquaintances might send him during the season of their feast (letter 775). In the following letter, the same advisor again recommends that his petitioner politely refuses to participate in a specific non-Christian festival, reinforcing his advice with reference to the commands and traditions of the holy Fathers (letter 776).

This double-sided approach to Jewish-Christian relations in Gaza is also evident in descriptions of Christian-pagan contacts in Gaza. When a petitioner asks about buying his necessaries from pagans in the marketplace, John the Prophet permits him to "engage in business transactions with pagans, buying whatever he needed from merchants peddling their wares at pagan festivals"[53] (letter 777). However, he also notes that Christians are not allowed to take part in the theatrical events and pagan feasts of the secular inhabitants of Gaza that promoted the ancient gods (such as *Brumalia* and *Rosalia*).[54] This direct prohibition is manifestly encapsulated in letter 836: "it is not proper for Christians and pious laity such as you to prefer human pleasures, which are harmful to the soul, rather than divine worship".

These sources indicate that both Barsanuphius and John of Gaza counselled their Christian petitioners to keep their exchanges with Jewish and pagan neighbors to an economic level, while specifically advocating that they refrain from having any connection in terms of religious matters.[55] This advice relating to

---

53 Hevelone-Harper, *Disciples of the Desert*, 83.
54 See Ashkenazi, "Sophists and Priests in Late Antique Gaza," 206. For pagan festivals in late-antique Gaza, see Nicole Belayche, "Pagan Festivals in Fourth-Century Gaza," in *Christian Gaza in Late Antiquity*, ed. Bitton-Ashkelony and Kofsky (Leiden; Boston: Brill, 2004), 5–22.
55 Hevelone-Harper, *Disciples of the Desert*, 81.

limiting the interactions with non-Christians most likely arises from the imperial and ecclesiastical bans against paganism in the late Roman Empire.[56]

2.2.3 Lay Christians and piety

The *Letters* of the Gazan ascetics also include references to diverse forms of pious practices of lay Christians performed as part of their daily life. For example, a devout layman asks various questions relating to his personal religious life. His queries range from topics such as the role of stillness (ἡσυχία) to church vigils and veneration for the sacred relics or altars in the shrines of martyrs or local churches (letters 739–742). In terms of actual Christian practices, some lay Christians appear to demonstrate their religious enthusiasm and an understanding of the Christian teaching in the *Letters* by offering their wealth and possessions (such as food and clothing) to those in need (letters 252, 253, 324, 326, 595, 625 and 635).[57] Other lay Christians are noted as entertaining travelers or the needy poor (letters 620, 635, 636, 681, 682, 691, 727, 728, 729 and 784).[58]

It is also apparent from the *Letters* that some pious laymen in Gaza actually implemented monastic practices, although not always successfully. Letter 745 deals with a lay Christian who initially followed the teachings of the monastic Fathers, but as a result of the actions of the devil we are told, he later became more indifferent to such things. In letter 771 a lay Christian is hesitant to bathe like monastic members because he believes such bathing would

---

56 On banning paganism and persecution in the later Roman Empire, see, *CTh* 16. 10; Ramsay MacMullen, *Christianity and Paganism in the Fourth to Eighth Centuries* (New Haven; London: Yale University Press, 1997), 1–31. For the survival of paganism after official banning, see Cameron, *The Mediterranean World in Late Antiquity*, 72–73; Timothy E. Gregory, "The Survival of Paganism in Christian Greece: A Critical Essay," *The American Journal of Philology* 107.2 (1986): 229–42.
57 For more detail, see section 4.2.
58 For more detail, see section 5.2.

offend those who might have expected him to refuse a bath because of his piety. This is clearly a reference to the practices of the ascetics of the eastern Mediterranean world, among whom there was an avoidance of washing (*alousia*) in order to reject worldly luxury and pleasure. Through such avoidance they sought to obtain "grace and godliness" and "the spirit's triumph over the body".[59] With regard to the layman who asks advice on rejecting a bath, John of Gaza recommends that he bathe, noting that it "is not forbidden for a layperson, at least whenever necessary" (letter 771).

The devout habits of lay Christians evidenced in the correspondence between the Gazan holy men and their lay interlocutors are not unique to Christianity in late-antique Gaza. Indeed, they are reported in many other Christian sources from the late Roman Empire.[60] In particular, the homilies of John Chrysostom reveal various practices among his congregation: performing almsgiving and fasting; attending church services; using biblical passages or Christian symbols as amulets to protect against evil spirits; purification of bodies through the washing of hands and ritual bathing; and even the rejection of marital sex, even though it was legitimate, before prayer.[61] Primary evidence also shows veneration of saints and their relics, as well as a focus on pilgrimages to sacred places—the Holy Land, shrines of saints, monasteries and hermitages of ascetics.[62]

---

59 See Fikret Yegül, *Baths and Bathing in Classical Antiquity* (Cambridge, MA: MIT Press, 1995), 318.
60 See Derek Krueger, ed., *Byzantine Christianity* (Minneapolis: Fortress Press, 2010), 19-78.
61 Jaclyn Maxwell, "Lay Piety in the Sermons of John Chrysostom," in *Byzantine Christianity*, ed. Derek Krueger (Minneapolis: Fortress Press, 2010), 22-30.
62 On the veneration of saints and their relics, see Peter Brown, *The Cults of the Saints: Its Rise and Function in Latin Christianity* (Chicago: University of Chicago Press, 1981). On pilgrimage in Late Antiquity, see Brouria Bitton-Ashkelony, *Encountering the Sacred: The Debate on Christian Pilgrimage in Late Antiquity* (Berkeley: University of California Press, 2005); Mariel Dietz, *Wandering Monks, Virgins and Pilgrims: Ascetic Travel in the Mediterranean World, A.D. 300-800* (University Park, Penn: Pennsylvania State University Press, 2005).

Although the instances are somewhat rare in the *Letters*, we also find a reference to one pious practice that lay Christian women pursued in their lives. Letter 595 deals with the laywomen who used to approach the monastery of Seridos with gifts. This is specifically in the context of Aelianos, as a new abbot, who appears concerned about their visits. He sends a letter to John of Gaza, to which John replies that only women who have a special purpose—be it to bring a donation, to meet their brothers or perhaps out of longing for God's words—are permitted to enter into the monastic community (letter 595). This is in contrast to Euthymius and Sabas from Byzantine Palestine who did not permit women to enter their monastic community under any circumstances.[63] This exchange between Aelianos and John of Gaza, suggests that laywomen occasionally visited the Gazan monastery so as to hear the word of God or to entrust the community with their possessions.

Other sources show some female believers more actively involved in devotional practices beyond material support for the poor Christians in their communities. According to Rufus, Peter the Iberian's parents Bakurios and Bakurduktia decided to follow the monastic life and dedicated their material resources to help the poor, and their own time to fasting and prayer.[64] According to Alice-Mary Talbot, laywomen engaging in such practices continue to be evident among the upper-middle classes in later centuries.[65] It is reasonable therefore to assume that pious laymen and women in late-antique Gaza were actively involved in merciful activities and even monastic practices.

---

63 Hevelone-Harper, *Disciples of the Desert*, 131.
64 John Rufus, *The Life of Peter the Iberian* in *John Rufus: The Lives of Peter the Iberian, Theodosius of Jerusalem, and the Monk Romanus*, intro. and trans. Cornelia Horn and Robert Phenix Jr (Leiden; Boston: Brill, 2008), 11–12. See Sebastian Brock and Susan Ashbrook Harvey, *Holy Women of the Syrian Orient* (Berkeley: University of California Press, 1987).
65 Alice-Mary Talbot, "The Devotional Life of Laywomen," in *Byzantine Christianity*, ed. Derek Krueger (Minneapolis: Fortress Press, 2010), 201–20.

Other letters indicate that some lay believers in Gaza chose to express their fervor and piety in intellectual ways. They sought to defend religious orthodoxy against those who attacked or distorted their faith. One example we have is of an anonymous layperson who perceived certain insults directed towards his orthodox faith, and became angry. He asks the Other Old Man how to respond to such insults. In reply, John tells his questioner to treat the persons with gentleness and patience, rather than to dispute with them (letter 658). Another letter gives the story of a man who wants to join a theological discussion among spiritual fathers and therefore asks whether he can talk over such matters with them (letter 694). In a subsequent letter, the same interlocutor also asks whether or not it is good to support an orthodox brother who is in dispute with a heretic (letter 695). Such enthusiasm for the defense of faith in terms of intellectual argument reflects a level of academic interest within the city as well as indicating the presence of conflicts with heretics in late-antique Gaza.

In addition to these, it is clear that certain lay believers had contact with Nestorians and Origenists who had been anathematized as a heretic. Letters 732 and 733 describe a layman who is worried about a friend who follows the heresy of Nestorius. John exhorts the man to support his friend to a degree that it is not harmful to his own soul, and to entrust the matter to God when it goes beyond his own limitations (letter 732). In the following letter, John counsels the same interlocutor to recommend to his heretical friend that he learn the orthodox faith. If the friend is willing to be open to the faith, the man should send him to the holy Fathers who would be capable of managing such a person. However, if the friend resists after several attempts at reform John suggests the man should break off the relationship (letter 733).

The *Letters* also mentions that the second Origenist contro-versy—the doctrine of pre-existence of souls and a final restoration—was a problem for monks in Gaza in the sixth century.[66] According to the letter 600, there were some Origenist works held in the monastery of Seridos. These include such as "the books of Origen and Didymus, as well as the *Gnostic Chapters* of Evagrius and the writings of his disciples" referring to the pre-existence of human souls and to *apokatastasis*. Moreover, another letter provides evidence of presence of some Origenist monks resident in the Gazan monastery who were regarded as good spiritual fathers (letter 603). With regard to the Origenists and their works in Gaza, Barsanuphius sternly warns their disciples to keep away from them, by condemning the doctrines of Origen and his disciples as follows: "These are the doctrines of the Greeks; they are the vain talk of people who claim to be something. Such words belong to idle people and are created through deceit" (letter 600). Likewise, he urges his interlocutor to avoid such doctrines: "Brother, if you want to be saved, do not preoccupy yourself with these things. For I bear witness before God that you have fallen into a pit of the devil and into ultimate death. Therefore, avoid these things and follow in the footstep of the fathers" (letter 600).

Then where did the Origenist monks came into Gaza? Hevelone-Harper suggests the possibility that the heretics origi-

---

66 Daniël Hombergen says that the Origenist controversy "is usually divided into two main phases: the first controversy at the end of fourth century and the second in the mid-sixth century". See Daniël Hombergen, "Barsanuphius and John of Gaza and the Origenist Controversy," in *Christian Gaza in Late Antiquity*, ed. Brouria Bitton-Ashkelony and Aryeh Kofsky (Leiden: Brill, 2004), 173. For more detail on the second Origenist controversy, see Hevelone-Harper, *Disciples of the Desert*, 23–25; Lorenzo Perrone, "Palestinian Monasticism, the Bible, and Theology in the Wake of the Second Origenist Controversy," in *The Sabaite Heritage in the Orthodox Church from the Fifth Century to the Present*, ed. Joseph Patrich (Leuven: Peeters, 2002), 245–59; Joseph Patrich, *Sabas, Leader of Palestinian Monasticism: A Comparative Study in Eastern Monasticism, Fourth to Seventh* (Washington, DC: Dumbarton Oaks Research Library and Collection Centuries, 1995), 331–48. See also Elizabeth A. Clark, *The Origenist Controversy: The Cultural Construction of an Early Christian Debate* (Princeton: Princeton University Press, 1992).

nated from the Judean monasticism, on the basis of the work of Cyril of Scythopolis. According to Cyril, Agapetus, a new abbot of the New Lavra, discovered "four Origenist monks" in his community around 514. He expelled them from the Lavra, and they were deported to Eleutheropolis and Ascalon, not too far from the region of Gaza.[67] Here she thinks that "some monks near Gaza heard of the teachings of Origen from the monks" expelled from the Judean monasticism.[68] However, while this is possible, we do not have any concrete evidence to prove the suggestion. Another possible source for Origenism in sixth-century Gaza, Champion claims, is the Origenist monks who lived in and near Caesarea. According to him, there were already numerous Origenists in Caesarea in the mid-fifth century,[69] and some of them may have moved down to Gaza and neighboring areas. Gaza's intellectual and geographical proximity to Caesarea supports this argument.[70]

As indicated above, the *Letters* suggest that Gazan Christians came into conflict with Nestorians and Origenists in the sixth century albeit intermittently. Interestingly, the advice of both John of Gaza and Barsanuphius with regard to interaction with the heresies is fairly passive and indirect. They suggest their readers avoid such heresies and instead focus on the correct teachings. In this regard their advice is not significantly different from that of the Desert Fathers. For example, when some Arians visited Abba Sisoes and began to criticize the orthodox faith, the Abba merely suggests his disciple take "the book of Saint Athanasius and read it" instead of conducting an argument or engaging in

---

67 See Patrich, *Sabas, Leader of Palestinian Monasticism*, 333; Hevelone-Harper, *Disciples of the Desert*, 24.
68 Hevelone-Harper, *Disciples of the Desert*, 24.
69 Patrich, *Sabas, Leader of Palestinian Monasticism*, 332.
70 For the connection between Gaza and Caesarea, see Champion, *Explaining the Cosmos*, 37.

the controversy.[71] Another Father, Abba Poemen, likewise has a similar response to heretics denouncing the archbishops of Alexandria. He asks his follower to "give them something to eat and send them away in peace".[72] It is tempting to suggest that such a stance by the Gazan fathers with regard to theological controversy arises not only from their concern that the conflict might distract them from their spiritual progress, but also that they wished to maintain the unity of their monastic community.

2.3 Monks in late-antique Gaza

2.3.1 Becoming a monk

Although little is known about how many pious laymen in Late Antiquity wanted to become monks, it is clear that that not all applicants were successful in obtaining a monastic habit, perhaps in certain cases because of ecclesiastical and imperial strictures. For example, according to the fourth canon of the Council of Chalcedon (AD 451), slaves were not allowed to become monks without permission of their masters.[73] One year after this council, Valentinian III ordered that no serf, slave, guild, member of city councils, or tax collector was permitted to become a cleric or monk.[74] This imperial policy, according to Charles Frazee, seems to arise from the Emperor's belief that the socio-economic services of those people were crucial to the provinces of the later Roman Empire.[75] The regulation was then slightly modified in the decree of Justinian, issued in 535: slaves and even criminals could be accepted into monasteries if they demonstrated that

---

71   Sisoes, *Sayings of the Desert Fathers*, 182.
72   Poemen, *Sayings of the Desert Fathers*, 150.
73   *The Acts of the Council of Chalcedon*, vol. 3, trans. Richard Price and Michael Gaddis, Translated Texts for Historians Volume 45 (Liverpool: Liverpool Press, 2005), 95–96.
74   *NVal* 35.3.
75   Charles A. Frazee, "Late Roman and Byzantine Legislation on the Monastic Life from the Fourth to the Eighth Centuries," *Church History* 51.3 (1982): 269.

they were suitable for monastic life during their three-year noviciate.[76] In addition, the councillors of cities, called *curiales*, were allowed to join monasteries "only if they had spent fifteen years in a monastery first, and were willing to surrender a substantial part of their estate".[77] Although slaves, criminal and civic officials were officially given a chance to become monks under the modified policy, not many from those groups appear to have taken up monastic habits.

Monastic postulants should be required to not only relinquish their biological families, but also to renounce their own property to the coenobium, after setting aside sufficient money for their family members.[78] The *Precepts* of Pachomius note that the candidates are required to relinquish their biological parents as well as their property and belongings.[79] Furthermore, the monastic rules of Shenoute offer evidence for the abdication of personal property ownership, and the sources record that whoever becomes a monk shall, first of all, renounce their own possessions when they are at the gatehouse and "sign over every article that they have brought, in accordance with the ordinances

---

76 Frazee, "Late Roman and Byzantine Legislation on the Monastic Life from the Fourth to the Eighth Centuries," 272.
77 Cameron, *The Mediterranean World in Late Antiquity*, 91.
78 See Rosa Maria Parrinello, "The Justinianean Legislation regarding wives of the monks and its context: The *Letters* of Barsanuphius and John of Gaza," in *Männlich und weiblich schuf Er sie: Studien zur Genderkonstruktion und zum Eherecht in den Mittelmeerreligionen*, ed. Christian Bourdignon, Matthias Morgenstern and Christiane Tietz (Göttingen: Vandenhoeck & Ruprecht, 2011), 196–97. Avshalom Laniado, "Early Byzantine State and the Christian Ideal of Voluntary Poverty," in *Charity and Giving in Monotheistic Religion*, ed. Miriam Frenkel and Yaacov Lev (Berlin: Walter de Gruyter, 2009), 15; Frazee, "Late Roman and Byzantine Legislation on the Monastic Life from the Fourth to the Eighth Centuries," 275–76.
79 Pachomius, *Precepts*, 49, in *Pachomian Koinonia*, vol. 2 (Kalamazoo, Cistercian Publications Inc. 1981), 152–53. See also James Goehring, *Ascetics, Society and the Desert: Studies in Early Egyptian Monasticism* (Harrisburg: Trinity Press International, 1999), 61–62.

of our fathers".[80] In addition to the monastic regulations in Egypt, the *Institutes* of John Cassian, who laid the foundation for western monasticism, also refers to the idea that when monastic candidates have been received in a coenobium, they are asked to relinquish all of their former possessions.[81]

Such a practice is likewise identified with reference to monastic candidates in the monastery of Seridos. In the *Letters,* a man called Dorotheos of Gaza reveals his desire to join the monastic life (letters 252–254). His correspondence with both John of Gaza and Barsanuphius outlines his concerns about becoming a monk of the Gazan coenobium: he asks how can he distribute his possessions and follow Jesus. Similarly, the letters of the wealthy Christian named Aelianos (letters 571–572), show that the abandoning of individual property and family connections was necessary in order to enter a monastery in sixth-century Gaza.

Once monastic candidates were accepted into monastic communities, they were required to stay in the monasteries as lay persons for a certain period of time. According to a regulation of Justinian, it is during this period of their novitiate that monastic abbots examined the prospective monks' motives and backgrounds: whether they were free men or slaves, and whether they were those who sought to be exempt from civil obligations. After this process was completed, the candidates would then start to learn the monastic rules, while still remaining as lay persons.[82]

The length of time and the individual program of probation were variable according to the differing situations of particular monasteries. Although the training period in a Syrian coenobium lasted three years, other monasteries in the Mediterranean East

---

80 Shenoute, *The Canons of Our Fathers:* Monastic Rules of Shenoute, trans. Bentley Layton (Oxford: Oxford University Press, 2014), 243.
81 John Cassian, *The Institutes,* annot. and trans. Boniface Ramsey (New York; Newman Press, 2000), 4.3.5.
82 *The Novel of Justinian,* 5.2. See Patrich, *Sabas, Leader of Palestinian Monasticism,* 260.

required somewhat shorter periods. For example, Basil notes that the length of training depends on the religious background and state of the novice, while Pachomian monasticism accepted a prospective monk only after a period of time.[83] With regard to Palestinian monasticism in general, while some prospective monks were accepted into monasteries after a period similar to Pachomian monasticism, others immediately received the monastic habit directly from their abbot.[84] According to an anecdote from the *Pratum Spirituale* of John Moschos, one day an anonymous robber visited Abba Zosimus and asked to be allowed into the Lavra of Abba Firminos. The abbot Zosimus gave the robber a monastic habit immediately after providing some instruction. A few days later, he sent the new monk off to the monastery of Dorotheos of Gaza. The novice learnt the whole Psalter and monastic rules for nine years, before returning to the Lavra of Abba Firminos.[85]

There were also differences in the way in which the monastic candidates were dressed. Some novices, as suggested in the story of Abbot Zosimus, learnt monastic rules and the Bible after wearing the monastic habit *schema*, while others followed the Justinian regulation which ordered monastic postulants to wear the *schema* only after learning the basic practices of the monastery over a three-year period.

2.3.2 Monks and education

Monasteries in the East were known to provide their monks with at least a primary education to enable them to read and write the Psalms and some parts of the New Testament, although some

---

83 Patrich, *Sabas, Leader of Palestinian Monasticism*, 259–60.
84 Hirschfeld, *The Judean Desert Monasteries in the Byzantine Period*, 72; Patrich, *Sabas, Leader of Palestinian Monasticism*, 262.
85 Moschos, *The Pratum Spirituale*, 166.

monks still remained illiterate.[86] This is because monks were expected to learn the Bible and to make a lifelong study of it through memorising, reading and writing.[87] According to the regulations of Pachomian monasticism:

> Whoever enters the monastery uninstructed shall be taught first what he must observe; and when, so taught, he has consented to it all, they shall give him twenty Psalms or two of the Apostle's epistles, or some other part of the Scripture. And if he is illiterate, he shall go at the first, third, and sixth hours to someone who can teach and has been appointed for him. He shall stand before him and learn very studiously with all gratitude... There shall be no one whatever in the monastery who does not learn to read and does not memorize something of the Scriptures. [One should learn by heart] at least the New Testament and the Psalter.[88]

Because Scripture was considered as a necessary prerequisite as well as a foundation of spirituality and central to the life of monks in coenobitic monasteries, Barsanuphius encourages his monastic interlocutor to strive to study the Psalter and learn the Psalms by heart (letter 215). He further exhorts his reader that to learn Scripture speedily is regarded as a great gift of God (letter 402).

However, it is significant to note that while the *Letters* recommend the reading and studying of Scripture, they do not recommend that individuals engage in interpreting Scripture. Instead, they suggest the pursuit of monastic virtues such as silence and contemplation. For example, when John is approached by an anonymous interlocutor who asks whether he join the

---

86 See Henry I. Marrou, *A History of Education in Antiquity*, trans. George Lamb (London: Sheed and Ward, 1956), 330–33.
87 See Lorenzo Perrone, "Scripture for a Life of Perfection. The Bible in Late Antique Monasticism: The Case of Palestine," in *The Reception and Interpretation of the Bible in Late Antiquity*, ed. Lorenzo DiTommaso and Lucian Turcescu (Leiden: Brill, 2008), 393–417.
88 Pachomius, *The Rules of Saint Pachomius* 139–40 in *Pachomian Koinonia*, vol. 2 (Kalamazoo: Cistercian Publications, 1981), 166.

discussion about the Scriptures, he encourages his questioner to keep silence rather than discussing issues related to the Bible (letter 697). Both John of Gaza and Barsanuphius dissuade their readers from teaching Scripture, judging that this "may be of no benefit" to them or "of less benefit than something else".[89] In letter 469, a monk asks whether he should tell good stories from the Bible or *Lives of the Desert Fathers*. In reply he is told that, because each individual person has a different measure for hearing and speaking in terms of such writings, some can successfully tell stories, while others cannot. As a result, the advisor recommends silence which "is always good and admirable above all else" (letter 469). The *Vie De Saint Dosithée*[90] records that when Dositheos entered into the monastery of Abba Seridos, the abbot entrusted him to Dorotheos. When Dorotheos later discovered that the new monk had learnt Scripture to meet his own intellectual curiosity, he sought to limit his reading of Scripture, noting that such learning was not beneficial to spiritual health. From the evidence above, it is obvious that although the Gazan ascetics believed study of Scripture to be important for monks, they did not allow their monastic followers to do anything which may cause spiritual damage. In this, their desire to nurture their disciples is clearly evident.

Monks in the coenobium of Seridos were also influenced by the *Apophthegmata Patrum*, presumably compiled in the southern district of Judea or in the Gazan area in the first-half of the sixth

---

89 Alexis Torrance, "Barsanuphius, John, and Dorotheous on Scripture: Voice from the Desert in Sixth-Century Gaza," in *What Is the Bible: The Patristic Doctrine of Scripture*, ed. Matthew Baker and Mark Mourachlan (Minneapolis: Fortress Press, 2016), 71–72.
90 Dorotheos, *Vie De Saint Dosithée*, 12 in *Dorothée de Gaza: Oeuvres spirituelles*, SC 92, ed. and trans. Lucien Regnault and J. de Preville (Paris: Editions du Cerf, 1963), 143; Perrone, "Scripture for a Life of Perfection," 400–1.

century.[91] Gazan anchorites certainly appear to have been familiar with the *Sayings of the Desert Fathers*. They explicitly or implicitly use numerous phrases and thoughts of the Desert Fathers as a basis for spiritual advice when consulting with monastic interlocutors.[92] Indeed, Barsanuphius recommends his disciples read and follow these works in order to acquire the monastic virtues of humility and perfect prayer (letters 143, 150, 469 and 600).

In addition to both Scripture and the *Apophthegmata Patrum*, Seridos' monks also appear to have, privately or collectively, had other more diverse books in their possession, because of geographical position of Gaza. These books include: several medical books (letter 327); theological books (letter 547); a commentary by John Chrysostom on the book of Matthew (letter 464); and some works of the Cappadocian fathers including the *Ascetical Works* of St. Basil (letters 318, 319 and 604), as well as those of Origen, Didymus the Blind and Evagrius of Pontus (letter 600). The existence of these different books not only reflects the spiritual and intellectual needs and characteristics of monks in the community of Seridos, but also indicates that sixth-century Gazan monasticism, like the rhetorical school of Gaza, was open to influences from outside monastic culture. These influences came from such different locations as Egypt, Antioch and Minor Asia.

2.3.3 Monks and the secular world

The walls surrounding a monastery or an individual cell secluded monks and other ascetics from people in the secular world, although the two groups often encountered and cooperated with

---

91 Rubenson, "The Egyptian Relation of Early Palestinian Monasticism," 35–46; John Chryssavgis, "The Road from Egypt to Palestine: The Sayings of the Desert Father: Destination and Destiny," *Aram Periodical* 15 (2003): 97–108.
92 See Chryssavgis, introduction to *Barsanuphius and John: Questions and Responses*, 11; Hevelone-Harper, *Disciples of the Desert*, 17.

each other according to mutual need. From a number of anecdotes in the *Sayings of the Desert Fathers*, we know that despite the fact that the Desert Fathers urged their followers to stay in their cells or shelters, they actually left their homes and thus had encounters with the secular world in different contexts: for example, monks and ascetics were known to go on pilgrimages to holy places; to sometimes visit to other monks or their own relatives; to go abroad on business trips; to engage in farming activities such as the gathering of a crop; and even to migrate.[93]

In contrast to those exhorted to stay at home, some Desert Fathers and monks in Egypt instead suggested the benefits of a wandering lifestyle. This was an attempt to acquire certain ascetic virtues such as *xeniteia* (ξενιτεία)[94] or *amerimnia* (ἀμεριμνία).[95] In other cases they were simply following the precedents of their forebears, including exemplars such as Antony the Great.[96] This mendicant lifestyle naturally brought them into interaction with those in the secular world. Indeed, some lay Christians invited spiritual fathers into their homes. Peter the Iberian and his friends often enjoyed the hospitality of devout ordinary Christians during their various journeys, such as: the magistrate of Oxyrhynchus Moses;[97] Elijah who loved Christ and saints as well as the poor and the stranger;[98] and the magistrate of Arca (or Arka) Maximus.[99] The previous discussion therefore shows that

---

93 Regnault Lucien, *La vie quotidienne des Pères du désert en Egypte au IVe siècle* (Paris: Hachette, 1990), 165-75.
94 The Greek word ξενιτεία means "wandering," "exile" or "travel in a foreign land," see Geoffrey W. H. Lampe, *A Patristic Greek Lexicon* (Oxford: Clarendon Press, 1961), 931-32, s.v. ξενιτεία.
95 The Greek word ἀμεριμνία means "freedom of care and anxiety," see Lampe, *A Patristic Greek Lexicon*, 86, s.v. ἀμεριμνία.
96 Daniel Caner, *Wandering, Begging Monks: Spiritual Authority and the Promotion of Monasticism in Late Antiquity* (Berkeley: University of California Press, 2002), 19-49.
97 John Rufus, *The Life of Peter the Iberian*, 86.
98 John Rufus, *The Life of Peter the Iberian*, 131.
99 John Rufus, *The Life of Peter the Iberian*, 141.

the relationship between monks and lay believers in the early Byzantine world was "not an absolute dichotomy, but rather a symbiosis" as described by Nicholas Marinides.[100]

Similarly, monks in late-antique Palestine and Gaza also maintained close links with their surrounding societies.[101] The *Letters* refer to monks encountering lay Christians in the monastery of Seridos in a variety of contexts. The laity are said to visit for the purpose of medical treatment (letters 313 and 314), to hear the word of God and even to meet their relatives (letter 595). The monastic members themselves are reported as meeting people outside the coenobium when they worship together in local churches (letter 712). They are also described as having meals together (letters 715 and 716).[102] Such encounters with the laity as noted in the *Letters* are likely not to be irrelevant in terms of the geographical proximity of the monastery of Seridos to its neighboring cities such as Tabatha (about 1 km) and Gaza (about 12 km).[103] Its geographical location is also significantly different from many other monasteries in Palestine, which were primarily settled in desert areas rather than in the vicinity of both large cities and small towns.[104] This proximity, undoubtedly, made it easier for monks to access the secular world and to be involved in the social and economic affairs of ordinary people in the city.[105]

Nevertheless, social interaction with laymen could be considered to be a double-edged sword for the monks. On the one hand, these encounters might help to meet monks' private or commu-

---

100 Nicholas Marinides, "Lay Piety in Byzantium, ca.600–730" (PhD diss., Princeton University, 2014), 2.
101 Doron Bar, "Rural Monasticism as a Key Element in the Christianization of Byzantine Palestine," *Harvard Theological Review* 98.1 (2005): 49–65; Leah Di Segni, "Monastery, City and Village in Byzantine Gaza," *Proche-Orient Chrétien* 55 (2005): 24–51.
102 See Hevelone-Harper, *Disciples of the Desert*, 96–98.
103 The distance between Tabatha and Gaza is seven miles. See section 3.1.1.
104 Hirschfeld, *The Judean Desert Monasteries in the Byzantine Period*, 3.
105 See Di Segni, "Monastery, City and Village in Byzantine Gaza," 33–49; Hirschfeld, "The Monasticism of Gaza," 61–88.

nity needs, but on the other hand they could be dangerous for monastics themselves in several ways. For instance, the correspondence between John of Gaza and Dorotheos of Gaza who worked as a monastic physician in the monastery of Seridos (letters 313 and 314) shows that Dorotheos felt uneasy about contact with people outside the monastery and hesitates to consult his patients, saying that such frequent contact disturbs him when he is trying to engage in ascetic practices such as silence. John advises Dorotheos to persevere in terms of encounter with the outsiders, noting that the medical work provides opportunities to demonstrate mercy towards others. Another monk's concern about the same issue is evident in the letter of an anonymous monk. This man wants to become friends with laypeople but is not sure that attempting such friendships is a good thing for him (letter 743). So he asks his spiritual father for advice, and John replies in the negative. John tells him that the making of a friendship outside the monastery will only bring affliction and inconvenience. However, if he wishes in spite of such difficulties, John simultaneously allows the monk to choose to keep company with others.

Gifts from laypeople were also a potential source of trouble for monks and ascetics and were seen by some to exert a bad influence on the monastic life. Marinides highlights three main areas of concern: firstly, the economic help potentially makes it easier for monks to live idle lives; secondly, the receipt of gifts may encourage greed and jealousy on the part of outsiders; finally, property or possessions which monks received from their followers may distract them from their holy duty.[106] However, it would be mistaken to assume that ascetic leaders entirely forbade monastics from receiving goods as gifts. On the contrary, they allowed their monastic followers to accept them as much as was necessary to maintain their religious life. In his work *The*

---

106 Marinides, "Lay Piety in Byzantium, ca. 600-730," 233-35.

Foundations of the Monastic Life, addressed primarily to monks in the early stages of their religious journey,[107] Evagrius of Pontus states explicitly:

> If you need food or clothing, do not be ashamed of accepting what another brings you, for this is a form of pride. But if you possess a surplus of these things, give to one who needs them. It is in this way that God wants his children to administer their property among themselves.[108]

Here the Egyptian monk allows his ascetic audience to take their necessities as needed, making sure to only take what is required and to spread the charity to others in need. In contrast, Augustine of Hippo is a little more strict and only permits his sick monks to receive a special diet and clothes from laypeople outside the monastic community.[109]

As has been demonstrated above, there were points of contact between monastics and those who lived in the secular world. However, there is still one central issue with regard to the relationship between monastic and lay Christians as raised in the *Letters* which has yet to be discussed, namely, the overarching perspective of both John of Gaza and Barsanuphius on the fundamental differences between lay and monastic Christians. From the very early years of the Church there existed a double-class system. According to the *Proof of the Gospel* of Eusebius,

> Two ways of life were thus given by the law of Christ to His Church. The one is above nature, and beyond common human living; it admits not marriage, child-bearing, property nor the possession of wealth, but wholly and permanently seperates from the common customary life of

---

107 See Robert Sinkewicz, introduction to *The Foundations of the Monastic Life: A Presentation of the Practice of Stillness* in *Evagrius of Pontus: The Greek Ascetic Corpus* (Oxford: Oxford University Press, 2006), 1.
108 Evagrius, *The Foundations of the Monastic Life: A Presentation of the Practice of Stillness*, 4.
109 For further discussion on this topic, see section 6.4.

mankind... Such then is the perfect form of the Christian life. And the other more humble, more human, permits men to join in pure nuptials and to produce children, to undertake government, to give orders to soldiers fighting for right; it allows them to have minds for farming, for trade, and the other more secular interests as well as for religion... And a kind of secondary grade of piety is attributed to them.[110]

Norman Baynes further elucidates the double standard apparent in this passage, noting the presence of a "double ethic which is of primary significance in East Roman life—the two standards: one for the ordinary Christian living in his life in the work-a-day world and the other standard for those who were haunted by the words of Christ" such as, in second century, confessors and martyrs.[111]

Such a double-standard system lasts well into late-antique ecclesiastical and ascetic leaders. To put it more concretely, they continue to support the existence of the double-class system, even while treating their secular disciples as almost equal to their religious counterparts. For example, while John Chrysostom has a tendency to extol the similarities between the monastic and lay life, he nevertheless draws a distinction between the two groups, with regard to celibacy representing a higher standard of faith.[112] A similar phenomenon is also found in the *Apophthegmata Patrum*. Although there are some references in the *Apophthegmata* in which the life of an ordinary Christian in the secular world is explicitly contrasted to the more worthy life of a reli-

---

110 Eusebius of Caesarea, *The Proof of the Gospel*, trans. W. J. Ferrar (London: S.P.C.K, 1920), I.8.29.
111 Norman Baynes, "The Thought-World of East Rome," in *Byzantine Studies and Other Essays* (1955; repr., Westport, CN: Greenwood Press, 1974), 26–27.
112 Jaclyn Maxwell, *Christianization and Communication in Late Antiquity: John Chrysostom and His Congregation in Antioch* (Cambridge: Cambridge University Press, 2006), 131.

gious,[113] a great many anecdotes suggest that the life of a pious lay Christian did not essentially differ from that of a monk in important aspects.[114] According to Graham Gould, lay people were also encouraged by the Desert Fathers to "cultivate: not only charity, hospitality, and chastity, but humility, detachment, freedom from anger, and the possession of a 'good will' in whatever state of life, lay or secular, married or unmarried".[115]

Such an attitude towards the relationship between lay believers and monks lasts to Gazan Christianity in the sixth century. As discussed in section 2.2.3 above, many devout laypeople represented in the *Letters* demonstrate diverse forms of pious practices and even monastic practices such as *alousia* and *hesychia*. Barsanuphius and John generally allow them to follow such ascetic habits, although they do not do *alousia*. For this reason, Hevelone-Harper asserts that some letters of the Gazan Old Men addressed to their lay disciples "could easily be mistaken for those written to monks" and that "Barsanuphius and John's message to lay Christian did not differ substantially from that given to monks, although the letters do show an appropriate sensitivity to lay people's concerns and obligations".[116]

Despite this, they clearly distinguish lay Christians from monastics, reinforcing the concept that these people are lay people and not religious. In one letter, a pious man asks John whether he could stand and sing the *Trisagion* (τὸ τρισάγιον) when he is with others in a church. John counsels him to act according to those who are present with him at the time. If he is with spiritual fathers or laypeople superior to himself, he should have a care not to offend them by joining in. When he is with his lay brothers

---

113 Graham Gould, "Lay Christians, Bishops and Clergy in the *Apophthegmata Patrum*," *Studia Patristica* 25 (1993): 398.
114 Gould, "Lay Christians, Bishops and Clergy in the *Apophthegmata Patrum*," 399–400.
115 Gould, "Lay Christians, Bishops and Clergy in the *Apophthegmata Patrum*," 399.
116 Hevelone-Harper, *Disciples of the Desert*, 80–81.

and sisters, he should stand up and sing the hymn loudly to encourage the rest of congregation to greater piety (letter 712). This distinction between laity and religious is further reinforced in a letter from another layman who asks whether he should bless the food (letter 716), after being asked by a spiritual father. He is advised to refuse the request, and to reply: "I am neither a clergyman, nor do I have the monastic habit, but I am merely a sinful layman; therefore, this is beyond me".

It is therefore apparent that while Barsanuphius and John encouraged lay Christians to pursue devout practices in their lives, they simultaneously distinguished their secular believers from their monastic followers. Such emphasis of the Gazan holy men on the distinction between the classes is most probably relevant to their intention to clarify the indistinct boundary between monks and lay Christians in sixth-century Gaza and especially Tabatha.[117]

2.4 A bishop in late-antique Gaza

2.4.1 The powers and role of a bishop

In the later Roman world, as the Church continued to grow, so bishops too gained more and more authority. In the early Church, a Christian bishop as a head of a local group was in charge of not only the ministry of the Word and the liturgy, but also of the pastoral care for his community.[118] These functions, as they were defined in the pre-Constantinian era, are attested in

---

117 For the flexible boundary between monks and lay Christians in sixth-century Gaza, See Hevelone-Harper, *Disciples of the Desert*, 100–1.
118 See Henry Chadwick, "The Role of the Christian Bishop in Ancient Society," in *The Role of the Christian Bishop in Ancient Society: Protocol of the 35th Colloquy, 25 February 1979*, ed. H. C. Hobbs and W. Wuellner (Berkeley: The Center for Hermeneutical Studies in Hellenistic and Modern Culture, 1980), 1–14.

the *Didascalia Apostolorum*, compiled in the third century.[119]

> He [a bishop] is a servant of the word and meditator, but to you a teacher, and your father after God, who has begotten you through the water. This is your chief and your leader and he is a mighty king to you. He guides in the place of the Almighty. But let him be honoured by you as God (is), because the bishop sits for you in the place of God Almighty.[120]

In his outline of the various roles of episcopal authority, the anonymous author of this third-century work then immediately draws our attention to a particular justification of a church leader as a redistributor in terms of offerings. The *Didascalia Apostolorum* encourages its readers to present offerings to their local bishops, either directly or indirectly because the bishops are "well acquainted with those who are afflicted and dispenses and give to each one as it is right for him".[121] Here the bishop is clearly not only the head of a local church, but also the patron of the destitute in his individual district.[122]

After the conversion of Constantine the Great, the power and influence of episcopal leaders grew. Specifically, the power of the bishops increased as a direct result of the diverse privileges which Constantine and his successors granted them. The manifestations of this power is exemplied in the growth in the number and power of episcopal courts (*audientia episcopalis*), the exemption for bishops from compulsory public duties and taxation, the direct gift of imperial subsidies, and the granting of the right to

---

119 For a discussion on the date of *Didascalia Apostolorum*, see R. Hugh Connolly, *Didascalia Apostolorum: The Syriac Version Translated and Accompanied by the Verona Latin Fragments* (Eugene, Oregon: Wipf & Stock, 2009), cv–cix.
120 *Didascalia Apostolorum in Syriac*, IX, trans. Arthur Vööbus CSCO 402 (Louvain: Secrétariat du Corpus (SCO), 1979), 100. For more detail on the dating of the documentation, see introduction to *Didascalia Apostolorum in Syriac*, IX, 23–32.
121 *Didascalia Apostolorum in Syriac*, IX.
122 Brown, *Poverty and Leadership in the Later Roman Empire*, 24–26.

appoint or depose their own church officials.¹²³ While the appointment and deposition of clergy was a traditional power the bishop already theoretically held, the other new and special privileges are significant.

The *audientia episcopalis* gave bishops the right to deal with civil suits and religious matters brought by inhabitants, either lay or clerical, within their own parish.¹²⁴ As part of this court system the local bishop was able to contact and deal with both insiders and outsiders to his Christian community, thereby extending his influence beyond his own local area.¹²⁵

The second and third privileges of taxation exemptions and direct economic support for the Church through imperial subsidies enabled ecclesiastics to accumulate wealth and control material resources. Christian emperors from Constantine onwards not only offered annual subsidies of food to Churches in order to help lower clergymen, widows and the poor,¹²⁶ but also decreed that bishops and their staff were exempted from taxation and public custom duties.¹²⁷ The economic benefits that flowed from both of these privileges contributed greatly to the fulfilment of "the Church's role as a carer for the poor and the sick: As a guardian of the 'poor', the bishop had wider and more comprehensive clientele than any traditional civic magnate".¹²⁸ Allen and Neil

---

123 Cameron, *The Mediterranean World in Late Antiquity*, 64; Jones, *The Later Roman Empire 284-602*, 89-91; J. H. W. G. Liebeschuetz, *Decline and Fall of the Roman City* (Oxford: Oxford University Press, 2001), 139-45; Brown, *Poverty and Leadership in the Later Roman Empire*, 67-73.
124 CTh 16.2.23. For more general information on episcopal courts in Late Antiquity, see John Lamoreaux, "Episcopal Courts in Late Antiquity," *Journal of Early Christian Studies* 3.2 (1995): 143-67; Pauline Allen and Bronwen Neil, *Crisis Management in Late Antiquity (410-590 CE): A Survey of the Evidence from Episcopal Letters* (Leiden: Brill, 2013), 175-79.
125 See Brown, *Poverty and Leadership in the Later Roman Empire*, 67-73.
126 Jones, *The Later Roman Empire 284-602*, 89-90.
127 CTh 16.2.2, 16.2.10, 16.2.11 and 16.2.14.
128 Liebeschuetz, *Decline and Fall of the Roman City*, 141. See also Brown, *Poverty and Leadership in the Later Roman Empire*, 72; Jay Bregman, *Synesius of Cyrene, Philosopher-Bishop* (Berkeley: University of California Press, 1982), 62-63.

also point out late-antique bishops as civil defenders revealed in episcopal correspondence,[129] showing that bishops played an important role in many diverse areas of life and society. They deal with issues ranging from theological controversies and ecclesiastical disputes to environmental disasters (earthquakes, epidemic diseases and famine) as well as socio-economic crises (population displacement, social abuses and the breakdown of structures of dependence).

The Roman Church also expected its bishops to bring its monks under episcopal control. In 451, the Council of Chalcedon clarified its policy on monastics. In particular, the fourth canon deals with it.

> Those who truly and sincerely enter on the solitary life are to be accorded due honour. But since some people use a cloak of monasticism to disrupt both the churches and public affairs, while they move around the cities indiscriminately and even try to set up monasteries for themselves, it is decreed that no one is to build or found a monastery or oratory anywhere contrary to the will of the bishop of the city. Those who practice monasticism in each city and territory are to be subject to the bishop, and are to embrace silence and devote themselves to fasting and prayer alone, persevering in the places where they renounced the world; they are not to cause annoyance in either ecclesiastical or secular affairs, or take part in them, leaving their own monasteries, unless indeed for some compelling need they be permitted to do so by the bishop of the city. No slave is to be accepted into a monastery as a monk contrary to the will of his master; we have decreed that the infringer of this our regulation is excommunicate, lest the name of God be brought into disrepute. The due care of the monasteries must be exercised by the bishop of the city.[130]

---

129 See Allen and Neil, *Crisis Management in Late Antiquity*.
130 *The Acts of the Council of Chalcedon*, vol. 3, 95–96.

It is seen that the canon gave bishops the episcopal authority over monks and monastic movements, which were expanding their influence on their local societies. On the other hand, it prevented monastic members from becoming involved in either church or secular affairs, although the rule was, as we know, not often executed as originally outlined.[131]

Canon eight of the same council also highlights the need for episcopal control of monks as well as clergymen "of almshouses, monasteries and martyria" and laymen. All of these groups were encouraged to obey their bishops. The penalties for failure to obey were strict: monks and laymen are to be excommunicated, while clerics are "to be subjected to the penalties of the canons" (canon 8).[132] Interestingly, the canons also required all clerics to enrol in their own churches and to remain satisfied with those churches where they originally served (canons 10 and 20). Taken together, although the evidence is lacking on the extent to which these contemporary ecclesiastical regulations were successfully implemented in local cities and towns in the Mediterranean East, the bishops presumably sought to exert much more authority over monks and the lower clergy.

As discussed above, the figure of the Christian bishops had, over time, became more and more respected. Bishops came to hold a place as ecclesiastical and civil leaders in the cities of the later Roman Empire. Gaza is one such city. The orations of Choricius tell us how Marcian, as bishop of Gaza, established the churches of St. Sergius and St. Stephen for the sake of fellow-citizens during the reign of Justinian.[133] He also fulfilled his duties as a civil leader. As well as providing support for the rhetorical

---

131 For more details, see L'Huillier, *The Church of the Ancient Councils*, 221.
132 *The Acts of the Council of Chalcedon*, vol. 3, 97.
133 Choricius of Gaza, *The First Encomium to Marcian Bishop of Gaza*, in Fotios K. Litsas, *Choricius of Gaza: An Approach to His Work* (Ph.D. Diss., University of Chicago, 1980), 30; Choricius of Gaza, *The Second Encomium to Marcian Bishop of Gaza*, in Litsas, *Choricius of Gaza: An Approach to His Work*, 28.

school in Gaza, he engaged in many and diverse social welfare activities and philanthropy including (re)constructing baths, alms-houses and even walls around the city in Gaza. He also protected the citizens from being abused by soldiers.[134] Such civil activities, however, do not mean that his authority superseded that of other civil officials in Gaza, who were responsible for water supply to the city and the repair of collapsed churches.[135]

Unlike Choricius' depiction of the Gazan bishop as a civil patron, the *Letters* of the two Gazan elders depict a bishop as a spiritual father and teacher. In letter 844, we have a bishop of Gaza, probably Marcian, asking Barsanuphius what he should do about the many people in his church that had been possessed by spirits, and were now uttering prophecies and speaking in tongues among church members. Barsanuphius offers the following response:

> Your holiness should suffer excessively with those who are afflicted. For this is the task of a spiritual father and teacher. Moreover, a good shepherd cares for and is vigilant over his sheep. Therefore, train people to cooperate with the supplication and prayer offered for their sake; for in this way, they shall be able to achieve great things, according to the Lord's commandment (letter 844).

Elsewhere, John builds on this image when he refers to a priest as "a spiritual physician", who seeks to cure those who are suffering from spiritual and bodily illness (letter 211).

2.4.2 The clergy and monks

Christianity in the Holy Land rapidly spread during the late-antique period. While in 325 there were three episcopal sees

---

134 Choricius, *The First Encomium to Marcian Bishop of Gaza*, 8 and 78; Choricius, *The Second Encomium to Marcian Bishop of Gaza*, 24. For more detail, see Ashkenazi, "Sophists and Priests in Late Antique Gaza," 201; Hevelone-Harper, *Disciples of the Desert*, 112–13.
135 Glucker, *The City of Gaza in the Roman and Byzantine Periods*, 80–81.

in Palestine, by Justinian's time there were "about 50".[136] This impressive growth naturally required more and more church staff to assist bishops as heads of their local church. In 518 Apamea, the metropolitan Archdiocese of Syria, had at least 17 priests, 42 deacons, three sub-deacons and 15 readers at this time, while the metropolitan see of Ravenna claimed to have "ten priests, eleven deacons, five sub-deacons, twelve acolytes, twelve readers and four singers".[137] In addition, Justinian ordered that 60 priests, 100 deacons, 90 sub-deacons, 40 deaconesses, 100 readers, 25 singers and 100 doorkeepers be appointed as clergymen attached to the Great Church of Constantinople.[138]

Before the fifth century, clerics were traditionally recruited from lay Christians and sometimes even existing members of monastic communities.[139] In 398, however, the Theodosian Code commanded bishops to recruit their assistant staff only from those wearing a monastic habit:

> If perchance the bishops should suppose that they are in need of clergy, they will more properly ordain them from the number of monks. They shall not incur disfavour by holding those persons who are bound by public and private accounts but shall have those already approved.[140]

This imperial decree is presumably the result of an attempt to protect imperial finance, given the fact that contemporary Christian clerics were exempt from compulsory public duties due to their divine service.[141] However, this policy also delivered a supplemen-

---

136 Claudia Rapp, *Holy Bishops in Late Antiquity* (Berkeley: University of California Press, 2005), 173.
137 Jones, *The Later Roman Empire 284–602*, 911.
138 Jones, *The Later Roman Empire 284–602*, 911.
139 For monks joining the clergy prior to the fifth century, see Rapp, *Holy Bishops in Late Antiquity*, 147.
140 *CTh* 16.2.32. See also Andreas Sterk, *Renouncing the World Yet Leading the Church: The Monk-Bishops in Late Antiquity* (Cambridge: Harvard University Press, 2004), 316 n. 27.
141 Exemption of clergymen, see *CTh* 16.2.1; 16.2.2.

tal benefit, in that those who had already adopted the monastic spirit then made their debut in the institutional church. The fact that many of the fifth-century bishops actually came from monastic backgrounds reflects how widely this law was executed.[142]

The recruitment of monks into priesthood was also common in Egypt from the mid-fourth century onwards and in Palestine and Syria from the fifth century onwards.[143] Late-antique Gaza seems to be no exception to this. Letter 790 mentions a bishop who was previously a monk, while letter 813, interestingly, refers to a person's journey from layperson and academic to a priest in Jerusalem, passing through intermediate stages as a monk and a deacon. Letter 789 also deals with a village priest (χωρεπίσκοπος) who wanted to quit his episcopal position and withdraw to a monastic life. Such bishops and priests as represented in the *Letters*, who came from monastic backgrounds, were familiar with monastic practices, including the need to consult with spiritual directors. This naturally fostered close ties between the two Gazan anchorites and their clergy.

However, some pious laypersons, rather than monastics, were occasionally ordained to the priesthood or episcopacy in Gaza. For example, Marcian, bishop of Gaza, did not come from a monastic or ascetic background, but rather from an upper-class family from Gaza. His family had previously "produced a government official, a lawyer, a teacher, and two other bishops".[144] Another evidence is letter 812 where Marcian consults with John of Gaza. When the bishop wondered if he should ordain his capable and pious secretary, John encourages him to ordain his own secretary with the fear of God.

---

142 Sung-Hyun Nam, "The Poor Euergetes in the Hagiographic Literature," *Journal for the Promotion of Classical Studies* 25 (2009): 332 [Korean].
143 See Rapp, *Holy Bishops in Late Antiquity*, 147–48.
144 Hevelone-Harper, *Disciples of the Desert*, 112; Ashkenazi, "Sophists and Priests in Late Antique Gaza," 119.

2.5 Conclusion

During the late-antique period, the city of Gaza emerged as a crucial trade, traffic and academic hub in the Mediterranean East. This was in large part due to its geographical location as well as social stability and economic prosperity in the late Roman Empire. The socio-economic and cultural prosperity of Gaza was the driving force behind the influx of diverse outside cultures including Hellenistic philosophy, medical knowledge and monasticism. The open and dynamic atmosphere of Gaza can be seen to have an effect on lay and monastic Christians in the first half of the sixth century.

In addition, the geographical proximity of the Gaza's monastery to its surrounding cities and villages made it easier for monks to make contact with those outside the walls of the coenobium, to exert influence and to be influenced themselves. Moreover, lay believers and clergymen did not seem to hesitate to access monks and the monastery of Seridos. Clergymen, lay believers and monastics were closely linked together in late-antique Gaza.

In this chapter, a picture of both the monastic and secular world in late antique Gaza has so far been described. The next chapter will consider in detail the history of Gazan monasticism during the late antique period, the portrait of Barsanuphius and John of Gaza in the *Letters*, and, finally, a consideration of their compiled letters as an historical source.

Chapter 3
Gazan Monasticism and the *Letters*

This chapter traces the history of Gazan monasticism and introduces the *Letters* of Barsanuphius and John of Gaza to provide a historical framework for this study. In the first section, we examine what is known of the monastic lives of leading monks in late-antique Gaza (St. Hilarion, Abba Isaiah and Peter the Iberian), with special attention given to their eleemosynary activities. The second section deals with the identity of Barsanuphius and John, their position in sixth-century Gaza, and their collection of approximately 850 letters addressed to monks as well as lay Christians and clergymen. These letters indicate that Barsanuphius and John saw themselves, and were seen by others, as spiritual fathers and teachers whose role was to care for and guide their diverse interlocutors by means of letter-exchanges.

3.1 The history of Gazan monasticism before the sixth century

3.1.1 St. Hilarion

The history of monasticism in the region of Gaza begins with St. Hilarion, the well-known monk of Palestine in Late Antiquity, who founded the earliest Gazan monastery.[1] Jerome and Sozomen say that St. Hilarion, who was born into wealthy family in the village of Tabatha to the south of Gaza in 291/2, spent several years learning both rhetoric in Alexandria and the ascetic lifestyle under Antony the Great in the Egyptian desert.[2] Returning

---

1 Jerome, *Life of Hilarion*, 14; Hirschfeld, "The Monasticism of Gaza," 67–68.
2 Jerome, *Life of Hilarion*, 2–3; Sozomen, *Ecclesiastical History*, 3. 14.

to his hometown in 308 and finding that his parents had died in his absence, he distributed their property to his brothers and to the poor of the town in memory of Ananias and Sapphira from the Acts of the Apostles.[3] He lived in a tiny hut for about ten years before later establishing a small cell "five feet high" and "slightly wider than his body" in the wilderness "seven miles from Majuma, the port of Gaza".[4] St. Hilarion's reputation as a holy man eventually attracted the attention of the people of Gaza and its surrounding areas, who came to him begging for his advice and help.[5] As a result of this attention, in later life, St. Hilarion fled to Sicily, followed by Dalmatia, and finally settled in Cyprus, where he died in 371.[6] His body, buried in Cyprus, was later brought back by one of his followers, Hesychas. He was buried at the site of his former monastery in the region of Gaza before being later converted into a shrine dedicated to the holy Hilarion.[7]

In terms of St. Hilarion's hermitage mentioned above, Elter René and Hassoune Ayman argue that a monastery they discovered at Umm el-'Amr is identical to the hermitage. The first piece of evidence to support this theory is the location of the site. The ruined hermitage in Umm el-'Amr is seven miles away from Gaza, which accords exactly with the distance given by Jerome in his *The Life of Hilarion* where he states that St. Hilarion's monastery was "seven miles from Maiuma". The second piece of evidence is a Greek inscription found in the sanctuary building of the site.[8]

---

3   Jerome, *Life of Hilarion*, 3.
4   Jerome, *Life of Hilarion*, 3, 9; Sozomen, *Ecclesiastical History*, 3.14. John Binns thinks that Hilarion returned to his hometown in 308. See John Binns, *Ascetics and Ambassadors of Christ: The Monasteries of Palestine 314–631* (Oxford: Clarendon Press, 1996), 154.
5   Jerome, *Life of Hilarion*, 38.
6   Sozomen, *Ecclesiastical History*, 5.10.
7   Jerome, *The Life of Hilarion*, 46; Sozomen, *Ecclesiastical History*, 3.14. See Rufus, *The Life of Peter the Iberian*, 137.
8   Elter René and Hassoune Ayman, "Le monastère de Saint-Hilarion à Umm-el-'Amr," *Comptes rendus des séances de l'Académie des Inscriptions et Belles-Lettres* 148.1 (2004): 368.

The inscription reads ΕΥΧΕΣ ΚΑΙ ΠΡΕΣΒΙΕΣ ΤΟΥ ΑΓΙΟΥ ΠΑΤΡΟΣ ΗΜΩΝ ΙΛΑΡΙΩΝΟΣ ΕΛΕΗΘΩΜΕΝ ΑΜΗΝ ("By the prayers and intercessions of our holy father Hilarion may we find mercy, Amen").

Their claim is, however, disputed by Leah Di Segni who notes that the archaeological evidence pertaining to the cell's size and location, and its close proximity to the sea, do not accurately correspond to the description of Hilarion's cell given by Jerome, although she acknowledges that the site is indeed seven miles away from Maiuma of Gaza.[9] Di Segni further suggests that the monastic complex in Umm el-'Amr may be more properly identified with the monastery of Abba Seridos, which became the coenobium under the influence of Barsanuphius and John of Gaza in the sixth century.[10] Consequently, she asserts that both the location of the ruin, which is near Tabatha south of Wadi Ghazzeh, and the presence of "a hostel and an infirmary" on the site, are in accordance with descriptions from the *Letters* of Barsanuphius and John of Gaza.[11]

In the *Life of Hilarion*, Jerome provides many anecdotes about St. Hilarion, with a focus on his miraculous healing abilities (see chapters 13–23 of the *Life of Hilarion*). He tells stories about the healing of a barren woman from Eleutheropolis (13), Aristaenete's children (14), a blind woman (15), some paralysed men (16, 19), and even men possessed by wicked demons (17–18). Through these anecdotes Jerome provides a picture of the saint as not only a miracle worker, but also as an exemplary monk. The saint is particularly noted for his ascetic practices as

---

9   See Leah Di Segni, "Late-antique Gaza: Hilarion, Choricius, Graffies, Mimes and Ecphrasis," review of *Gaza Dans L'Antiqué Tardive. Archéologie, Rhétorique et Historie. Actes du Colloque International de Poiters (6–7 mai 2004)*, ed. Chatherine Saliou, *Journal of Roman Archaeology* 20 (2007): 647–50.
10 Di Segni, "Late-antique Gaza: Hilarion, Choricius, Graffies, Mimes and Ecphrasis," 650.
11 On a hospice and infirmity in the monastery of Seridos, see Hirschfeld, "The Monasticism of Gaza," 76.

well as being a welcoming person who helped those in difficulty. However, the work of Jerome is, in general, silent on the topic of St. Hilarion's almsgiving. Indeed, the only reference we have regarding any actual charitable giving is the story of the distribution of his parents' wealth.

3.1.2 Abba Isaiah of Scetis

Abba Isaiah (d.491) was one of the most influential monks in the world of late-antique Gazan monasticism. According to Zachariah Rhetor and John Rufus, he was originally trained in the monasteries of Scetis in Egypt desert. As a result of his fame he was besieged by a host of admirers and forced to make a move to Palestine in 452–453. This was when Peter the Iberian was a bishop of Maiuma.[12] He dwelt for some time in the desert near Eleutheropolis before withdrawing to Beth Daltha near Gaza in 485, spending his last few years supervising monks in the surrounding neighbourhoods.[13] Interestingly, he kept in touch with the outside world through his disciple Abba Peter from that time until his death in the monastery in 491.[14] This pattern of communication was echoed, about a century later, by Barsanuphius and John of Gaza. The Gazan anchorites, like their predecessor Abba Isaiah, enclosed themselves in their cells and only communicated through their disciples (Abba Seridos and Dorotheos).[15]

Abba Isaiah and his companion, Peter the Iberian, were famous figures in the non-Chalcedonian camp of late-antique

---

12 Zachariah Rhetor, *Vita Isaiae Monachi*, 4; Rufus, *The Life of Peter the Iberian*, 138.
13 Zachariah Rhetor, *Vita Isaiae Monachi*, 6; Rufus, *The Life of Peter the Iberian*, 138.
14 Rufus, *The Life of Peter the Iberian*, 138. On the date of his death, see Bitton-Ashkelony and Kofsky, *The Monastic School of Gaza*, 21; Bitton-Ashkelony and Kofsky, "Gazan Monasticism in the Fourth-Sixth Centuries," 33; Derwas. J. Chitty, "Abba Isaiah," *Journal of Theological Studies* 22.1 (1971): 50. Hirschfeld actually suggests that Abba Isaiah died in 489. See, Hirschfeld, "The Monasticism of Gaza," 74.
15 For more details, see section 3.3.2.

Palestine.¹⁶ In an effort to achieve reconciliation between the Chalcedonians and the non-Chalcedonians, the emperor Zeno (425–491) dispatched Cosmas the Eunuch to bring both men to Constantinople. He wanted them to both sign the *Henotikon* (482) which was designed to resolve the doctrinal issues between the two camps.¹⁷ However, Isaiah of Scetis refused to obey the emperor's summons, giving as a pretext his illness and inability to travel, while Peter the Iberian was not interested in participating and escaped to Phoenicia prior to the eunuch's arrival in Gaza.¹⁸

It is interesting to note that although the Egyptian monk was indeed an ardent supporter of the non-Chalcedonian tradition, his *Ascetic Discourses*,¹⁹ including monastic teachings, were accepted by Chalcedonians and non-Chalcedonians alike, unlike those of Peter the Iberian.²⁰ In addition, his Greek *Discourses* were translated into Syriac some time during the sixth century, and seemed to have exerted a continuing influence on the Syrian tradition. Indeed, Dadisho, the seventh-century Syrian monk, wrote

16 For the relationship of Abba Isaiah to the non-Chalcedon beliefs, see Pseudo-Zachariah Rhetor, *The Chronicle of Pseudo-Zachariah Rhetor*, trans. Robert Phenix and Cornelia Horn, Translated Texts for Historians Volume 55 (Liverpool: Liverpool University Press, 2011), V. 9. b.
17 For more details about the *Henotikon* of Emperor Zeno, see Pseudo-Zachariah Rhetor, *The Chronicle of Pseudo-Zachariah Rhetor*, 198 n. 121.
18 Pseudo-Zachariah Rhetor, *The Chronicle of Pseudo-Zachariah Rhetor*, VI. 3. a–b; Rufus, *The Life of Peter the Iberian*, 140–41.
19 Abba Isaiah, *Les cinq recensions de l'Ascéticon syriaque d'Abba Isaïe*. CSCO 289–290, 293–294, Syr. 120–123 (Louvain: Secrétariat du Corpus SCO, 1968). For the English translation, see Abba Isaiah, *Abba Isaiah of Scetis: Ascetic Discourses*, ed. and trans. John Chryssavgis and Pachomios Penkett (Kalamazoo: Cistercian Publications, 2002).
20 Chryssavgis and Penkett, introduction to *Abba Isaiah of Scetis: Ascetic Discourses*, 35–37; Chitty, "Abba Isaiah," 70. Because the term "Nestorian" was "originally devised as opprobrious epithet, and implies the holding of heretic opinions," Sebastien Brock claims that it is better to call this the "Church of the East". Nevertheless, I have chosen to use the term "Nestorian" for the sake of convenience. See Sebastian P. Brock, *Introduction to Syrian Studies* (Piscataway, NJ: Gorgias Press, 2006), 67.

a commentary on the work.²¹ Abba Isaiah's avoidance of theological polemics in his ascetic teachings may go some way towards explaining this phenomenon. In particular, Bitton-Ashkelony and Kofsky note:

> Abbah Isaiah normally avoids theological dialectics and polemics, and even warns against dabbling with theology, yet his work also contains some element of theorizing speculation, which creates a solid basis and an ideological framework for the practical, sophisticated struggle against the multifaceted manifestation of sin within the ascetic psyche.²²

The *Ascetic Discourses* of Abba Isaiah offer practical advice on the ascetic life including the following: solitude and isolation, silence, work, perfection, prayer, passions, humility and discernment, and balance.²³ Abba Isaiah of Scetis also demonstrates a clear attitude towards those in need. He advises his readers to offer warm hospitality to their guests. He suggests that if the visitor is "a brother for the sake of God", accept him gladly and, when the guest is leaving, send away the person with what he needs if necessary".²⁴ However, Abba Isaiah recommends that if the visitor is an itinerant monk, help him with the love of God, but hide the presence of the monk from their neighbors.²⁵

---

21 Sebastian P. Brock, *Spirituality in the Syriac Tradition*, 2nd ed. (Kottayam: St Ephrem Ecumenical Research Institute, 2005), 29–30, 33. For more information on his works, see also Sebastian P. Brock, *A Brief Outline of Syriac Literature*, rev. ed. (Kottayam: St Ephrem Ecumenical Research Institute, 2009), 47.
22 Bitton-Ashkelony and Kofsky, "Gazan Monasticism in the Fourth-Sixth Centuries," 37. See also Chryssavgis and Penkett, introduction to *Abba Isaiah of Scetis: Ascetic Discourses*, 24.
23 Chitty, "Abba Isaiah," 69, also suggests that "we remember that Zacharia in his *Chronicle* twice (v.9 and vi. 3) describes the Abba Isaiah as πρακτικός. And this describes well the character of our Corpus—a practical guide for the monk on the way, in prayer and work, towards the one unchanging goal—to attain to accordance with the Nature of Jesus."
24 Isaiah, *Ascetic Discourses*, 3.
25 Isaiah, *Ascetic Discourses*, 3.

What is interesting here is that while Abba Isaiah distinguishes the ordinary traveling monk from the wandering monk, he nevertheless advises his readers to give alms to all of them. This somewhat ambivalent attitude in Isaiah's *Discourses* towards itinerant monks, who were sometimes viewed negatively by others, is not much different from the views put forward by John of Gaza in the *Letters*. The sixth-century Gazan anchorite recommends that an abbot, who is concerned about an itinerant monk, ask the monk to leave his community after providing him with some food.[26] Isaiah and John's cautious stance may be considered as a necessary response to contemporary negative attitudes towards wandering monks. Ecclesiastical and monastic policy banned the practice of migration for late-antique monks, unless they had the permission of their individual bishop.[27]

Abba Isaiah of Scetis emphasises offering help to the poor in his instructions on ascetic life. He suggests that such charitable activity actually works to save monks from succumbing to evil desires such as the sin of avarice: "[d]ear brother... [l]et us learn to love the poor, because this may save us from avarice when it approaches us".[28] He also promotes charity as a sensitive barometer of a person's spiritual condition: "lack of charity shows that a person has no inner virtue".[29] As a result, giving alms to the poor is itself then regarded as an act of love and demonstrative of one of the virtues to which monks are expected to aspire.[30] Charity, from an ascetic's perspective, is therefore a crucial means to free oneself from secular desires and to achieve monastic virtue.

---

26 See letters 588–589.
27 For more details on wandering monks and policies on monks' traveling, see section 5.3.3.
28 Isaiah, *Ascetic Discourses*, 16.
29 Isaiah, *Ascetic Discourses*, 16.
30 See Isaiah, *Ascetic Discourses*, 21.

3.1.3 Peter the Iberian

Peter the Iberian (413/417–491), an Iberian prince, spent his youth in Constantinople as a political hostage. When he was still young, he and his friend John the Eunuch made a pilgrimage to Jerusalem where they encountered Melania the Younger and her family. He then began his monastic career as a novice in Gerontius's monastery on the Mount of Olives.[31] Together Peter and John later established a monastery which also functioned as a hostel for pilgrims. They did this not long after embarking on a rigid ascetic life.[32] Their monastery was converted into a *xenodocheion*, further highlighting the monks' desire to imitate their chosen role model, the blessed Passarion. Famous for his good deeds, Passarion was known as "the great lover of the poor and lover of strangers".[33] After spending some time caring for pilgrims and the poor in the *xenodocheion*, they were advised by their spiritual father Zeno to leave the hostel and return to their monastic community.[34] The empress Eudocia visited the monastery and expressed a desire to meet Peter after hearing that he dwelt there.[35] This request caused Peter and John to hand over their monastery to other monks and to make a journey to a small town between Gaza and Maiuma.[36] The *Life of Peter the Iberian* notes that Maiuma was "full of many holy men, monks bearing their cross" when Peter the Iberian and John made their journey to the region.[37] Peter and his companion, according to Horn and Phenix, arrived in Gaza in 444.[38] However, we can

---

31 Rufus, *The Life of Peter the Iberian*, 40–48. For more detail, see Patrich, *Sabas, Leader of Palestinian Monasticism*, 259–60.
32 Rufus, *The Life of Peter the Iberian*, 64–66. Horn and Phenix Jr suggest that Peter's monastery as it was founded in Jerusalem was "a solitary monastery." See Horn and Phenix Jr, introduction to *John Rufus: The Life of Peter the Iberian*, lxxvii.
33 Rufus, *The Life of Peter the Iberian*, 52.
34 Rufus, *The Life of Peter the Iberian*, 67–68.
35 Rufus, *The Life of Peter the Iberian*, 71.
36 Rufus, *The Life of Peter the Iberian*, 72.
37 Rufus, *The Life of Peter the Iberian*, 72.
38 Horn and Phenix Jr, introduction to *John Rufus: The Life of Peter the Iberian*, lxxxvii.

assume that Rufus' depiction of Maiuma as "full of many holy men" may indeed be exaggerated, taking into consideration the gradual growth in terms of the monastic movement in the coastal city at least after the mid-fifth century, as discussed above (chapter 2.1.1).

Peter the Iberian, who had fled to Maiuma seeking solitude, was then appointed as bishop of Maiuma by Paul, the Monophysite bishop of Maiuma.[39] Six months later, he was exiled to Egypt under an imperial decree banishing all anti-Chalcedonian bishops in Palestine, resulting from pressure applied to the Emperor by the Chalcedonian Christians.[40] Returning to Palestine after two decades of exile, he settled in a village called Palaea, which was not far from Ashkelon. He still continued to act as a key figure among non-Chalcedonians in Palestine before being forced to take flight again as a result of Zeno's *Henotikon*.[41] He escaped to Phoenicia before taking a long journey across Palestine and Arabia and settling in the city of Jamnia near Ashkelon at some distance from Gaza.[42] Despite a subsequent request from his followers to return to his previous settlement, Peter spent the remainder of his life in Jamnia.[43] After his death his disciples secretly brought his body back to his old monastery in Maiuma.[44]

In the *Life of Peter the Iberian*, Rufus depicts his protagonist, Peter, as a monastic hero "realizing the monastic ideal of *xeniteia*" and stresses the ideal that spiritual motivation caused Peter to

---

39   Rufus, *The Life of Peter the Iberian*, 75.
40   Rufus, *The Life of Peter the Iberian*, 78–82. For more details about background of Peter the Iberian, his ordination and persecution of anti-Chalcedonian clergy, see, Pseudo-Zachariah Rhetor, *The Chronicle of Pseudo-Zachariah Rhetor*, III, 3–5. Horn suggests that the date of his flight to Egypt is 455. See Horn, *Asceticism and Christological Controversy in Fifth-Century Palestine*, 93.
41   Rufus, *The Life of Peter the Iberian*, 105, 140. Horn thinks that he returned to Palestine from Egypt in 475. See, Horn, *Asceticism and Christological Controversy in Fifth-Century Palestine*, 101.
42   Rufus, *The Life of Peter the Iberian*, 141–70.
43   Rufus, *The Life of Peter the Iberian*, 164.
44   Rufus, *The Life of Peter the Iberian*, 181–83.

remain in Jamnia despite the request of his followers.[45] Aryeh Kofsky, however, in examining the religious and social circumstances of non-Chalcedonians in late-antique Palestine, observes that ecclesiastical politics were perhaps the reason behind Peter's reluctance to return.[46] He notes that such religious exiles faced a spiritual dilemma with regard to returning to any of the holy places from which they had previously been expelled by Chalcedonian authority:

> The sincere Monophysite living in the holy places must make his bitter choice either to abandon his attraction to and veneration of the holy places thereby remaining true to his faith and brethren or to retain communion with the "heretical" Chalcedonians.[47]

Given such a complicated situation, it seems reasonable to assume that ecclesiastical politics were the motivation behind Peter's decision on remaining in Jamnia.

When examining the charitable activities of Peter the Iberian and his companion John, it is best to start with their monastery in Jerusalem. Rufus describes how, after building their coenobium near the Tower of David, they lived an ascetic life in their monastery, distributing the money they had brought with them from Constantinople to monks and the needy. He also notes that they entertained pilgrims visiting holy places in Jerusalem.[48] Rufus compares their hospitality with that of Abraham from the book of Genesis:

> Although they already had distributed the greater part of it in every place to holy monks and to the poor, with the

---

45 Aryeh Kofsky, "Peter the Iberian: Pilgrimage, Monasticism and Ecclesiastical Politics in Byzantine Palestine," *Liber Annuus* 47 (1997): 221–22.
46 Kofsky, "Peter the Iberian: Pilgrimage, Monasticism and Ecclesiastical Politics in Byzantine Palestine," 216.
47 Kofsky, "Peter the Iberian: Pilgrimage, Monasticism and Ecclesiastical Politics in Byzantine Palestine," 217.
48 Rufus, *The Life of Peter the Iberian*, 64–66.

rest they planned to conduct good business, receiving and refreshing the pilgrims and the poor who were coming from everywhere to worship in the holy places. While they were thus able to provide enough for [their] necessities, they received pilgrims in Abrahamic manner, they [who themselves were] pilgrims and foreigners and who had no experience at all of such services.[49]

Rufus' reference to them as loyal followers of Abraham's style of hospitality is most likely an attempt to justify the faith and authority of Peter and John the Eunuch in non-Chalcedonian circles.[50] As well as describing their hospitality towards pilgrims, Rufus is at pains to demonstrate to his readers that the two monks continued to maintain their own ascetic lifestyle in the coenobium.[51]

However, according to other evidence, it appears that both Peter and John were actually not able to maintain a balance between their work and the ascetic life. As a result, their spiritual father, Abba Zeno, recalled them to the monastery, saying "you have become experienced in the reception of pilgrims, come, labour [in] the monastic way of life, [and] be instructed in a [coenobitic] monastery, for this is more profitable for those who are still children in age".[52]

3.1.4 Some features of Gazan monasticism before the sixth century

The spiritual leaders discussed above offer some interesting insights on several of the conspicuous features of Gazan monasticism in Late Antiquity. First of all, a major characteristic of the coenobium in Gaza is its close connection with monastic centers in Egypt. As noted above, Abba Isaiah came from the Egyptian

---

49 Rufus, *The Life of Peter the Iberian*, 66.
50 See Horn, *Asceticism and Christological Controversy in Fifth-Century Palestine*, 277.
51 Rufus, *The Life of Peter the Iberian*, 66.
52 Rufus, *The Life of Peter the Iberian*, 67–68.

desert, while both St. Hilarion and Peter the Iberian visited Egypt and stayed in Egypt for reasons of education and as a result of exile. While the geographical proximity of Gaza to Egypt is obviously important, the theological and doctrinal connections are also significant. The migration of monastics between the two locations resulted in a level of theological proximity between Scetis desert and Gazan monasticism, which in turn influenced the strength of non-Chalcedonian belief in the area. Important non-Chalcedonians included both Abba Isaiah and Peter the Iberian in late-antique Gaza. In contrast, Judean desert monks can be seen to more readily follow the teachings of the Council of Chalcedon.[53]

Secondly, the ascetics in the Gaza monasteries, although dwelling in cells or monastic communities, were usually not completely separated from the secular world. They often encountered lay followers inside as well as outside the walls of their coenobium. This proximity to the outside world, as be expected, made it easier to be involved in the social and economic affairs of ordinary people in the city. According to Di Segni, such interaction between monks and laypeople in the region of Gaza was the result of two important considerations: the monks' material need, and social and spiritual matters in the local community.[54] In other words, while the monks gained economic benefit from their encounters with lay people in surrounding areas, the lay people also gained benefits from the monks who acted as arbitrators, intercessors or spiritual teachers for lay believers, fulfilling necessary roles in the community. In this they were encouraged by the actions of their spiritual leaders.

Finally, the *Life of Hilarion*, the *Ascetic Discourses* and the *Life*

---

53   Horn and Phenix Jr, introduction to *John Rufus: The Life of Peter the Iberian*, xlix. For more detail on non-Chalcedonism in Gaza, see Jan-Eric Steppa, *John Rufus and the World Vision of Anti-Chalcedonian Culture*, 2nd ed. (New Jersey: Gorgias Press, 2005), 15–24.
54   Di Segni, "Monastery, City and Village in Byzantine Gaza," 49.

of Peter the Iberian all stress that their protagonists were primarily involved in helping those in need, such as sick people, poor travelers and pilgrims, and the destitute in their community. However, their charity was not unlimited nor at the expense of any spiritual ideals. On the contrary, as Abba Zeno mentioned above, Gazan monasticism tended to emphasize a good balance between a monk's ascetic life and merciful activities. Indeed, Isaiah of Scetis promotes such moderate charity in his *Discourses*, as noted by Chryssavgis and Penkett:

> The most striking feature and spiritual foundation of Abba Isaiah's writing is *balance*. Any excessive measure—even in the treatment of his favourite topics like the gift of tears—is attributed to the demonic, though he is also mild in his concept of demons. Isaiah clearly enjoyed a wide reputation for discernment. He was moderate and modest, while at the same time not mediocre in his discipline and doctrine.[55]

3.2 Barsanuphius and John of Gaza

3.2.1 The identity of Barsanuphius and John of Gaza

Little is known of the personal background of Barsanuphius. The *Letters* just reveal that he had at least one biological brother (letter 348) and he suffered from occasional weakness of faith (letter 512). In his youth he claims to have been tempted by demons (letter 58). In addition, some information about his eating habits can be gleaned. Like other monks of his day, he ate bread as a staple food (letter 78). He recommends his ordinary monastic followers to consume one bowl of cooked food and one cup of wine each day, advising them to increase to two full cups of wine when sick (letter 159). Bitton-Ashkelony and Kofsky, who

---

55 Chryssavgis and Penkett, introduction to *Abba Isaiah of Scetis: Ascetic Discourse*, 27.

studied monastic communities in the region of Gaza, assume that monks in the monastery of Seridos generally ate not merely some bread and wine for their food, but also some food, which cooked with fruits and vegetables produced on the garden of their monastery.[56] This does not mean, nevertheless, that such a style of ascetic diet was adopted by Gazan holy men Barsanuphius and John because appropriate eating is a private and subjective matter for ascetics.

It is not known when or why Barsanuphius came to live in the southern region around Gaza. However, he lived the life of a recluse there from the early sixth century, surrendering his cell to his disciple Abba John sometime between 525 and 527, and moving to a new cell.[57] Barsanuphius and his colleague John, as Samuel Rubenson notes, lived as anchorites "physically isolated in cells within or outside a monastery".[58] So he, like his predecessor Abba Isaiah, kept in touch with the outside world through his disciple Abba Seridos, while John the Prophet communicated through his disciple, Dorotheos of Gaza.[59]

Biographical data on John the Prophet is even scarcer than on Barsanuphius, and as a result, the identity of the Gazan hermit remains obscure. The relation between John of Gaza, also known as "the Other Old Man", and John of Beersheba has been the matter of much debate among modern scholars. Chitty and Rapp believe that the two men are different figures although both from the region of Palestine. They base this assumption on the fact that both men are mentioned in a couple of the same letters (letters 3

---

56 Bitton-Ashkelony and Kofsky, *The Monastic School of Gaza*, 185.
57 Chryssavgis and Penkett, *Abba Isaiah of Scetis: Ascetic Discourse*, 6.
58 See Samuel Rubenson, "Asceticism and Monasticism, I: Eastern," in *The Cambridge History of Christianity*, vol. 2: *Constantine to c. 600*, ed. Augustine Casiday and Frederick W. Norris (Cambridge: Cambridge University Press, 2007), 645.
59 See 3.1.2.

and 9).⁶⁰ However, Hevelone-Harper and Chryssavgis identify John of Beersheba as John of Gaza.⁶¹ Interestingly, Hevelone-Harper uses the same two letters, mentioned above, to identify John of Beersheba and John the Prophet. One of these letters was supposedly sent to John of Beersheba by the Other Old Man, which is a title often accorded to John the Prophet (letter 3). Hevelone-Harper argues that one manuscript "names Euthymius as the author of this letter", and on this basis, "it is possible that John inherited the title "The Other Old Man" from Euthymius, Barsanuphius' first colleague in Tawatha".⁶² Letter 9 is correspondence from Barsanuphius to John of Beersheba, in which Barsanuphius says to his scribe Seridos "My child, write to our brother John, greeting him in the Lord on my and your behalf, as well as on behalf of our brother John". Chitty and Rapp posit that the first "our brother John" is the recipient, John of Beersheba, while the second is John of Gaza. However, Hevelone-Harper argues that it is not impossible to infer that John of Beersheba is identical with John the Prophet because the second "our brother John" is only mentioned here "in the series of letters to John of Beersheba and may have been a later addition intended to distinguish John of Beersheba from Barsanuphius' colleague".⁶³

Chryssavgis suggests that around 525 John the Prophet, a Palestinian monk, joined Barsanuphius' seclusion at Tabatha.⁶⁴ We can think that John of Beersheba may have already been a well-known hermit in Beersheba before joining the monastic

---

60   Chitty, *Barsanuphius and John: Questions and Responses*, 453; Claudia Rapp, "'For next to God, you are my salvation': Reflection on the Rise of the Holy Men in Late Antiquity," in *The Cult of Saints in Late Antiquity and the Middle Ages*, ed. James Howard-Johnston and Paul Antony Hayward (Oxford: Oxford University Press, 1999), 74 n. 43.
61   Chryssavgis, "The Identity and Integrity of the Old Men of Gaza," *Studia Patristica* 39 (2006): 311; Hevelone-Harper, *Disciples of the Desert*, 38–44.
62   Hevelone-Harper, *Disciples of the Desert*, 39.
63   Hevelone-Harper, *Disciples of the Desert*, 39–40.
64   Chryssavgis, "The Identity and Integrity of the Old Men of Gaza," 308.

community of Abba Seridos, on the basis of that Barsanuphius first recommended John to "semi-eremitic life within the monastery" (letter 32) and then permitted him to live a completely solitary life (letter 36) combined with the work of directing others (letters 37–43). However, he did not become a prominent monk there. As Chryssavgis points out, if John was already well known as a hermit in the region of Beersheba, there would have been no need for him to require any particular guidance before offering spiritual counsel to others.[65] It is, therefore, plausible to assume that John was elevated from coenobitic life to solitary life after joining the monastic community of Abba Seridos.[66] Barsanuphius sets John up as another spiritual authority in the monastery of Seridos, and accepts John as an equal (letter 224). Afterward, Barsanuphius and John were likey to have had similar spiritual leadership in late antique Gaza in terms of their reputations (letters 221 and 783).

To add to the potential for confusion, there is also debate about the identity of Seridos, abbot of the monastery of Seridos and scribe of the letters of Barsanuphius. Neyt et al. suggest that Abba Seridos was already abbot of a monastic community and invited Barsanuphius to dwell in proximity to that community.[67] In contrast, Chryssavgis presumes that the monk was one of those monks who had come to Barsanuphius seeking his spiritual counsel, and had been appointed by the Gaza anchorite as his mediator, as well as an abbot to oversee a monastic community in Gaza.[68]

---

65 Chryssavgis, "The Identity and Integrity of the Old Men of Gaza," 311.
66 Chryssavgis, "The Identity and Integrity of the Old Men of Gaza," 310–11.
67 François Neyt, Paula de Angelis-Noah and Lucien Regnault, introducion to *Barsanuphe et Jean de Gaza: Correspondance*, 37.
68 Chryssavgis, "The Identity and Integrity of the Old Men of Gaza," 308.

3.2.2 The roles of Barsanuphius and John

Barsanuphius and John of Gaza are often analysed within the framework of the "holy man" in late-antique society.[69] This term has been widely used since the publication of Peter Brown's foundational article, "The Rise and Function of the Holy Man in Late Antiquity",[70] in which the phrase "holy man" indicated certain Christian ascetics who had a significant impact on society in the eastern Roman Empire. According to him, the holy man acted as a healer, a mediator, an intercessor, and even a civil patron in local societies. Through such functions of the saints, they emerged as "a man of power" in later Roman society.[71] In the Mediterranean East during Late Antiquity, a significant shift "occurred in the locus of civic and religious power from temples and institutions to the 'holy man' as a 'blessed object' mediating between the divine and the human".[72] Brown's original notion of the holy man has been revised in his later works. In other words, the holy man is not only an exemplar who was regarded as an imitator of Christ, but also an arbiter mediating between the divine and humanity, as well as between high-ranking officials and the lower class, and indeed, between Christians and pagans.[73]

Rapp builds her study of holy men in the fourth to sixth centuries as represented in epistolary sources in Syrian, Egyptian and Palestinian monasteries, on the foundations of Brown's defini-

---

[69] See Bitton-Ashkelony and Kofsky, *The Monastic School of Gaza*, 82–106; Alexis Torrance, "Standing in the Breach: The Significance and Function of the Saint in the Letters of Barsanuphius and John of Gaza," *Journal of Early Christian Studies* 17.3 (2009): 459–73; Rapp, "'For next to God, you are my salvation'," 63–81; Peter Brown, *Authority and the Sacred: Aspects of the Christianisation of the Roman World* (Cambridge: Cambridge University Press, 1995), 57–78.

[70] Peter Brown, "The Rise and Function of the Holy Man in Late Antiquity," *The Journal of Roman Studies*, 61 (1971): 80–101.

[71] Brown, "The Rise and Function of the Holy Man in Late Antiquity," 87.

[72] Susanna Elm, introduction to *Journal of Early Christian Studies* 6.3 (1998): 343.

[73] Peter Brown, "The saint as Exemplar in Late Antiquity," *Representations* 2 (1983), 1–25; Brown, *Authority and the Sacred*, 57–78; Rapp, "'For next to God, you are my salvation'," 66.

tion of the holy man from the late Roman Empire.[74] In particular, she highlights the holy man as a spiritual father and an intercessor. Monks were typically men who renounced their biological families, replacing them with new spiritual family members as found in monastic communities. The relationships in monastic communities are defined in kinship terms such as father, Abba, son, child and brother. Abbots and senior monks were seen to care for novices and younger ascetics in much the same way as parents cared for their children, including praying for them and offering spiritual direction.

The image of holy men as spiritual fathers and intercessors can clearly be seen in the letters of the Gazan anchorites addressed to both lay and monastic interlocutors. The correspondence between Barsanuphius and John of Beersheba[75] often employs "the kinship designations appropriate to their relative status".[76] John calls the Great Old Man "father" (letters 17 and 23), while Barsanuphius refers to John as both "brother" (letters 2–4, 6, 8, 10, 12–17, 19, 21–23, 26–30, 34–36, 39, 42,45, 47, 49 and 52–54) and "child" (letters 9, 24–25 and 31). This pattern is also frequently observed in the letters of the Gazan holy figures that are addressed to their fellow-monks and lay believers.[77] According to Rapp, letters sent to their monastic followers are "permeated by the idea that a fraternal relationship based on mutual prayer and the bearing of each other's burdens".[78] In addition to performing the role of a spiritual father, the *Letters* indicate that the two men saw themselves as intercessors, praying not only for their monastic disciples (letters 105, 107 and 113), but also for contemporary lay believers (letters 643, 784 and 778a). Such

---

74 Rapp, "'For next to God, you are my salvation,'" 63–81.
75 The correspondence between Barsanuplus and John of Beersheba is found in letters 1–54.
76 Rapp, "'For next to God, you are my salvation,'" 74.
77 Rapp, "'For next to God, you are my salvation,'" 76 n. 60.
78 Rapp, "'For next to God, you are my salvation,'" 76.

intercessory prayers were deemed necessary to help those in difficulty, supporting them to endure hardship (letters 105 and 107), and relieving patients' suffering (letters 643 and 784), although not always being able to resolve the questioner's actual problem (letter 778a).

Interestingly, the correspondence between the Gazan hermits and other priests or bishops indicates a slightly different attitude, which Rapp ignores in her study. Both Barsanuphius and John treated certain episcopal characters as their spiritual sons and prayed for them (letters 213 and 790). They also exercised a certain spiritual authority over bishops and priests, similar to that which they demonstrate over their lay and monastic disciples, and were thus expected to act as spiritual fathers.[79] On the other hand, the *Letters* also indicate the importance of maintaining both roles in a balanced style: being able to act as spiritual adviser while at the same time remaining in the subservient role in recognition of their interlocutors' superior position within the church. In one example John replies to an anonymous priest who, being elected bishop of his city, asks John whether or not he should carry out the episcopal duty. John begins his advice by noting, "Brother, you are asking me something that is beyond me; for I am the least significant person and have not reached such a measure" (letter 788). In another letter, John replies to a clergyman with spiritual directions regarding monastic and sickness issues, and then asks the interlocutor to forgive and pray for him to God because he does not deserve to advise others (letters 211 and 212). Here we can see that although Barsanuphius and John had profound influence on the clerics in their community, both high and low, they did not use their authority to openly challenge the church hierarchy.[80]

---

79 For more on the influence of the Gazan holy men on the church and its clergymen, see Hevelone-Harper, *Disciples of the Desert*, 106–18.
80 See Hevelone-Harper, *Disciples of the Desert*, 113, 118.

In addition to Brown and Rapp, Bitton-Ashkelony and Kofsky categorise Barsanuphius and John "as teachers of monks and laymen occupying a central place in their society".[81] The questioner of letter 23, John of Beersheba, explicitly calls Barsanuphius "father and teacher". This is similar to the ethos of Egyptian monasticism in which "the primary responsibility of the Abba and 'old man' (γέρων) is to teach his disciple how to live the monastic life and to face up to the problems and temptations to which any monk is exposed".[82] The role of the Gazan holy men as teachers becomes even more apparent when the topics touched on in the *Letters* are noted: examples of lay believers asking for instruction or guidelines on such diverse topics as slave-trading (letter 649), dealing with a sick slave (letters 765–766), engaging in social connections with non-Christians (letters 686, 775–777 and 836), marriage (letter 646), and legal and economic matters, including how to deal with property.[83] On the basis of these wide-ranging topics from religious matters to legal and social, it can be estimated that the holy men as leaders played a pivotal role in their community.

3.3 The *Letters* of Barsanuphius and John of Gaza

3.3.1 Communication through letters

In general terms, the spiritual direction of an Abba or spiritual father, as defined in the *Sayings of the Desert Fathers,* is based upon interpersonal interaction between the fathers and their followers.[84] Lay and monastic disciples who approached their masters seeking a "word" in terms of direction would most likely have

---

81 Bitton-Ashkelony and Kofsky, *The Monastic School of Gaza*, 105.
82 Gould, *The Desert Fathers on Monastic Community*, 26–27.
83 See also Hevelone-Harper, *Disciples of the Desert*, 89–92.
84 See Jennifer Hevelone-Harper, "The Letter Collection of Barsanuphius and John," in *Late Antique Letter Collection: A Critical Introduction and Reference Guide,* ed. Christiana Sogno, Dradley Storin and Edward Watts (California: University of California Press, 2017), 419.

received an oral response, of which we have no record. However, the spiritual direction of Barsanuphius and John of Gaza was predominantly conveyed in a different way. Petitioners brought messages or letters to Seridos and Dorotheos in the coenobium of Seridos, and these agents then conveyed the messages to their spiritual mentors (letter 761). The holy men, who lived in seclusion, dictated their replies to scribes rather than responding directly to the petitioners.[85]

From the correspondence between Barsanuphius and an Egyptian monk who wanted to meet with him, it is clear that the holy men did not want a direct form of communication between themselves and their interlocutors (letter 55). On this occasion, the monk in question eagerly asks for a personal meeting with Barsanuphius, but the respected saint politely refuses and instead dictates his response to Seridos in Greek, not Coptic, which was both his and the questioner's native language. This is presumably because his scribe Seridos did not know Coptic.[86] The reason why the Gazan anchorites desired to maintain such an indirect method of communication is most likely related to a desire to uphold their separation and silence, while also allowing an avenue for connection to the secular world.[87]

As the prologue to the *Letters* points out, Barsanuphius and John of Gaza indeed corresponded with a multitude of people, ranging from anchorites and coenobites to priests as well as ordinary believers.[88] Di Segni calculates the proportion of monks, clergy and laypeople mentioned in the *Letters* on the basis of the Italian edition published in 1991: around 64% of the *Letters*

---

85 For Seridos and Dorotheos as a scribe, see section 3.3.2.
86 See Hevelone-Harper, *Disciples of the Desert*, 45.
87 See Choat, "The Epistolary Culture of Monasticism between Literature and Papyri," 234; McNary-Zak, *Letters and Asceticism in Fourth-Century Egypt*, 8–9.
88 "Μέλλοντες δὲ ἐντυγχάνειν τοῖς γεγραμμένοις ἐν ταύτῃ τῇ βίβλῳ, εἰδέναι ὀφείλομεν ὅτι τὰ μὲν πρὸς ἀναχωρητὰς ἐρρέθη, τὰ δὲ τοῖς ἐν κοινοβίοις, ἄλλα δὲ τοῖς ἐν συμφωνίᾳ, ἕτερα δὲ ἱερεῦσι καὶ φιλοχρίστοις λαϊκοῖς."

were sent to monks or solitaries, 4.5% to priests, and approximately 31.5% to laymen.[89] Letters addressed to the laity therefore comprise a somewhat large portion of the preserved correspondence. This reflects the Gazan holy men's close connection with lay Christians in the secular world of Gaza in the first half of sixth century.

Although the *Letters* do at times make passing references to the presence of women, no direct letters sent to women are, significantly, preserved in the collection. This phenomenon seems not to say that "women were excluded from communicating with the anchorites", as Hevelone-Harper argues.[90] Rather, it is more plausible that the compiler intentionally omitted or excluded correspondence with female questioners, given that the *Letters* of Barsanuphius and John were compiled with the purpose of educating not only lay but also monastic Christians in Gaza regarding diverse matters which they faced in their lives.[91]

3.3.2 A scribe of the *Letters*

The letters of the Gazan holy figures were not written by the anchorites themselves, but rather by their scribes. Some of the letters reveal the fact that Seridos, head of the monastery of Seridos at Tabatha, wrote letters as the scribe of Barsanuphius. In the correspondence between the Great Old Man and Abba John, before he joined the monastery of Seridos, we find a commentary from the abbot describing this process:

> I, Seridos, moreover, tell you [Abba John] something else wonderful. As the Old Man said this, I thought to myself: "How can I remember all these things in order to write them down? Had the Old Man so wanted, I could have brought here some ink and paper, heard his words one by

---

89 Di Segni, "Monastery, City and Village in Byzantine Gaza," 26.
90 Hevelone-Harper, *Disciples of the Desert*, 80.
91 For more details, see section 3.3.3.

> one, and then recorded them". But he knows what I was thinking, and his face shone like fire, and he said to me: "Go ahead, write; do not be afraid. Even if I tell you ten thousand words, the Spirit of God will not let you write even one letter too much or too little. And not because you so wish, but because it is guiding your hand to record these things in a coherent manner (letter 1).

This passage describes that Seridos, as the scribe, is particularly afraid that he cannot write down every word which Barsanuphius uttered. This also reveals something of Barsanuphius' attitude towards recording his own thoughts and words as a spiritual director of others. He recommends that his scribe not write down exactly what he says, but rather reproduce, at a later stage, something which reflects the sense of the spiritual direction he seeks to convey, according to the guidance of the Holy Spirit.

However, there is a danger in such a method, that some recipients of the letters of the Gazan holy men may be concerned they are not receiving the true words of the holy men, but instead the interpreted views of the scribes. One example shows an addressee who appears to be suspicious of the authenticity of the letter he receives from Barsanuphius. This is a letter addressed to a monk supposedly in response to questions relating to sleeping on his seat and certain eye problems (letter 225). Barsanuphius comforts the questioner, telling him that the issues are of benefit and will cause him to be humble. Then he adds that this letter has "been dictated by me for you, and written down by means of my son [Seridos]" (letter 225). In the following letter, the monk begins to doubt whether this letter really has come from Barsanuphius himself or whether it has been written by the abbot under the name of the Great Old Man. Upon hearing this news, the Gazan elder orders his recorder Seridos to stand by the door of his cell and read the letter addressed to the monk out loudly (letter 226). By this action, he seeks to prove to the doubting monk that the letter as recorded by the abbot is correct and authentic, after both he and the monk are to hear his recorded words together.

In contrast to the letters of Barsanuphius, there is no information about the scribe (or scribes) of the letters of John of Gaza. Hevelone-Harpered assumes that Dorotheos carried the letters of John to recipients, on the basis of the fact that he served the Gazan holy man for nine years.[92] It is also considered possible that Dorotheos acted as his scribe while serving him as his personal attendant, much like Seridos did for Barsanuphius. As a mediator between John and the outside world, his role may have included writing down the instructions of the holy man. However, there is an issue with considering Dorotheos as John's scribe, for he was in charge of the hostel at the monastery of Seridos, and it may seem open to question whether he actually had time to engage in this occupation as well as being John's scribe, for this scribal role would have involved a substantial quantity of time.

As seen in the letters discussed above, Seridos did not record every word which Barsanuphius uttered in response to issues raised in request letters, and Barsanuphius himself thought that the spiritual master, at least to some extent, empowered his scribe to write and modify the words and expressions of the reply. The scribe of Barsanuphius can therefore be categorised as *an editor* according to the taxonomy of scribal roles.[93] It is tempting to suggest that because Barsanuphius and Seridos were together for a long time, the scribe knew well the spiritual father and could reveal exactly the intention of his spiritual direction in writing.

3.3.3 A compiler of the *Letters*

As well as that of the scribe, the identity of the compiler of the *Letters* of the Gazan holy men also needs to be considered. There

---

92 Hevelone-Harper, *Disciples of the Desert*, 72.
93 See section 1.3.4.

is insufficient evidence to reveal the actual identity of the redactor of the correspondence. But the *Letters* provide a clue towards revealing the redactor's identity. The anonymous compiler not only reproduced the correspondence, but "also commented upon each letter, occasionally naming the recipient, describing the situation that prompted the correspondence, and usually summarized or quoted" diverse questions—from everyday issues to spiritual or religious matters—in the original letters addressed to the Old Men".[94] This leads us to assume that, as the compiler and commentator, he had received a certain level of higher education and some understanding of the fields of philosophy and rhetoric.

Another clue regarding the identity of the compiler is the fact that some letters include the deaths of both Seridos and John the Prophet (letters 599 and 599b), as well as events after their death.[95] The compiler must therefore have been someone who had a greater familiarity with the coenobium of Seridos both before and after the deaths of these men. In addition, the letters from outside the monastery and the Gazan hermits' replies must also have been kept on file at the monastery by abbot Seridos himself or someone appointed by him. They were obviously held until they were put together for publication. When taking all of these facts together, Dorotheos of Gaza is most likely to have been the person involved in editing and compiling the letters of Barsanuphius and John: as one of the elite monks in the coenobium of Seridos and someone who outlived both Seridos and John.[96] He perhaps attempted to preserve the teachings of his spiritual fathers.

As mentioned above, there are three kinds of compilations with regard to letters: documentary, literary and fictitious compi-

---

94 Hevelone-Harper, *Disciples of the Desert*, 19.
95 See Hevelone-Harper, *Disciples of the Desert*, 168 n. 58; Bitton-Ashkelony and Kofsky, "Gazan Monasticism in the Fourth-Sixth Centuries," 17 n. 12.
96 See Hevelone-Harper, *Disciples of the Desert*, 76–77; Chitty, *The Desert a City*, 140; Chryssavgis, introduction to *Barsanuphius and John: Questions and Responses*, 7–8; Torrance, "Barsanuphius, John, and Dorotheous on Scripture," 70–71.

lations.[97] According to these classifications, the *Letters* of Barsanuphius and John are not fictitious, being based on genuine correspondence between the Gazan anchorites and their diverse interlocutors through their disciples (Seridos and Dorotheos). The *Letters* are also not to be categorised as documentary letters, because they were collected and edited by the unnamed redactor with a pedagogical purpose, as outlined in the prologue:

> As we are about to read this book, however, we are obliged to know that some of these words were spoken to anchorites, others to cenobites, still others to those living together and yet other to priests and Christ-loving laypersons. Moreover, some were intended for younger monastics or novices, other for those already advanced in age and disciplined in their habits, and still others for those approaching the perfection of virtue—as each was able to receive the words. For not all the same teachings are suitable for everyone...So we must not receive as a general rule the words spoken in a loving way to particular people for the sake of their specific weakness; instead, we should immediately discern that the response was surely addressed by the saints to the questioner in a very personal way...I have, by God's help, transmitted here in writing these response for the benefit of the those who read them with fear of God (prologue).

Having discounted the fictitious and documentary forms, the *Letters* can be considered as *a form of literary text*. At this point, it should be remembered that the collection of letters of Barsanuphius and John of Gaza was not a simple reproduction of their whole corpus of letters.[98] Rather the texts must have been edited with the precise purpose of creating a text designed for the education of lay and monastic Christians of the community.

---

97 See 1.3.5 Compilation of the collected letters.
98 For issues regarding compilation of letter-collection, see Allen et al., *Preaching Poverty in Late Antiquity*, 47–49.

As such it deals with how to approach the many diverse matters which they may face in their lives.

Nevertheless, it remains realistic to suppose that the texts in their final form do deliver something which truly represents the thoughts and ideals of both Barsanuphius and John on certain subjects. The anonymous compiler collected and edited the letters for both lay and monastic Christians, gathering together the letters with important and essential content and making choices about inclusions in his work. One of the main topics of the work as whole is the nature and purpose of charity.

In addition, the compiler of the *Letters* appears to have included general background details on monastic life in early sixth-century Tabatha. He provides detail regarding the guesthouse and hospital. He also outlines the connection between Barsanuphius and John of Gaza, as well as their contact with outsiders through the agency of Seridos. All of this helps to reconstruct the contemporary backgrounds of Barsanuphius and John, and their letters.

3.4 Conclusion

The purpose of this chapter was to deal with three issues: the history of Gazan monasticism, the background information on Barsanuphius and John of Gaza, and their compiled letters. Gazan monasticism was located in geographical and theological proximity to Egypt during the late-antique period. This goes some way towards explaining why some prominent monks in Gaza including Isaiah and Peter the Iberian connected with sixth-century Egypt. In this they were following the majority of monks in Egypt, many of whom followed the teachings of Monophysitism and argued against the Christology of the council of Chalcedon, which claimed that Jesus Christ had both human and divine natures.[99]

---

99 For the council of Chacedon, see Binns, *Ascetics and Ambassadors of Christ*, 2–6.

In addition to this, both St. Hilarion and Peter offered charity to those in need in person, while Isaiah advised his monks to help others because charity was an antidote for avarice and a virtue which monks should strive to achieve. According to Peter the Iberian, charity was also a means by which to help the destitute and to justify spiritual authority. As part of this promotion of the ideals of charity and care for others, both Barsanuphius and John of Gaza, like their predecessors, did not hesitate to have contact with ordinary people in neighboring towns and villages, although they kept themselves in strict seclusion near the monastery of Abba Seridos. This was well revealed in their abundant letters addressed to monks as well as lay Christians outside their monastery.

The holy men of Gaza employed the technique of letter-writing in order to communicate with the outside world through mediators, instead face to face meeting. Such an indirect method of communication is a result of a compromise between their desire to separate themselves from the world and their necessity to connect others. Although the collected letters do not represent everything the two saints dictated, they at least provide a partial but essential picture of their understanding of charity. With this in mind, the next three chapters will touch on a more detailed examination of the nature of charity as contained in the *Letters* of Barsanuphius and John of Gaza. Particularly, the chapter four plans to analyze pastoral care which the Gazan elders offered with regard to giving gifts on the situation in the Middle East.

Chapter 4
Giving Gifts in the *Letters*

As Adolf von Harnack outlines in his monumental work *The Mission and Expansion of Christianity in the First Three Centuries*, diverse kinds of charity were undertaken by the early Christians: general private almsgiving and almsgiving during church worship; gift-giving for the support of church teachers and officers; caring for widows and orphans, as well as for the sick; support for the weak and the disabled; support of various prisoners, including people sentenced to work in the mines; money set aside for the burial of the poor; caring for slaves; caring for those facing great calamity; providing employment for brethren; caring for those on a journey; and supporting the church in peril, either at home or in other places.[1] Among these categories, giving gifts to the poor, caring for or entertaining the poor and strangers, and caring for the sick are all explored in the next three chapters respectively.

This chapter, in particular, concentrates on the practice of giving alms to the indigent and occasionally to poor travelers in early Byzantine Gaza and its neighbouring areas, on the basis of the compiled letters of the Gazan holy men. The *Letters* include vivid examples of giving alms as implemented by lay Christians, monks and bishops in early sixth-century Gaza. This chapter will also pay special attention to Barsanuphius and John of Gaza's guidance and attitude towards giving alms to those in need. This evidence will help seek to reveal the rationale behind their spiri-

---

1 Adolf von Harnack, *The Mission and Expansion of Christianity in the First Three Centuries*, ed. and trans. James Moffatt, 2nd rev. and enl. ed. (New York: G.P. Putnam's Sons, 1908), 147–98.

tual directions and its implications in the context of the eastern Mediterranean world.

There are five sections to this chapter. The first section discusses the diverse forms of almsgiving found in the Greco-Roman and Jewish world. Section two touches on almsgiving by the laity as represented in the *Letters* with special attention to the relationship between direct and indirect giving, two special types of almsgiving (that is, voluntary renunciation of wealth by prospective monks and deathbed offerings), a case study of a stingy giver, and finally discussion of the potential rewards of almsgiving. The third section deals with evidence of almsgiving undertaken by individual monks as well as institutional almsgiving through the gatehouse in the monastery of Seridos. In the fourth section, this explores the issue of how a Gazan bishop could protect his congregation and the poor from the actions of government officials and the military. In the conclusion to this chapter, we offer an analysis of the Gazan holy men's attitude towards almsgiving by lay and monastic Christians, as well as episcopal almsgiving.

4.1 Giving gifts in the Ancient World

4.1.1 Giving gifts in Greco-Roman antiquity

Numerous texts and documents pertaining to gifts in the ancient Greek and Roman world attest that many imperial authorities and notables distributed gifts to their citizens in a variety of different ways.[2] These gifts included such things as corn, oil and money. In his monumental work *Bread and Circuses*, Paul Veyne suggests two kinds of gifts offered by wealthy aristocrats or municipal officers in ancient Greece and Rome: *largesse* (or

---

2 See Arthur R. Hands, *Charities and Social Aid in Greece and Rome* (London: Thames and Hudson, 1968); Arjan Zuiderhoek, *The Politics of Munificence in the Roman Empire* (Oxford: Oxford University Press, 2009).

liberality) and *euergetism*.³ The former is primarily related to the offering of gifts to those who are deemed worthy of receiving generosity in order to make amicable connections. Thus the liberality is not given to the destitute or social inferiors, but rather to the benefactor's acquaintances and fellow citizens.⁴ *Largesse*, as a result, "was to be discriminating and selective".⁵ In contrast, *euergetism*, involves gifts which notables give to their city and fellow citizens as the expression of their political superiority and distinctiveness, and sometimes as a way in which to enhance one's own honour and standing.⁶ In terms of *largesse* and *euergetism*, it appears that ancient benefactors primarily offered such gifts and money in anticipation of some kind of benefit, either political or with regard to social standing and honour.⁷

In addition to political gain and social connection, as well as increasing ones' own honour, some benefaction was also based on civil obligations on the part of social leaders.⁸ An example is recorded in the inscriptions from Corfinium in central Italy:

> To help the corn supply he (Q. Avelius Priscus) donated 50,000 sesterces to the state of Corfinium… (to offer) many feasts and distributions of money to the whole body of citizens from his own funds, and *frequently he gave financial assistance to meet the heavy obligation of the state*.⁹

However other sources show that, although rare, a few benefactors in the ancient world also made special provision (such as

---

3   Paul Veyne, *Bread and Circuses: Historical Sociology and Political Pluralism*, trans. Barin Pearce (London: Allen Lane, 1990), 75.
4   Roman Garrison, *Redemptive Almsgiving in Early Christianity*, Journal for the Study of the New Testament Supplement Series 77 (Sheffield: Sheffield Academic Press, 1993), 40–41.
5   Garrison, *Redemptive Almsgiving in Early Christianity*, 41.
6   Veyne, *Bread and Circuses*, 75.
7   Hands, *Charities and Social Aid in Greece and Rome*, 79–80.
8   Gary Ferngren, *Medicine and Health Care in Early Christianity* (Baltimore: John Hopkins University Press, 2009), 88–90.
9   Hands, *Charities and Social Aid in Greece and Rome*, 186–87, D.24. Italics mine.

corn and money) for the marginalized people including poor travelers, the sick and disabled citizens.[10] An inscription from Stratonicea in Asia Minor attests to this:

> Theophilus son of Theophilus of Hierakome and priestess Tryphera… [opened] the sacred refectory of the god to every class and age and to out-of-town visitors with the most ready goodwill and lavish generosity, entertained also the body of elders in the city with food to be carried away.[11]

Evidently, the destitute were not always ignored in their ancient societies. However, although the Greeks and Romans seem to have distributed direct benefactions to those in need, such as the poor, orphans, widows and the sick, this does not imply that they took a personal concern for the marginalised of society.[12] Indeed, for the ancients, a feeling of pity "was reserved not for the indigent but for those—mostly members of the upper classes—who had experienced a reversal of fortune that had reduced them to poverty; because the lower classes had never experienced a catastrophic fall, they could not deserve pity".[13] Moreover, civil generosity in the Greco-Roman world "clearly made but little difference to the situation of the poor".[14]

4.1.2 Giving gifts in early Jewish and Christian tradition

In comparison to the ancient Greeks and Romans, the attitude towards the poor and needy found in the Scriptures is quite different. The Hebrew Scriptures give high praise to the giving of aid to the impoverished. God commends his people, the

---

10 See Hands, *Charities and Social Aid in Greece and Rome*, 95–96.
11 Hands, *Charities and Social Aid in Greece and Rome*, 190, D.33. The [opened] in the quotation is mine.
12 Ferngren, *Medicine and Health Care in Early Christianity*, 87.
13 Ferngren, *Medicine and Health Care in Early Christianity*, 87. For more detailed explanation, see section 6.1.1.
14 Zuiderhoek, *The Politics of Munificence in the Roman Empire*, 34.

Israelites, to show kindness to those in need in their communities (for example, Deut. 15:7–11; Isa. 1:17), while his prophets note that those who exploit the destitute (including widows and orphans) will be punished (Amos 2:6–7; Mic. 2:1–2). This view of the poor, as Roman Garrison points out, arises from the theological understanding that "the poor are identified as God's people", and that Yahweh is the father or God who helps the poor and needy (Ps. 68:5, 10; 109:31; Isa. 41:17) and who executes justice for them (Ps. 140:12).[15] Further, many passages in the Old Testament also promise abundant rewards for those who care for the needy and marginalised.[16] In particular, Psalm 41 indicates that benefactors or givers will earn divine protection as well as spiritual and physical benefits.

> Happy are those who consider the poor; the Lord delivers them in the day of trouble.
> The Lord protects them and keeps them alive; they are called happy in the land.
> You do not give them up to the will of their enemies.
> The Lord sustains them on their sickbed; in their illness you heal all their infirmities (Ps. 41:1–3).

In addition, almsgiving is understood in the Old Testament as a means by which to earn the forgiveness of sin. The doctrine of redemptive almsgiving is explicitly found in the book of Daniel. In Daniel 4, in particular, Daniel says to Nebuchadnezzar that the king will have a chance of escaping divine judgement through giving alms to the marginalized: "O king, may my counsel be acceptable to you: atone for your sins with righteousness, and your iniquities with mercy to the oppressed, so that your prosperity may be prolonged" (Dan. 4:27).

With regard to this, Garrison points out that "Daniel contains

---

15 Garrison, *Redemptive Almsgiving in Early Christianity*, 46.
16 See Garrison, *Redemptive Almsgiving in Early Christianity*, 49–51.

one of the earliest uses of 'righteousness' to refer to charity, and the clearest passage to support redemptive almsgiving in the Hebrew Scripture".[17]

The doctrine of atoning almsgiving in the book of Daniel extends not only to the New Testament as mentioned below, but also to rabbinic literature during the Tannaitic period (approximately 10–220 CE). In the Jewish milieu in particular, atoning almsgiving seemed to be "accelerated by the destruction of the Temple".[18] According to Gary Anderson and Peter Brown, during the Second Temple period there was a significant change in terms of traditional images of *sin* and *God* in Jewish writings.[19] In other words, the notion of sin as "a load that could be lifted only by the heavy rituals of sacrifice" was substituted with the idea of sin as a debt, and God himself thus emerged as a "debt manager".[20] Thus one can remit one's own debts through implementing charity.

In addition to the Old Testament, the custom of aiding those in need by giving alms is also prevalent in the New Testament.[21] For instance, the authors of the Synoptic Gospels (Matt. 6:1-4, 25:31~46; Mark 10:2; Luke 10:35, 11:41) and Paul (Acts 20:32-35; 2 Cor. 8:1-9; 1 Tim. 6: 17-19) all exhort their listeners to offer their wealth as alms to the needy. Apart from these authors, the Epistles to the Hebrews and of James and Peter also include several passages pertaining to the practice of giving gifts to the poor (Heb. 13:1-4, 16; Jas.1:27, 2:14-17; 1 Pet. 4:8). Among them, the Gospel of Matthew in particular suggests that alms

---

17 Garrison, *Redemptive Almsgiving in Early Christianity*, 51.
18 Garrison, *Redemptive Almsgiving in Early Christianity*, 59.
19 Gary Anderson, *Sin: A History* (New Haven: Yale University Press, 2009), 9, 27; Peter Brown, *Ransom of the Soul* (Massachusetts: Harvard University Press, 2015), 96–97.
20 Brown, *Ransom of the Soul*, 97.
21 See John M. G. Barclay, *Paul and the Gift* (Grand Rapids: Eerdmans, 2015), 11–65; David J. Downs, *Alms: Charity, Rewards, and Atonement in Early Christianity* (Waco: Baylor University Press, 2016). Particularly, Barclay understands giving gifts and benefaction as grace.

should be given in secret (Matt. 6:1-4), and encourages those who give aid to the impoverished, reminding them that aiding the beggars means aiding Jesus because he disguises himself as the impoverished (Matt. 25:35-45). In the context of his farewell to the Ephesian elders in Acts 20, Paul's exhortation concludes with a call for the elders to imitate his example of working to support himself, his colleagues and the needy, by citing the injunction of Jesus in verse 35 "It is more blessed to give than to receive" (Acts 20:32-35). Although not prohibiting receiving alms from others, Paul places much more emphasis on the act of giving gifts to the impoverished than receiving. Finally, the Letter of James says that genuine faith is shown through and is completed by merciful works like clothing and feeding hungry and naked brothers and sisters (Jas. 2:14-17). For James, faith without aiding the poor is unimaginable.

Concerning the practice of giving gifts to the needy in the New Testament, diverse rewards for a donor or benefactor, which exerted a continuing influence on early and late antique Christian writers, need to be mentioned. According to Downs, early Christian authors frequently recommend the merciful practice, alluding to the fact that providing material assistance to the poor will be in diverse ways rewarded by God. In Particular, Luke 11:37-41 and 1 Peter 4:8 allude to redemptive almsgiving, which means that almsgiving can serve as a means of atoning for sins of those who aid the poor and marginalized.[22] The concept of atoning almsgiving is adopted and developed by many early Christian writings including *1 and 2 Clement, Shepherd of Hermas, Works and Almsgiving (De operre et eleemosynis)* of Cyprian of Carthage, and *Didascalia Apostolum*.[23] In the *Work and Alms* of Cyprian in

---

22 Down, *Alms: Charity, Rewards, and Atonement in Early Christianity*, 103-41.
23 For more details on redemptive almsgiving in early Christianity, see Garrison, *Redemptive Almsgiving in Early Christianity*; Down, *Alms: Charity, Rewards, and Atonement in Early Christianity*, 175-201.

particular, written in the middle of third century, almsgiving is regarded as a means to wash away post-baptismal sin in the frame of love of God because the flame of sins can be extinguished by almsgiving and faith.[24]

In contrast, the letters of Paul do not touch on the notion of atoning almsgiving, but instead they promise other recompense for generous benefactors. Paul's letters addressed to Corinthians indicate exemption from divine judgement (1 Cor. 11:27-32),[25] receiving material aid from others (2 Cor. 8:13-15), and the way to imitate self-giving love of Christ (2 Cor. 8:1-9). According to other Pauline letters, it is through such sharing with the needy that one can secure their lives from eternal death (1 Tim. 6:17-19).

Compared to almsgiving as a merciful activity in the Scriptures, the rabbinic writings generally appear to place great emphasis on considering "not only their physical needs, such as food and clothing, but also less tangible factors, including respect for the poor person's time, safety and feelings".[26] Some of them advise their followers to implement gift-giving in secret, as the teaching of Jesus did (Matt. 6:1-4), while some others advise the provision of loans for the poor rather than giving gifts because they give "the recipient the dignity of reciprocating the donation" and can "easily and quietly be converted into 'gifts'" if repayment is impossible.[27] In addition, God himself is, according to some rabbinic texts, involved in giving to beggars, and rewards or punishes benefactors according to their actions.[28] In other rab-

---

24 Cyprian, *Works and Almsgiving*, trans. R.J. Deferrari, FC 36 (Washington DC: Catholic University of America Press, 1958; repr., 2007), 1-2.
25 In the passage, Paul negatively expresses exemption of divine judgment as the result of caring for the poor.
26 Yael Wilfand, *Poverty, Charity and the Image of the Poor in Rabbinic Texts from the Land of Israel* (Sheffield: Sheffield Phoenix Press, 2014), 184.
27 Susan Homan, *The Hungry Are Dying* (Oxford: Oxford University Press, 2001), 47.
28 Wilfand, *Poverty, Charity and the Image of the Poor in Rabbinic Texts from the Land of Israel*, 177-78.

binic texts, the giving is considered as a means to imitate God as well as to secure a donor's life from death.[29]

In sum, the practice of giving alms to the poor found in both Greco-Roman and biblical tradition (including Jewish texts) has shown that different approaches to almsgiving between both parties depended on their understandings of the socially disadvantaged and the notion of almsgiving. Pagan Greeks and Romans generally thought the poor as the destitute, the inferior or social outsiders to their communities to be cared for if possible, while the Christian scriptures regarded them as God's people and Jesus in disguise, or as spiritual donors who offered spiritual gifts to their benefactors. Moreover, whereas showing mercy to the needy was treated as a means by which to reinforce one's political impact and social responsibility for the ancient Greco-Roman world, charitable activity was viewed as keeping the divine injunction to care for the poor, and as a method to gain various spiritual and material rewards in the biblical tradition.

4.2 Laypeople and gift giving

4.2.1 Direct and indirect giving

In the late-antique Christian world, the expressed ideal was that everyone (particularly the wealthy) was expected to look after those in distress in their local community.[30] In particular, caring for the poor is regarded as one of the main duties of pious laypeople in early Syriac Christianity.[31] In addition, the practice of giving alms to the needy was a frequent topic in homilies of the eastern and western Church Fathers, indicating its importance. For example, both Maximus of Turin and St. Augustine try to persuade their congregations to offer provisions to the poor

---

29 Wilfand, *Poverty, Charity and the Image of the Poor in Rabbinic Texts from the Land of Israel*, 178–80.
30 Brown, Poverty and Leadership in the Later Roman Empire, 9, 51.
31 Brown, *Treasure in Heaven*, 58–59, 73.

including travelers and widows during the penitential seasons of the liturgical year such as Lent and Advent.[32] John Chrysostom also preached a sermon on almsgiving in his homily XLIII on First Corinthians:

> And let us make a little chest for the poor at home; and near the place at which you stand praying, there let it be put: and as often as you enter in to pray, first deposit your alms, and then send up your prayer; and as you would not wish to pray with unwashed hands, so neither do so without alms... if you have this little coffer, you have a defence against the devil, you give wings to your prayer, you make your house holy, having meat for the King (S. Matt. xxv.34.) there laid up in store. And for this reason let the little coffer be place also near the bed, and the night will not be troubled with fantasies. Only let nothing be cast into it, which is the fruit of injustice. For this thing is charity; and it cannot be that charity should ever spring out of hardheartedness.[33]

Here the Antiochian Father persuades his congregation to prepare alms to the poor by outlining the marvellous efficacy to be gained in collecting money and giving to those less fortunate. Although, from a modern perspective, his references to magic and fantasy can seem a little strange, it reveals much about late-antique Christians' beliefs as well as their attitude towards merciful work. He certainly draws attention to the link between charity in giving tangible gifts and charitable thought.

In terms of the practicalities of almsgiving, some Christians collected alms at their homes and then distributed these gifts to the poor "at the door of their homes and especially at church

---

32 Finn, *Almsgiving in the Later Roman Empire*, 101; Maximus of Turin, *The Sermons of St. Maximus of Turin*, trans. Boniface Ramsey (New York: Mahwah, Newman Press, 1989), 60. For discussion of the Church Fathers' preaching on charity, see Allen, Neil and Mayer, *Preaching Poverty in Late Antiquity*.
33 John Chrysostom, *The Homilies on First Corinthians* XLIII. 7 (NPNF1 12:262).

entrances on their way to the Sunday *synaxis*".[34] Also, some believers would also, at times, give money, food or clothing directly to the indigent at pilgrimage centers, while others gave alms through agents such as bishops, clerics or monks.[35]

Such eleemosynary activity is frequently reported in the compiled letters of Barsanuphius and John of Gaza. Some benefactors in the *Letters* offered their wealth as alms to needy people in person. For instance, letter 625 includes a pious lay believer who asked how he should distribute a small amount of money to the poor. Another reference shows a lay person who questioned what he should give to poor visitors who approached his house (letter 635).

Concerning the practice of giving alms found in the correspondence of the Gazan mentors, the Gazan ascetics appear to place more emphasis on giving gifts to the poor through agents such as monasteries or churches rather than giving them directly, although direct and indirect almsgiving was from time to time practised by the Gazan inhabitants during Late Antiquity. For example, when Dorotheos asks John whether he should distribute his property through a monastic abbot, John recommends indirect distribution. To support his suggestion, he mentions the almsgiving practices of the first Christians in the Acts of the Apostles (Acts 4:35):

> They did not distribute the money by themselves, but rather through the Apostles. Indeed, they were freed of care and money and vainglory. So if you desire to reach that measure and to enjoy being carefree, as well as to find the time to care about God, then you should do the same (letter 252).[36]

---

34 Finn, *Almsgiving in the Later Roman Empire*, 99.
35 Finn, *Almsgiving in the Later Roman Empire*, 99–103.
36 Chryssavgis says that the 'another brother' in letter 252 is Dorotheos of Gaza on the basis of manuscript 1307 of Iveron Monastery on Mt. Athos. See Chryssavgis, *Barsanuphius and John: Questions and Responses*, vol. 2, 256 n. 1.

In the next letter, there is in response to a query about the distribution of property through the abbot. Barsanuphius, the Great Old Man, replies that if you want to be free from care and anxiety, and do not want to be troubled by self-will, then you must "Simply say that you wish to donate to the monastic community, and in your will reserve whatever you wish for the poor, and then be carefree. For this is obedience: not having control of oneself" (letter 253). From the letters 252 and 253, clearly the Gazan anchorites provided advice on giving gifts via an agent in order to protect the lay donors from secular passions which would disturb their spiritual life.

Such advice of the Gazan elders might be based on the premise that their lay and monastic Christians experienced spiritual, psychological or financial difficulties (such as vainglory, pride and anxiety) relating to possession distribution. The question section of letter 324 states that Dorotheos of Gaza sometimes gives some of his property to monks in person and that, when distributing his alms directly, however, he is tempted into vainglory. So he asks John of Gaza whether he should entrust his property to the abbot. On this occasion, John suggests that while both direct and indirect gift-giving do retain the possibility of causing vainglory, the latter is better and less likely to lead to spiritual pride. He notes that an indirect giver cares only for the gift while a direct donor often takes care of his or her own heart as well as that of those on the receiving end of the charity (letter 324). Dispensing alms to the needy appears to have brought about complications for benefactors, and the Gazan anchorite provided advice on giving gifts via an agent in order to protect the lay donors from secular passions which would disturb their spiritual life.

Such a preference for indirect giving was already common in early Christian sources before the *Letters*. The anonymous author of the *Didascalia Apostolorum* exhorts lay-readers to distribute their possessions to the marginalized through bishops or deacons. This is because the clergy were better acquainted with the circumstances of their congregations and could thus properly distribute offerings according to need.[37] Another piece of evidence is a letter from Heracleidas, sent to his friend Amphilochius, including the instructions of Basil the Great, Bishop of Caesarea, with regard to almsgiving. The Cappadocian bishop expresses the same opinion:

> And he [Basil] added to these words that it was not necessary for anyone to take upon himself the distribution of his goods, but only to commit this task to him to whom the management of the alms of the poor had been entrusted. And he proved this from the Acts, to wit: "Selling their goods they took and laid the price of the things before the feet of the Apostles, and distribution was made by them to everyone according as he had need". For he said that experience was necessary for distinguishing between the man who is truly in need and the man who begs through avarice.[38]

Basil directs the people in the alms-house to entrust their goods to an agent who can properly distribute alms to everyone in terms of their need, but who has sufficient experience to distinguish between the real poor and the fraudulent beggars. Both the *Didascalia Apostolorum* and Basil emphasise the use of trustworthy agents to give gifts to the poor, indicating that use of an agent was closely identified with appropriate distribution and seen as a way to avoid misuse and misdirection of alms.

The rationale behind indirect charity, as promoted by these sources, seems to be quite different to that of the two elders as represented in the *Letters*. While Basil and the author of the *Didascalia Apostolorum* encourage their congregations to per-

---

37 *Didascalia Apostolorum in Syriac*, IX (p.100). See also Brown, *Treasure in Heaven*, 24–25.
38 Basil of Caesarea. *Letters*. Roy J. Deferrari, trans. (Cambridge, MA: Harvard University Press, 1926), 150.

form indirect almsgiving in order to ensure that all gifts be properly distributed to persons in need, the Gazan holy men seem much more concerned with the spiritual wellbeing of the giver. The advice of the Gazan ascetics to the laity in their community with regard to almsgiving, indicates that their main concern was for the spiritual health of their lay benefactors rather than the distribution of alms in itself. In this way, they fulfil their role as spiritual fathers who are concerned about the spiritual perfection of their followers. Likewise, the holy men desired to edify and defend their lay disciples through spiritual direction as teachers and defenders (see 3.2.2). This attitude is also expressed by Barsanuphius and John of Gaza in contexts other than that of charitable giving. For example, they are careful not to let their lay-disciples become involved in theological controversies because they do not want their followers to be tempted into sin, such as the sin of anger (letter 658), or because they believe that taking part in theological debate is not beneficial for their followers (letters 694 and 695).

This emphasis on almsgiving through a monastery must have contributed to the accumulation of monastic wealth. The *Letters* and other sources show that this charity was then redistributed to the needy in the region of Gaza.[39] However, there is no evidence to suggest that monastic gifts in any way surpassed those of contemporary Gazan bishops and other elite benefactors.

Charitable activities in sixth-century Gaza were indeed conducted by the Gazan bishops and other wealthy councillors. As Hands and Zuiderhoek note, wealthy elites have voluntarily contributed to their communities since ancient times.[40] Their activities included such philanthropic works as building and repairing infrastructure (roads and bridges) as well as civil facilities (such

---

39 See 4.3.2.
40 Hands, *Charities and Social Aid in Greece and Rome*; Zuiderhoek, *The Politics of Munificence in the Roman Empire*.

as baths and theatres) in various cities of the Roman Empire. In return, these wealthy philanthropists received both socio-political (positions of power and authority) and psychological rewards (such as mental satisfaction). Furthermore, we have records of civil officials in sixth-century Gaza who were not only in charge of the water supply for the city, but also "responsible for the repairs of a dangerously dilapidated church, and were the subject of much public criticism when they neglected to deal with matters".[41] In addition, one early sixth-century bishop, Marcian, is reported to have established facilities for worship and engaged in additional philanthropic activities related to the poor and other citizens.[42] Here, what is clear from the evidence is that Marcian and city councillors of Gaza appear to have directed their philanthropic funds more towards establishing social and ecclesiastical facilities in Gaza itself. In contrast, the monastery of Seridos seems to have regularly distributed its gifts to the poor of the wider region as well as needy travelers passing through at a gatehouse[43] and a guesthouse or hospice called a *xenodocheion*.[44]

4.2.2 Self-dispossession of prospective monks

According to the teachings of the Gospels, voluntary abdication of material possessions for the marginalised was highly valued in Christian tradition. For example, in the discourse between Jesus and a rich young man (Matt. 19:21; Mark. 10:21 Luke. 18:22): "Jesus answered, 'If you want to be perfect, go, sell your possessions and give to the poor, and you will have treasure in heaven. Then come, follow me.'" The story of Ananias and Sapphira (Acts 5:1–11) takes this issue of abdicating material possessions one step further. In this example, the Apostle Peter questions both

---

41 Glucker, *The City of Gaza in the Roman and Byzantine Periods*, 81.
42 See 2.4.1.
43 See 4.3.2.2.
44 See 5.3.1.

Ananias and his wife, Sapphira, about their charitable giving. He challenges them, saying that they have kept back a part of their possessions for themselves instead of giving it all to the church. Upon being challenged they both fall down dead. The implication in this story is that, although the first Christians acknowledged the importance of renouncing possessions completely for charitable giving, it was not always so easy for them to do this in reality. Such a thing at times reoccurs in the early church. Thus, in his study on charitable works by wealthy Christians prior to Constantine's era, Countryman asserts that while the wealthy in the early church were concerned with the renunciation of possessions, the idea of renouncing everything "never became a norm for Christians".[45]

The situation, however, appeared to change after the advent of the monastic movement. Complete renunciation of all secular property and wealth (or self-dispossession) had become, in theory, a crucial principle of the monastic movement at least by the fourth century.[46] For example, Basil of Caesarea articulates detailed guidelines regarding the self-dispossession necessary before embarking on the ascetic life. In his view, complete renunciation of money and possessions was not merely an active display of one's desire to seek estrangement from all demons, but also a denial of one's own cravings of the flesh, bodily relationships and worldly cares. So the monastic candidate should, according to Basil, begin with the abdication of worldly goods and the customary manner of life, because such things prohibit the monk from becoming a citizen of heaven and imitating Christ.[47]

---

45 Countryman, *The Rich Christian in the Church of the Early Empire*, 209.
46 Laniado, "The Early Byzantine State and the Christian Ideal of Voluntary Poverty," 18; Toda, "Pachomian Monasticism and Poverty," 194. On renunciation in the works of the Desert Fathers, see Douglas Burton-Christie, *The Word in the Desert* (Oxford: Oxford University Press, 1993), 214–22.
47 Basil, *Longer Rules*, 8, in *The Asketikon of St. Basil the Great*, ed. and trans. Anna M. Silvas (Oxford: Oxford University Press, 2005).

The Cappadocian Father then touches upon the manner of distribution of the individual candidate's possessions. The property that the novice forsakes should be consecrated to God, and the one appointed to manage it is required to administer it with care. According to Basil, if such a property owner can be trusted to administer his own wealth, he should distribute it directly. Otherwise, he should entrust the task to "those who have been chosen for the work after extensive testing and have given proof of their capacity for trustworthy and wise administration".[48] Here the self-dispossession as the Christian ideal expressed in the New Testament was transformed from a mere relinquishing of one's own possessions into a formal distribution of gifts either directly to the needy or indirectly through the agency of a monastery.[49] Voluntary renunciation of wealth thus became a prerequisite for those seeking to wear the monastic habit (σχῆμα) in late-antique monasticism.

However, not all monks in Egypt and Palestine accepted the ideal of total self-dispossession in reality, as some monastic sources from the Mediterranean East indicate.[50] There are examples from Greek papyri found in Egypt which indicate (contrary to what might be expected) that, although some Egyptian monks indeed renounced the world, others still retained their private

---

48 Basil, *Longer Rules*, 9.
49 For more details on voluntary abdication of one's own possessions before assuming the monastic habit in Late Antiquity or early Byzantium, see Marinides, "Lay Piety in Byzantium, ca. 600–730," 237 n. 751; Hevelone-Harper, *Disciples of the Desert*, 63 n. 10. For examples of voluntary poverty among late-antique bishops, see Allen, Neil and Mayer, *Preaching Poverty in Late Antiquity*, 96–102, 146–47, 195–96, 219–23; Augustine, *Praeceptum* 1.3–1.4 and 1.7 in Adolar Zumkeller, *Augustine's Ideal of the Religious Life*, trans. Edmund College (New York: Fordham University Press, 1986), 289.
50 See James Goehring, *Ascetics, Society and the Desert: Studies in Early Egyptian Monasticism* (Harrisburg: Trinity Press International, 1999), 60–68; Roger Bagnall, *Egypt in Late Antiquity* (Princeton University Press, 1993), 298. On the issue of personal property ownership in Byzantine monasticism, see Alice-Mary Talbot, "A Monastic World," in *A Social History of Byzantium*, ed. John Haldon (Malden, Mass.: Wiley-Blackwell, 2008), 258–62.

property such as money and estate.[51] The *Sayings of the Desert Fathers* and *Pratum Spirituale* also indicate that some ascetics and monastics kept their own property and sometimes even a slave for reason of their own health problem or ascetic discipline.[52]

The *Life of Peter the Iberian* of John Rufus, contains more decisive evidence regarding the possessions of monks. When Peter the Iberian and his companion John the Eunuch arrived in Jerusalem and received the monastic *schema* in the monastery of Gerontius on the Mount of Olives, they nevertheless retained a considerable amount of the money they had brought with them from Constantinople.[53] With this considerable wealth, they were able to not merely establish a monastery called "the Monastery of the Iberians", but also to create and maintain their *xenodocheion*, which had been converted from their monastic community.[54] It is obvious in this case that there was a gap between theory and reality in respect of the complete abdication of property as a prerequisite condition for a prospective monk in the Mediterranean East.

Similarly, the two Gazan anchorites of the *Letters* do not appear to have firmly stuck to the cardinal rule that all wealth and property is renounced. Like Peter the Iberian, they instead suggest potentially more beneficial acts in consideration of the institutional and personal circumstances of both their lay petitioners and their community. It is therefore important to consider in detail the correspondence between the Gazan mentors and those monastic candidates who desired to follow the radical instruction of Jesus and give up their wealth, but were not able to do this completely due to personal considerations. The import-

---

51 Goehring, *Ascetics, Society and the Desert*, 63.
52 See Antony the Great, 20; Cassian, 7; an Abba of Rome, 1; John Moschos, *Pratum Spirituale*, 221/ Nissen 2.
53 Rufus, *The Life of Peter the Iberian*, 66.
54 Rufus, *The Life of Peter the Iberian*, 64–66. Horn and Phoenix suggest that Peter's monastery erected in Jerusalem was "a solitary monastery." See *John Rufus*, lxxvii. For *xenodocheion* in the fourth century, see Brown, *Poverty and Leadership in the Later Roman Empire*, 33–44.

ant letters to examine are 252–254 and 571–572.

Before becoming a monk of the Gazan coenobium, a wealthy Christian, Aelianos, asked John of Gaza whether he should renounce all of his property to become a monk or whether he could leave some property for the sake of his aged wife and children (letter 571). In his reply, John tells him that while it is a cardinal principle to completely abandon one's own possessions when entering the monastery, when necessary, it is allowable to keep some portion of the property for the maintenance of the man's family. In the following letter, the same interlocutor asks the other Gazan elder, Barsanuphius, about renunciation of worldly goods and money. The Great Old Man strongly urges the addressee to help his elderly wife to settle down and then to turn immediately away from everything (letter 572). He cites scriptural passages (Luke. 9: 60–62; Matt. 10:37) in support of his recommendation. He also suggests the questioner follow the instruction already sent by John of Gaza. Such advice to a postulant is consistent with the legislation of Justinian who commanded that, before a person assumes the schema, they should donate their own property to the coenobium where they enter. However, they were also required to ensure the availability of sufficient funds for any spouse or children still living.[55]

While Dorotheos of Gaza, like St. Antony,[56] desired to follow the perfect renunciation which Scripture (Matt. 19:27) suggests, his physical condition would not allow him to do this. Thus, he

---

55 *The Novel of Justinian*,123. 40. See Rosa Maria Parrinello, "The Justinianean Legislation regarding Wives of the Monks and Its Context: The Letters of Barsanuphius and John of Gaza," in *Männlich und weiblich schuf Er sie: Studien zur Genderkonstruktion und zum Eherecht in den Mittelmeerreligionen*, ed. Christian Bourdignon, Matthias Morgenstern, and Christiane Tietz (Göttingen: Vandenhoeck & Ruprecht, 2011), 196–97; Avshalom Laniado, "Early Byzantine State and the Christian Ideal of Voluntary Poverty," 15; Frazee "Late Roman and Byzantine Legislation on the Monastic life from the Fourth to the Eighth Centuries," 275–76.

56 Athanasius, *The Life of Saint Antony*, trans. Robert T. Meyer (New York: Newman Press, 1978), 2.

asks whether or not he should keep a portion of his wealth for his own nourishment (ἀποτροφή) to sustain him in his ill health. Barsanuphius responds by saying that ordinary people, who have not yet approached perfection, do not need to care about such matters. He advises Dorotheos to keep such necessary money and possessions because complete renunciation is really only for those who have already achieved perfection (letter 254). That is, while the Gazan mentors know what the ideal pertaining to self-dispossession of prospective monks should be, they are nevertheless mindful of the individual's personal needs and conditions to modify the principle. It is apparent that he applied the rule in a flexible way, thus compromising between the monastic regulations and the specific circumstances of his lay-questioners.

The adaptable and moderate style of spiritual guidance that the Gazan holy men offered probably functioned as a quite attractive element to inhabitants in Gaza who sought to renounce their property and accept monastic life. It can only be conjectured whether or not it consequently enabled more candidates to enter into the monastic community, having satisfied their concerns for their family and dependents as well as their own health needs.

4.2.3 Deathbed offerings

For Byzantines, death was not just the end of life, but rather the beginning of a new life.[57] This interpretation of death forced people on their deathbed to prepare for the afterlife by confessing sins, receiving the Communion, and being baptised, if necessary.[58]

---

57 Nicholas Constas, "Death and Dying in Byzantium," in *Byzantine Christianity*, ed. Derek Krueger (Minneapolis: Fortress Press, 2010), 139. On death in the late Roman Empire, see Éric Rebillard, "The Church, the Living, and the Dead," in *A Companion to Late Antiquity* (Chichester; Malden, MA: Wiley-Blackwell, 2009); Éric Rebillard, *Care of the Dead in Late Antiquity* (Ithaca: Cornell University Press, 2009).
58 Constas, "Death and Dying in Byzantium," 125–26. On special rites for the dying people (the penitential psalms, baptism and Eucharist), see Éric Rebillard, "The Church, the Living, and the Dead," 221–22.

Within this framework, the ideal of the deathbed offering (or almsgiving) was viewed as an important means by which to prepare for the next life.[59] It is not rare for late-antique Christians to seek to persuade people on their deathbed to distribute their own possessions to those in need. For example, Cyril of Scythopolis records that Abba Sabas helped Sophia, a woman who lived in Jerusalem and was in possession of a considerable sum of money to abandon all her possessions upon her deathbed and to give them to the church. After her death, he established "the guest-house at Jericho with gardens" with her money. He also purchased a water-supply for his companions, "built the guest-house in the lavra to serve the fathers, and achieved much else besides".[60]

In the homilies of John Chrysostom on the Gospel of St. John, he urges his congregation to persuade others in the community when they are dying to leave money to those in need:

> When therefore one is about to die, let the friend of that dying person prepare the obsequies, and persuade the departing one to leave somewhat to the needy... These are the right sort of funerals, these profit both those who remain and those who depart. If we be so buried, we shall be glorious at the Resurrection-time, but if caring for the body we neglect the soul, we then shall suffer many terrible things, and incur much ridicule. For neither is it a common unseemliness to depart without being clothed with virtue, nor is the body, though cast out without a tomb, so disgraced, as a soul appearing bare of virtue in that day.[61]

He preaches on the benefit of the death gift as the best method by which to prepare one's own life after death. Indeed, he links the practical preparations made by those left behind to care for the body of the deceased following death with the spiritual

---

59 Finn, *Almsgiving in the Later Roman Empire*, 106–7.
60 Cyril of Scythopolis, *The Lives of the Monks of Palestine*, 109.3–109.17.
61 Chrysostom, *The Homilies on the Gospel of St. John* LXXXV. 6 (NPNF1 14: 627–28).

preparations which a good friend should make to ensure that the dying person has the best change of resurrection.

John of Gaza appears to approach this issue in a slightly different way, suggesting that it is better to give away possessions prior to the final moment and not wait for the deathbed offering. According to letter 617, a layperson asks about giving alms before his death. When he questions the Gazan anchorite about whether he should dispense his property to the needy gradually or all at once, John cautiously but resolutely counsels him that selling all his property and distributing it to the poor immediately is the best way to reach perfection. To support his argument, John quotes biblical references on the sharing of wealth (Prov. 3:28; Matt. 19:21). Simultaneously, he also suggests that each person should share his wealth in proportion to his own measure, in an echo of the letters discussed above regarding the need to remember to care for dependents. John goes on to exhort the layperson as follows:

> Therefore, let us strive to do what is good before we are seized at the hour of death—for we do not know on what day we shall be called—lest we be found unprepared and be shut out with the five foolish virgins, who did not take oil in their flasks with their lamps. Let us do our best according to our weakness, and the Master of all is good; he shall lead us with the wise virgins into his wedding-chamber and into the ineffable joy that is with Christ (letter 617).

While John suggests that the deathbed offering leads one to achieve perfection, he also sounds a note of warning about leaving things too long because of potentially dying before an offering can be made. In suggesting the two options to choose regarding death offering, he attempts to persuade the prospective donor to prepare for his death by making a deathbed offering in a timely fashion. This eschatological advice seems to convince the donor to do good works in contemplation of his own death, to "acknowledge that his life is uncertain" and to make sure his actions and choices in life are based on sound eschatological judgement.[62]

Although deathbed offerings were emphasised in late-antique Christianity, it seems to have been difficult for those on their deathbed to be able to personally distribute their possessions to the poor through the agency of churches and monasteries. This is sometimes because of conflicts between those on their deathbed who wanted to offer their money to the church and their families or heirs. It is also because death-gift wills were potentially "vulnerable by the standards of strict Roman law".[63] In other words, some donors made testaments in relation to leaving property to churches and monasteries, using vague terms that named the recipients as "a holy and venerable council", "Christ" or even "the poor". These vague terms did not satisfy the legal status of wills under Roman law and "were to be avoided as a potential cause of litigation".[64] When this happened the testament might very well not take effect properly even though the pious believer in reality wanted to make a charitable offering.

In summary, deathbed gifts to the church or monasteries were, in reality, a somewhat problematic area. While there were many who clearly wanted to make such donation, they may have been thwarted by a sudden death or perhaps hampered by the needs or demands of their dependents, or the requirements of Roman law.

4.2.4 A stingy giver and those with little

In addition, not all lay Christians were willing to participate in eleemosynary activities, although ecclesiastical and monastic leaders in Late Antiquity emphasised them. There is a variety of

---

62 Jonathan Zecher, *The Role of Death in the Ladder of Divine Ascent and the Greek Ascetic Tradition* (Oxford: Oxford University Press, 2015), 146.
63 Brown, *Through the Eye of a Needle*, 486.
64 Brown, *Through the Eye of a Needle*, 486–87.

excuses made by wealthy members of particular congregations as to why they were reluctant to offer alms to the indigent: being without a servant, being a long way from home, being too far from a money-changer and even the age-old excuse that they had already given charity previously.[65]

Some of the *Letters* also present images of lay people who are reluctant to give alms. In letter 626, John the Prophet receives a letter from a lay believer who states that he would like to conduct almsgiving, but has not done so due to doubts about the giving. John suggests that, if his hesitation is driven by stinginess, he should actually add more money to that which he initially planned to donate. Furthermore, in letter 335 John clearly demonstrates his views on the matter in detail:

> If stinginess afflicts you, restraining you from giving something to your neighbour in need, then act according to the situation. If you possess a lot, give a little more; if you possess a little, give exactly the needed amount. If you wish to give according to vainglory or to please people, then do not give more than necessary, but only give precisely whatever is required.

John not only advises the one who is stingy to give more to compensate for his lack of enthusiasm, but he is also realistic about the amounts a person can give. He suggests a person with little money only give what is required and warns against those who give for the purpose of increasing their own prestige.

For the novice almsgiver, John has different instructions. In letter 623, he reminds the beginner that God recompenses those who give according to what they sow. He also suggests a soft and gradual approach towards giving alms. Those who are unaccustomed to giving alms should start with small amounts and gradually increase their donation, so as to eventually be able to "reach

---

65   Finn, *Almsgiving in the Later Roman Empire*, 100–1.

perfect measures", which means that they are taken from all earthly things and "become one in spirit with heavenly things" (letter 623).

This evidence allows a fair certainty that both John's response to the novice giver and the person who hesitates to give alms at all indicates a sensitive and gradual approach to his followers and those who ask his advice. John does not provide uniform direction to all interlocutors without regard to their personal circumstances. Rather he offers different solutions to different people, always seeming to take account their mental and spiritual situation or status. This style of spiritual direction is echoed in the works of John Cassian who learnt Egyptian asceticism. According to him, a spiritual father is a helper who sets his disciples "on the road to spiritual perfection" and guides them on the basis of his discernment and their obedience.[66] In order to fulfil his spiritual responsibilities, the spiritual father needs to assess his disciple's spiritual and physical condition, and suggests appropriate gradual steps for their journey on the road to spiritual development. The father helps his disciples to achieve spiritual growth through frequent communication and direction.[67]

4.2.5 The rewards

In order to encourage their readers to participate in giving alms, many late-antique ecclesiastical and monastic elites raise the issue of the diverse rewards available and the potential positive effects of almsgiving. These include expiation of sins, a promise of salvation, and even protection from demonic influences.[68] It is in the *Letters* that giving gifts to the poor is also seen as a channel through which a benefactor receives spiritual profit. The first

---

66 George Demacopoulos, *Five Models of Spiritual Direction in the Early Church* (Notre Dame: University of Notre Dame Press, 2007), 114–15.
67 Demacopoulos, *Five Models of Spiritual Direction in the Early Church*, 115–16.
68 See Lampe, *A Patristic Greek Lexicon*, "D. effect" in s.v. ἐλεημοσύνη.

spiritual reward of merciful work recognized in the *Letters* is divine protection. In one letter a layperson, who suffered unfairness at the hands of a high-ranking official, asks John of Gaza whether it is good to ask another influential person to protect him and his property (letter 785). John replies:

> Do not purchase the protection of any mortal and corruptible person; for today that person is here, but tomorrow he is not. If you give away your property and your protection dies, then you will have lost your property as well as your protection. Do you want to purchase a protection that is incorruptible? Then purchase the protection of the immortal and incorruptible king and God, namely, by [giving money to] the poor; indeed, he receives unto himself whatever is done to the poor: "For I was hungry and you gave me food to eat" (letter 785).

In the passage, John advises the man to seek the protection of God as superior and longer-lasting than any potential protection available from influential, but necessarily transitory, figures in the community. Then he goes on to say that he can achieve this by giving charity to the poor. In this point, it is for the Gazan mentor that the poor were no longer receivers, but instead became spiritual donors in a sense, able to give spiritual gifts to their benefactors.

Secondly, giving gifts to the poor became a means of ensuring entry to the heavenly kingdom. As Brown indicates, giving gifts to the poor, especially the holy poor, in the context of Late Antiquity, was already regarded as a means to obtain salvation and blessing.[69] However, John of Gaza reveals a slightly different stance with regard to the reward for giving alms to the marginal-

---

69 Brown, *Treasure in Heaven*, xiv. For Brown, holy poor are "person who received alms and other forms of support" because "they had abandoned their usual means of support so as to pursue the hightes aims of the Christian life." See Brown, *Treasure in Heaven*, xii.

ized. He notes that offering alms to the poor with a pure motive ensured the giver of access to the Kingdom of Heaven (letter 627), thereby putting emphasis on the inner condition of givers, not the identity of beneficiary. Such an understanding of almsgiving as a method by which to attain salvation is rooted in the Jewish Scriptures including the Psalms, Proverbs and Isaiah.[70] The concept had already become prominent in western Christian by the end of the fourth century.[71] Thus the existence of redemptive almsgiving in the *Letters* is neither new nor strange.

Given the role of John the Prophet as a spiritual father and counsellor in Gaza and its outskirts, it is enough to assume that the promise of spiritual profits and incentives in the correspondence of John the Prophet to his lay-followers must have, to a greater or lesser degree, motivated almsgivers, although it is impossible to measure the degree of influence of the rewards. He intended to persuade his followers (including hesitant and stingy donors) to take part in doing the right thing, and suggested spiritual or psychological incentives to encourage such good practice.

4.3 Monks and gift giving

4.3.1 Giving gifts and monks before the *Letters*

For monastic Christians, possession of personal property was a double-edged sword. On the one hand, material possessions could absolutely help the monastics to offer alms to the needy, when they themselves supposedly had nothing except the bare necessities demanded for their ascetic lifestyle. On the other hand, possessing property was also seen as an impediment to spiritual growth. The *Apophthegmata Patrum* repeatedly expresses

---

70   See section 4.1.2.
71   Boniface Ramsey, "Almsgiving in the Latin Church: The Late Fourth and Fifth Centuries," *Theological Studies* 43.2 (1982): 226.

warnings against having material possessions because they were perceived to have a negative effect on the ascetic lifestyle.[72] One anecdote of St. Antony encapsulates this attitude. It tells of a brother who relinquished the world but yet who kept some possessions for his personal expenses. The story describes what happened when he visited the great monk St. Antony of Egypt and consulted him about the issue:

> He went to see Abba Anthony. When he told him this, the old man said to him, "If you want to be a monk, go into the village, buy some meat, cover your naked body with it and come here like that". The brother did so, and the dogs and birds tore at his flesh. When he came back the old man asked him whether he had followed his advice. He showed him his wounded body, and Saint Anthony said, "Those who renounce the world but want to keep something for themselves are torn in this way by the demons who make war on them.[73]

This anecdote clearly indicates that St. Antony thought that material goods were the means by which demons could ensnare ascetics. This viewpoint is in keeping with the instruction of Pachomius who also warns of the hazards of wealth, suggesting that Satan could snatch the soul of a greedy ascetic away through any riches he might retain:

> We are assailed by [the temptation of] the love of money. If you wish to acquire riches—they are the bait on the fisher's hook—by greed, by trafficking, by violence, by ruse, or by excessive manual work that deprives you of leisure for the service of God—in a word by any other means—if you have desired to pile up gold or silver, remember what the Gospel says, *Fool! They will snatch away your soul during*

---

72 See Theodore of Pherme, 1, in *Sayings of the Desert Fathers: The Alphabetical Collection*, trans. Benedicta Ward (London: Mowbrays, 1975), 63; Isidore the Priest, 3 in *Sayings of the Desert Fathers*, 91.
73 Antony the Great, 20, in *Sayings of the Desert Fathers*, 4.

> the night! Who will get your hoard? Again, *He piles up money without knowing to whom it will go.*[74]

With regard to the relationship between an ascetic lifestyle and wealth, the fourth-century Evagrius of Pontus goes further. He first distinguishes material goods themselves from the holding of such goods. His view is that the goods themselves are not evil, but rather that the holding of such possessions is potentially problematic. This is because ownership causes a monk to acquire evil thoughts such as continual anxiety and worry about his possessions.[75] For this reason, any monastic with many possessions is not easily free from care and may display a tendency to live his life shackled to such items. On the relationship of wealth to the ideal monastic lifestyle, Evagrius writes in his work *On the Eight Thoughts* that the wealthy monk is indeed like "a heavily laden boat that easily sinks in a sea storm. Just as very leaky ship is submerged by each wave, so the person with many possessions is awash with his concerns".[76] He further states that "the monk with many possessions has bound himself with the fetters of his worries, as a dog is tied to a leash, even when he is forced to move off elsewhere".[77]

However, this does not mean that Evagrius entirely prohibits monks from receiving gifts from others. Rather, he allows his disciples to receive their necessities as required from others, while also urging them to share their surplus money and possessions with other needy people.[78] His advice in relation to wealth

---

74 Pachomius, *Instruction of Pachomius*, 1. 52, in *Pachomian Koinonia* vol. 3, trans. Armand Veilleux (Kalamazoo: Cistercian Publications, 1982), 37.
75 For more detail on the hazard of possessions in Evagrius, see Brakke, "Care for the Poor, Fear of Poverty, and Love of Money: Evagrius Ponticus on the Monk's Economic Vulnerability," 78–82.
76 Evagrius, *On the Eight Thoughts*, 3. 3, in *Evagrius of Pontus: The Greek Ascetic Corpus*, ed. and trans. Robert Sinkewicz (Oxford: Oxford University Press, 2006), 78.
77 Evagrius, *On the Eight Thoughts*, 3. 7.
78 See Evagrius, *The Foundations of the Monastic Life*, 1.

undoubtedly arises from his concern to protect the ascetics from demonic attacks, as recorded in his monastic instruction:

> This should be your attitude towards almsgiving. Therefore, do not desire to possess riches in order to make donations to the poor, for this is a deception of the evil one that often leads to vainglory and casts the mind into occasions for idle preoccupation.[79]

It is clear that although Evagrius sees giving alms to the poor as an important duty for monks, he does not view it as a primary duty.[80] Indeed, he is careful to point out the pitfalls of giving for the purpose of pride and self-worth, which in themselves are as dangerous as the desire to possess material items for their own sake.

However, the monastic attitude towards material wealth underwent a change as the monastic movement itself developed. Individual monks were still prohibited from receiving material goods for themselves alone, but monasteries were allowed to receive such gifts. Indeed, some coenobitic leaders in the East in the fourth and fifth centuries actually created a special position within their monastic communities for an official who was responsible for receiving and distributing incoming wealth. Basil of Caesarea appointed a special monk to be in charge of offering charity to those who came to the coenobium, making it a rule that anyone else who was to distribute alms to the poor was to function under the authority and control of this one person.[81] Basil warned the appointed one to share the monastic gifts only with appropriate guests, not everyone who visits the monastery.[82]

---

79 Evagrius, *The Foundations of the Monastic Life*, 4.
80 For further discussion in this contentious issue, see Brakke, "Care for the Poor, Fear of Poverty, and Love of Money," 82–87.
81 Basil, *Short Rules*, 100.
82 Basil, *Short Rules*, 101.

Some monastic sources from the Egyptian desert also propose that, from at least the end of fourth century onwards, monastic leaders should designate special agents called deacons to collect and distribute gifts to the needy.[83] According to the canon of Shenoute, monastic members of the *diakonia* were only allowed to take gifts from people outside their coenobium with the permission of the monastic abbot.[84] Other monks were prevented from receiving secret items—food, cords, sandal-thongs or anything—either from their families or others.[85] At the *diakonia* in the White monastery, the deacons were to take care of the sick while gatekeepers performed any almsgiving and hospitality towards beggars and guests at the gatehouse.[86] In addition, the *Historia Ecclesiastica* of John of Ephesus provides other information regarding the deacons:

> Among the various charitable institutions at Constantinople which had sprung from Christianity, no mean place was held by the diaconates, which were institutions for the care of the sick and persons in distress. The utility of them was the greater, because, while the hospitals were attended only by clergy, monks and nuns, the diaconates gave an opportunity to pious laymen to devote themselves to works of active benevolence: numerous ladies, who might otherwise have found no fitting field for their energies,

---

83 For *diaconiae* in eastern monasticism, see Ariel G. López, *Shenoute of Atripe and the Uses of Poverty*, 170 n. 106; Andrew Ekonomou, *Byzantine Rome and the Greek Popes* (Lanham: Lexington Books, 2009), 207–11; Hendrik Dey, "Diaconiae, xenodochia, hospitalia and Monasteries: 'Social Security' and the Meaning of Monasticism in Early Medieval Rome," *Early Medieval Europe* 16.4 (2008): 398–422, esp. 402–3, 405–6, 413–14. Ekonomou suggests that "by the end of the fourth century and the beginning of the fifth century" monastic *diaconiae* started to appear in Lower Egypt, see Ekonomou, *Byzantine Rome and the Greek Popes*, 208.
84 Shenoute, *The Canons of Our Fathers*, 288.
85 Shenoute, *The Canons of Our Fathers*, 15, 18.
86 Layton, introduction to *The Canons of Our Fathers*, 55. For the duties of gatekeeper in the monastery of Choziba, see Hirschfeld, *The Judean Desert Monasteries in the Byzantine Period*, 163.

piously tended the suffering members of Christ's flock.[87]

In the sixth-century Constantinople, a deacon needed to cooperate with pious laypeople in his task of caring for the sick or in performing other eleemosynary activities. By contrast, contemporary hospitals were normally operated by clergy, monks, and nons only.

4.3.2 Gift Giving and monks as described in the *Letters*
4.3.2.1 Personal giving by individual monks

Gazan inhabitants often brought goods and money with them to the coenobium of Seridos. The correspondence between John of Gaza and Aelianos, as the new abbot of the monastery of Seridos, indicates that the abbot was concerned about laypeople bringing possessions and money with them to his coenobium (letter 594). In addition to laymen, the *Letters* also show that pious laywomen donated some of their possessions to the monastery of Seridos (letter 595).[88]

Some of those gifts to the monastery might have been spent in buying necessary items or erecting (or extending) monastic facilities such as a hospice, as they were in other monasteries in early Byzantine Palestine. According to Cyril of Scythopolis, when a wealthy officer offered "a huge and uncountable" amount of alms to the blessed Sophronius, a superior of the monastery of Theodosius, the superior used the money to expand the monastery and erect a church to the Virgin Mary on the site.[89] Elsewhere, Cyril describes another story of a pious officer called

---

87 John of Ephesus, *Historia Ecclesiastica* (=*The Third Part of the Ecclesiastical History of John Bishop of Ephesus*), 3.2.14, trans. R. Payne Smith (Oxford: Oxford University Press, 1860), 113–14.
88 For devout women's interactions with monks through visits, gifts and appeal related to socio-economic matters in Late Antiquity, see Erica Mathieson, *Christian Women in the Greek Papyri of Egypt to 400 CE* (Belgium: Brepols, 2014), 154–65.
89 Cyril of Scythopolis, *The Lives of the Monks of Palestine*, 240-240.24.

Acacius. Upon hearing of the excellent reputation of Abba Theodosius, he came to visit the holy man with one hundred *solidi*.[90] He sat down before Abba Theodosius to hear his spiritual instruction and immediately realized that the Abba would not receive anything personally for himself. Therefore, the visitor buried the money, which he had taken to the elder, in the cave of Theodosius, and returned to his home. The day after his departure, the anchorite found the hidden money and spent it in founding a coenobium and hospice, as well as buying two little asses to carry necessary provisions.[91]

However, some other gifts were redistributed to those in need. In the coenobium of Seridos in Tabatha, there were the two kinds of almsgiving: personal almsgiving by individual monks and institutional almsgiving through the charitable facilities (that is, a gatehouse or a guesthouse) of the monastery. In terms of the former, John of Gaza basically tries to dissuade new monks from taking donations from the laity outside the monastery and personally disposing of them to the poor and beggars. In response to a question about accepting such property on behalf of a layman, and in order to redistribute it, John persuades a particular monk to "not take part in the distribution of another person's possessions" because of the dangers inherent in what seems to be a simple charitable task (letter 619). This position is reconfirmed in epistolary correspondence between John and an anonymous monk who asks whether he should take money from others to redistribute to the poor. John replies that although the merciful work is, in principle, a charitable virtue which every monk should perform, receiving and redistributing alms is not allowed to all monks. He further states that "only those who have reached stillness and mourning for their own sins" are able to

---

90 An average worker in the sixth century could earn approximately seven solidi a year. See Jones, *The Later Roman Empire 284–602*, 858.
91 Cyril of Scythopolis, *The Lives of the Monks of Palestine*, 238–238.19.

dispense alms to the poor, because such charity could in fact tempt the redistributors into worldly passions such as vainglory and avarice (letter 618). The limitation he places on the redistribution of alms within the coenobium reflects his concern that such charity could distract immature monks from the correct focus of their ascetic lives.

When monks are actually allowed the authority to dispense gifts to those in need, there are still more restrictions and they do not do so at their own discretion. John suggests a clear guideline which all redistributors of alms should necessarily keep in mind. According to the letter 631, if someone is to be appointed as a distributor of others' alms, he must first of all perform in accordance with the intention of the donor. However, he can only help those in need at his own discretion when the original benefactor has not indicated any particular persons as beneficiaries or cited any particular wishes.

In contrast, in response to another layman who was willing to hand over money to someone else as agent, John notes that it might be more prudent to entrust the money to someone who is experienced in giving alms to the needy. This is because entrusting someone with wealth or possessions could actually prove to be a burden to the receiver (letter 629). So those who are asked to receive alms from a donor are also to decline the offer politely for precisely this reason (letter 629). However, once a donor allows someone else to distribute his money, he should not doubt the motives and actions of the distributor. Rather he is directed to leave the matter up to God who will direct the individual distributor (letters 629 and 632). The point made here is that unless the almsgiver trusts the person to whom he has given discretionary control of his money, he should not have assigned him to distribute the money in the first place.

John's attitude towards redistribution of alms given to the monastery is similar to one of his predecessors. In the *Life of Peter the Iberian,* Peter and his companion are shown as trying to care for pilgrims visiting holy places in Jerusalem, while also attempting to maintain their ascetic practices.[92] However, they failed to balance the two halves of their lives. At that time, Abba Zeno, the spiritual father of Peter the Iberian, advised both Peter and John the Eunuch to return to their monastery "to receive further training through obedience and humility" because this spiritual training was more profitable for the spiritually immature.[93]

Both John of Gaza and Abba Zeno display a tendency to differentiate senior monks from junior ones, and to consider that only mature monks should be placed in charge of distributing alms and offering hospitality. Both appear keen to help their immature monastics to focus on their ascetic practices, rather than to get involved in charitable tasks. Such guidance on redistribution of wealth, although it may not have been the intention of John of Gaza, leads to senior monks monopolizing donations and monastic property within their monastic communities. This contributed towards strengthening the positions of the mature monks within the coenobitic communities of Seridos and Zeno.

4.3.2.2 Institutional giving

In addition to any individual redistribution of alms by particular monks, the monastery of Seridos in the *Letters* must have also performed institutional almsgiving through its gatehouse, like that of other monastries. However, the *Letters* provide very little information about the charitable facility. What we just know is that the gatehouse was probably located outside the walls of the monastery (letters 288, 359–360), and that the gatekeeper (θυρωρός) was required to possess "wisdom, prudence, knowledge, strength, assistance, and discernment" in order to perform his work well (letter 360). So it is necessary to explore other

---

92 Rufus, *The Life of Peter the Iberian*, 66.
93 Rufus, *The Life of Peter the Iberian*, 67–68.

monastic sources that detail the functions of gatehouses in the Mediterranean East, if we are to conjecture viably about the gatehouse of Seridos.

Gatehouses in Judean monasteries were, according to Hirschfeld, not merely entrances for the purpose of checking who went in and out. They also functioned as social and commercial places in which to "meet females, who were not allowed into monastery, or to help the drivers unload".[94] In addition, the monastic rules of Shenoute provide more detailed information on the role of the gatehouse in Egyptian monasticism. These rules attest that the gatekeeper should extend "cordial hospitality including food and lodging to visitors", "conduct commercial transactions", "incarcerate sinful monks", and receive monastic candidates.[95] The rules further order the gatekeepers in this Egyptian monastery to provide their guests with lodging and two meals per day.[96] Such treatment of strangers was quite generous, particularly when we compare it to the treatment of ordinary monks of the coenobium of Shenoute who were "served one meal per day".[97] The last monastic source that we should touch on here is the *Pratum Spirituale* of John Moschos, which providess us with an example of how monastic distribution to the poor and marginalized happened at the gatehouse of a monastery:

> It used to be the custom for the poor and the orphans of the region to come here [the Skopelos monastery] on Maundy Thursday to receive half a peck of grain or five loaves of blessed bread, five small coins, a pint of wine and half a pint of honey.[98]

---

94 Hirschfeld, *The Judean Desert Monasteries in the Byzantine Period*, 161–65.
95 Layton, introduction to *The Canons of Our Fathers*, 53.
96 Shenoute, *The Canons of Our Fathers*, 180, 181, 370–73.
97 Shenoute, *The Canons of Our Fathers*, 195.
98 Moschos, *Pratum Spirituale*, 85. For more detail on the Holy Thursday, see Derek Krueger, "Christian Piety and Practice in the Sixth Century," in *The Cambridge Companion to the Age of Justinian*, ed. Michael Maas (Cambridge: Cambridge University Press, 2005), 292–97.

Taking into consideration the evidence of other monasteries, the gatehouse in the coenobium of Seridos probably functioned not only as a physical entrance that provided a location for social and commercial activities, but also as one of the charitable centers in sixth-century Gaza. For this reason, the Great Old Man Barsanuphius suggests, as mentioned above, that a gatekeeper should be wise, prudent, and mature to manage his own duty (letter 360).

4.4 Ecclesiastical leaders and gift giving

Christian bishops in the Later Roman Empire played a crucial role in supporting the poor as well as their local cities (as mentioned in section 2.4.1 above). This episcopal support helped to establish their authority within society. In *Poverty and Leadership in the Later Roman Empire,* Brown explores the role of the late-antique bishop, and calls him variously a "lover of the poor", a "guardian of the poor", a "governor of the poor" and even a "protector of the weak".[99]

Late-antique bishops exercised authority over personnel affairs within their bishoprics, and served as arbitrators in religious or socio-economic disputes. They also had special rights in terms of dealing with ecclesiastical revenue.[100] With revenue in particular, the ecclesiastical leader or someone whom he appointed as a manager to deal with church money,[101] was supposed to spend the money in supporting his clergy, maintaining ecclesiastical and charitable buildings, and caring for the poor.[102] In the *Letters*, we find similar depictions of bishops as episcopal

---

99   Brown, *Poverty and Leadership in the Late Roman Empire*, 1–73.
100 Jones, *The Later Roman Empire 284-602*, 874–75.
101 In the East, a bishop appointed one of his priests as a manager to deal with church revenue in order to "avoid the bishops being involved in any financial scandal" after the Council of Chalcedon. See Jones, *The Later Roman Empire 284-602*, 902.
102 Jones, *The Later Roman Empire 284-602*, 894.

leaders who strove to aid and protect the poor, either directly or indirectly, and who had control of the revenue necessary to perform these actions. According to letter 828, there was a certain bishop who was anxious about keeping the accounts of the church (τὰ λογάρια τῆς Ἐκκλησίας).[103] He therefore asked Barsanuphius for advice. In response, the Great Old Man reminds the bishop that to keep the church accounts is to keep God's accounts, and advises him that he should feed and clothe the poor as part of his role as the administrator of such accounts.

However, it was not always easy for bishops to disburse church money for the purpose of helping the needy. Sometimes they were hampered by the intervention of municipal officials. Letter 830 is concerned with the difficulties faced by one such bishop. According to the text, one day many tax-collectors (πράκτορες) came to the city of the questioner, demanding contributions from his church. The bishop then asked Barsanuphius whether or not he should give them any material resources which by rights belonged to the poor. Barsanuphius exhorts the bishop to be more afraid of God than human authorities, and instead to confront the authority figure and to encourage him to do the right thing.

In order to figure out the situation, we need briefly to mention a tax imposed on the Church. Churches in the early fifth century "paid regular land tax, the *canonica inlatio*, but enjoyed tax exemptions related to all additional payments", as well as the public service on repair of roads and bridges.[104] Moreover, Valentinian III (425–455) had exempted "ecclesiastical properties once and for all from public taxation", although some of the taxes were in fact later restored.[105] When a land-tax was imposed

---

103 Hevelone-Harper argues the bishop in letters 829–830 was Peter Patriarch of Jerusalem. See Hevelone-Harper, *Disciples of the Desert*, 117.
104 Jones, *The Later Roman Empire 284–602*, 898.
105 Frazee, "Late Roman and Byzantine Legislation on the Monastic Life from the Fourth to the Eighth Centuries," 267.

on the Church with regard to its estates, it paid the levy, but otherwise, it did not need to pay. Therefore, the governmental official mentioned in letter 830 can be said to have been demanding illegal payments from the bishop.

Evidence is limited on the question of how often bishops gave alms to the poor, as well as how much they were expected to contribute. However, what is clear from the *Letters* is that Barsanuphius regarded a bishop as a protector of the poor. The advice of the Gazan saint is therefore closely linked to his understanding of a bishop as a "spiritual father and teacher" and a shepherd who cares for his sheep (letter 844).[106]

Interestingly, although the Gazan anchorites appear to have had spiritual authority over any local bishops, they repeatedly urge the episcopacy to protect and care for their poor congregations, using a tone of encouragement and exhortation rather than forcible command—although they do become more forceful when their recommendations are ignored. For example, one day some farmers in the region of Gaza were abused by soldiers of the governor.[107] Both a bishop and other senior municipal officials were expected to inform the emperor of this incident, but hesitated for fear of the governor's reprisal (letter 831). Barsanuphius' response to their seeking advice on the matter is: "If you believe that God truly cares for the poor, then take a courageous stand on this matter. For the one who cares for the poor will certainly lead those who struggle on behalf of the poor" (letter 831). He also assures them that they are right to protest and take this information to the governor, paraphrasing Matthew 25:45: "Just as you did it to one of the least of these, you did it to me" (letter 831).

However, the bishop and other senior municipal officials

---

106 For the Gazan anchorites' understanding of roles of a bishop, see section 2.4.1.
107 Chryssavgis regards the term "governor" (δούξ) as used to indicate "military administrator" in the Gaza area. See *Barsanuphius and John: Questions and Responses*, vol. 2, 315 n. 148.

were still afraid of the governor and took no action. Barsanuphius therefore followed up with another letter, delivering a stern rebuke to them for keeping their silence: do not "betray the work of God" and "struggle for the sake of truth until death" (letter 832). In a subsequent letter, John of Gaza also admonishes the bishop about fighting on the side of the poor so as to gain the reward of mercy on the day of last judgement. Significantly, John tells the church leader not to be afraid of either the emperor or the governor because God and the Great Old Man are both involved in this matter (letter 833).

4.5 Conclusion

This chapter has dealt with the many facets of the practice of giving gifts to the poor as observed in the *Letters* of Barsanuphius and John of Gaza, in the context of the nature of almsgiving in the eastern Mediterranean world. It discussed diverse issues related to almsgiving: the relationship between direct and indirect almsgiving, the complicated concept of self-dispossession for prospective monks, deathbed offerings, the nature of the rewards of almsgiving, the failure to give alms, requirements relating to almsgiving in the monastic context, and the usage of accounts of the church.

While providing ideal guidelines regarding almsgiving, the respected advisors also simultaneously recommend practical and moderate charity. In other words, they advise their lay interlocutors to offer charity in proportion to their own spiritual ability and personal conditions. Furthermore, they put emphasis on giving gifts through agents rather than direct almsgiving. This style of spiritual direction can be said to be intimately connected to the holy men's overwhelming concern for the spiritual and psychological health of their lay and monastic interlocutors. For example, they urge their lay questioners to give alms to the poor through agents so as to gain greater spiritual benefit and to avoid the dangers of vainglorious almsgiving. For both prospective monks and people on their deathbeds, they suggest almsgiving according each individual's own measure.

They also apply the same considerations to monastic almsgiving. They differentiate novice or immature monks from mature ones, and seek to protect immature ascetics from worldly passions by recommending only advanced monks redistribute gifts to poor. They also consistently encourage their local bishops to carry out their charitable duties as defenders of the poor, in the face of potentially stiff opposition, promising personal support and spiritual rewards. In this chapter, the concept of giving gifts as outlined in the *Letters* was, so far, explored. The following chapter in this book will probe into the question of hospitality (ξένια), that is, the custom of welcoming a guest or traveler.

Chapter 5
Entertaining the Stranger in the *Letters*

After the conversion of Constantine the Great, there was a marked increase not only in the number of private benefactors, but also of imperial and civil officials who began to directly and indirectly devote their efforts and money toward supporting the virtue of entertaining the stranger.[1] Likewise, the practice of welcoming a guest occupied a prominent place in the monastic lists of virtues during the late-antique period.[2] Ascetic literature in the late-antique East, including the *Apophthegmata Patrum*, reveals that ascetics themselves were perhaps more involved in entertaining those in need than might have been expected.[3] Some

---

1 Olivia Remie Constable, *Housing the Stranger in the Mediterranean World: Lodging, Trade and Travel in Late Antiquity and the Middle Ages* (Cambridge: Cambridge University Press, 2003), 11–39; Demetrios Constantelos, *Byzantine Philanthropy and Social Welfare* (New Jersey: Rutgers University Press, 1968), 186–95.

2 Constantelos, *Byzantine Philanthropy and Social Welfare*, 152–71, 185–95; Andrew Arterbury, *Entertaining Angels: Early Christian Hospitality in Its Mediterranean Setting* (Sheffield: Sheffield Phoenix Press, 2005); Constable, *Housing the Stranger in the Mediterranean World*, 11–39; Wendy Mayer "Welcoming the Stranger in the Mediterranean East: Syrian and Constantinople," *Journal of Australian Early Medieval Association* 5 (2009): 89–106; Luke Lavan, "Religious Space in Late Antiquity," in *Objects in Context, Objects in Use: Material Spatiality in Late Antiquity*, ed. Luke Lavan, Ellen Swift and Toon Putzeys (Leiden: Brill, 2008), 194–7. For Christian hospitality in the eastern Mediterranean world during Late Antiquity, see Amy Oden, ed., *And You Welcomed Me* (Nashville: Abingdon Press, 2001); Vööbus, *History of Asceticism in the Syrian Orient*, 361–83. For archaeological evidence of hospitality in Palestine, see Hirschfeld, *The Judean Desert Monasteries in the Byzantine Period*, 196–200; Hirschfeld, "The Monasteries of Gaza: An Archaeological Review," 76–77. For literary sources pertaining to hospitality in Palestine, see Binns, *Ascetics and Ambassadors of Christ*, 54–55, 95–96; Patrich, *Sabas, Leader of Palestinian Monasticism*, 165–66; Horn, *Asceticism and Christological Controversy in Fifth-Century Palestine*, 273–99; Hevelone-Harper, *Disciples of the Desert*, 133–4.

3 For hospitality in Egyptian monasticism during the late-antique period, see Regnault, *La vie quotidienne des Pères du désert en Egypte au IVe siècle*, 153–63.

monasteries provided food and accommodation for their visitors who came from a distance while others offered medical help to sick guests in their hospices.[4] The *Letters* of Barsanuphius and John of Gaza also include multiple references to both laity and monks welcoming guests.

This chapter deals with how ordinary Christians and monks in sixth-century Gaza entertained strangers, following the injunction of Jesus to offer hospitality to the marginalized (Matt. 25:31–46).[5] It will analyze how the Gaza holy men responded to diverse questions related to hospitality, arguing that although Barsanuphius and John of Gaza believed in general terms that hospitality should be given to the poor, they did not suggest even and equal hospitality, but rather prudential forms of hospitality, differentiated according to the condition and status of those on the receiving end. By this distinction they sought to protect both benefactors and beneficiaries. Furthermore, with regard to monastic hospitality in particular, the chapter will argue that the primary concern of the Gazan holy men was to protect their monastic followers from problems that might arise as a result of providing hospitality and welcoming strangers into their community. This meant guarding against the specific danger incurred in welcoming unidentified visitors themselves, while also protecting the monks from the more significant risk of a potential distraction from the ascetic life.

The chapter begins by exploring the customs of hospitality in Greco-Roman and early Jewish and Christian societies, which were the basis for the style of hospitality undertaken by pious lay persons in early sixth-century Gaza. It then moves a discussion of

---

4 For monasteries with medical facilities in Palestine, see Hirschfeld, *The Judean Desert Monasteries in the Byzantine Period*, 198–99; Hirschfeld, "The Monasteries of Gaza, 76–77.
5 For further discussion on the influence of Matthew 25:31–46 on early Christians, see Meeks, *The Origins of Christian Morality*, 104; Arterbury, *Entertaining Angels*, 111–13.

the nature and purpose of monastic hospitality, paying specific attention to the *xenodocheion* (ξενοδοχεῖον) in the coenobium of Seridos, and the practice of entertaining both ordinary Christians and monks, including wandering monks.

5.1 Hospitality in the ancient world

5.1.1 Hospitality in Greco-Roman antiquity

People in the ancient world, although not as much as modern ones, migrated or travelled for diverse reasons, including political, religious, administrative, military, economic or personal purposes.[6] Migration was often fraught with difficulty and potentially dangerous, and was a particular challenge, especially for the poor. Travelers had to be ready not only to protect themselves from the dangers posed by bandits and thieves, but also to source provisions and lodging.[7] As a result, many inns and lodging-houses were erected both in main cities and rural areas of the classical world to cater for this movement of people.[8] For those without the necessary funds to spend on commercial food and accommodation, hospitality from family, friends and fellow-citizens increased in importance.

In ancient Greece and the Roman Republic, the practice of entertaining the stranger was commented upon by contemporary writers. It was even seen as sacred by some Roman writers. Cicero thinks of hospitality as "a most hallowed thing" which the gods devised for humans, while Seneca mentions that "hospitality" and "close relationships" are the most sacred two things among

---

6   See Lionel Casson, *Travel in the Ancient World* (London: Allen & Unwin, 1974); Mariel Dietz, *Wandering Monks, Virgins and Pilgrims*, 11–42.
7   Dietz, *Wandering Monks, Virgins and Pilgrims*, 21; Constantelos, *Byzantine Philanthropy and Social Welfare*, 185.
8   See Constable, *Housing the Stranger in the Mediterranean World*, 18–39.

human beings.⁹ Furthermore, some ancients believed, although it was rare, that Zeus cared for strangers and beggars.¹⁰

Welcoming outsiders was also considered to be a basic responsibility of civilized persons in the ancient world. In other words, charity, including hospitality, was primarily not "a part of social ethics but rather an element of social policy", used to maintain social and political order.¹¹ Because of such an understanding of hospitality, the wealthy in the ancient Greco-Roman world generally tended to spend their money in erecting hospices and practising charitable virtue to benefit the cities in which they lived as well as their fellow-citizens, relatives, and acquaintances. In contrast, there was not the same interest in helping the poor themselves on the road.¹²

According to Andrew Arterbury, if pagan hosts in the ancient world perceived that there were guests approaching their homes, they would ask for their identities and, being satisfied with the answers and fearing no danger, would then bring the travelers into their homes. Typically they offered a bath, a meal, sometimes new clothes, and even short or long term of lodging based on the individual requirements of the travelers and the conditions of their journey.¹³ Taking a step forward, some hosts, when the guest-friends were leaving, provided the travelers with provisions and perhaps even escort them to an exit for the towns.¹⁴

---

9   John Nicols, "Hospitality among the Romans," in *The Oxford Handbook of Social Relations in the Roman World*, ed. Michael Peachin (Oxford: Oxford University Press, 2011), 424–25. See Oden, ed., *And You Welcomed Me*, 18.
10 Homer, *Odyssey, Volume I: Books 1–12*, trans. A. T. Murray and rev. G. E. Dimock, LCL 104 (Cambridge, MA: Harvard University Press, 1919), 9.269-71; Homer, *Odyssey, Volume II: Books 13–24*, trans. A. T. Murray and rev. G. E. Dimock, LCL 105 (Cambridge, MA: Harvard University Press, 1919), 14. 55.
11 Frank M. Loewenberg, "On the Development of Philanthropic Institutions in Ancient Judaism: Provisions for Poor Travelers," *Nonprofit and Volunteer Sector Quarterly* 23.3 (1994): 204.
12 Loewenberg, "On the Development of Philanthropic Institutions in Ancient Judaism," 204; Constantelos, *Byzantine Philanthropy and Social Welfare*, 11.
13 See Arterbury, *Entertaining Angels*, 15–54.
14 Arterbury, *Entertaining Angels*, 52–53.

This Classical view of hospitality was, as the hosts and guests all knew, performed in anticipation of some kind of benefits accruing to the host at a later time. Waterbury argues that the reciprocal nature of this relationship meant that some visitors expected their hosts to entertain them well, usually in accordance with their status and position in society.[15] It was therefore natural for both hosts and visitors to select their counterparts in such a way as to gain advantage through the custom of hospitality.[16]

5.1.2 Hospitality in early Jewish and Christian tradition

For ancient Jews, the practice of hospitality also held a special place. Like the ancient Greeks and Romans, it was viewed as a means by which to maintain many socio-religious norms. Indeed, the Mosaic Law itself required that Israelites demonstrate a loving and compassionate attitude towards fellow Jews as well as foreign residents or visitors in their communities (Exod. 20:10; 23:12; Deut. 24:14–15).[17] In addition to this idealistic view of hospitality, there was a more practical justification. According to a rabbinic text, charity was considered as a form of insurance for oneself and one's family in an unstable and uncertain world. Poverty could happen to anyone and thus the one who gave to others in charity might one day be a recipient of charity themselves.[18]

Within an ancient Jewish context, travelers, as Arterbury indicates, tended to seek hospitality from their relatives and fellow Israelites if possible, and hosts generally checked the identities of any unknown visitors and tried to extend their hospitality mostly to other Jews wherever possible.[19] Jewish hosts were also

---

15 Arterbury, *Entertaining Angels*, 53.
16 Arterbury, *Entertaining Angels*, 132.
17 Oden, *And You Welcomed Me*, 17–18; for more detail on Jewish hospitality, see Arterbury, *Entertaining Angels*, 55–93.
18 Loewenberg, "On the Development of Philanthropic Institutions in Ancient Judaism," 204.
19 Arterbury, *Entertaining Angels*, 91–92.

encouraged to provide visitors with the practicalities of proper provisions including meals, water and oil, and lodging.[20] Moreover, some hosts seem to have expected at least a degree of reciprocity in reward for their sacrifice, much as ancient Greeks and Romans did, although it appears to be much less prevalent.[21]

However, in contrast to the situation described above in relation to the ancient Greeks and Romans, the Jewish hosts seldom gave expensive gifts to their guests as part of their hospitality, although they did entertain guests lavishly (Gen. 18:1–33).[22] Another difference is in the nature of lengths of stay. With regard to lodging, guests in Jewish sources were recommended to stay "for shorter lengths of time, often only for a meal", while the length of stay for guests in Greco-Roman sources appears to vary from one or two nights to many weeks, depending on the status and condition of the visitor.[23]

In addition to the Old Testament and rabbinic texts, a variety of the actions related to extending hospitality to strangers are observed in the New Testament (Matt. 15:32-39, 25:31-46; Luke 10:1-9, 38-42; John 4:3-43, 6:8-13; Acts 9:43, 16:11-15, 21:3-16; Rom. 12:13, 15:7, 16:1-2; Gal. 4:13-14, 6:10; 1 Tim. 3:2; Titus 1:8: Heb. 13:2; 3 John 5-8, etc.).[24] In the four Gospel in particular, Jesus himself entertains the needy with pity on the one hand (Matt. 15:32-39; John 6:8-13); he is received by diverse hosts on the other hand (Luke 14:1, 19:5-10; John 12:2). He also deals directly with the significance of hospitality in the final judgement of the nations in Matthew 25:31-46, in which the

---

20 Arterbury, *Entertaining Angels*, 91.
21 Arterbury, *Entertaining Angels*, 92.
22 Arterbury, *Entertaining Angels*, 58. The practice of gift-giving is recorded "in Hellenistic Jewish texts" such as the Book of Tobias and Josephus, see Arterbury, *Entertaining Angels*, 92.
23 For the length of stays in Greco-Roman hospitality, see Arterbury, *Entertaining Angels*, 52. For that of Jewish hospitality, see Arterbury, *Entertaining Angels*, 58.
24 See Arterbury, *Entertaining Angels*, 94–181. Here biblical passages related to receving guests in the New Testament are thoroughly analyzed.

Son of Man separates the sheep from the goats, and puts the former on his right and the latter on the left. According to the passage, he praises those on his right, saying that "I was a stranger, and you invited Me in" (Matt 25:35), and promises eternal life (25:46). It is through the last judgement discourse that Jesus showed how important hospitality was for early Christians.

In addition to the four Gospels, other epistles include comments related to extending hospitality. In his epistles, Paul recommends his listeners to strive to extend hospitality to travelers and outsiders who need assistance (Rom 12:13; 1 Tim. 3:2; Titus 1:8). He also compliments Galatian believers on their wonderful hospitality. In Galatians 4, Paul recalled his first visit to Galatia and explained how they received himself. According to the apostle, the Galatian Christians welcomed himself "as angel of God" or "Jesus Christ Himself" (4:13-14). The author of Hebrews (13:2) wants the recipients of their letters to welcome strangers, reminding them that Abraham and other hosts in the Old Testament unknowingly extended hospitality to divine messengers (Gen. 18:2-5, 19:1-14; Judg. 6:11-18). In brief, charitable activity in the New Testament was considered as a means to keep teachings of Jesus, "a moral imperative and a prized custom" for early Christian communities.[25]

Because of the sociocultural atmosphere of the New Testament, it would be mistaken to expect that a meritorious host would help any visitor who needed assistance. Some hosts might, as Jewish tradition did, offer hospitality to Christian guests only after checking the identities of visitors. In 2 John, the elder urged his listeners not to implement hospitality to those who denied the fact that Jesus Christ had came in flesh, because to receive heretical teachers was to agree with their false teaching (7-11). Here, it is apparent that the author thought that orthodox beliefs

---

25 Arterbury, *Entertaining Angels*, 94.

about Christianity was much more significant than hospitality as upholding contemporary cultural custom, with a view to protecting the congregation from the dangers inherent in welcoming guests.[26]

This brief overview of hospitality in both the Greco-Roman world and early Jewish and Christian tradition has identified three important elements. First, for ancient Greeks and Romans the welcoming of a stranger was seen as crucial in maintaining social order, as was helping fellow-citizens, although a few sources depicted the poor as being protected by Zeus. In contrast, ancient Jewish and Christian hospitality generally appeared to have been based on divine injunction combined with the practical and realistic considerations of a potentially uncertain future when the favor might need to be returned. Secondly, both Jewish and pagan hosts customarily sought to verify the identities of their guests. This was to set some limit on welcoming people on the basis of their individual socio-economic and religious status, as well as a means of protecting against dangers. For Greeks and the Romans in particular, the visitors were likely to select their counterparts on the basis of their own status and wealth. Thirdly, it was traditional for hosts in the ancient world to anticipate some form of reward for their sacrifice, even if such expectations varied.

5.2 Laypeople and entertaining strangers

5.2.1 Practising moderation

The *Letters* of Barsanuphius and John of Gaza contain references to laypersons who sought advice about entertaining strangers who might visit their homes. According to letter 635, a man questions John of Gaza about what he should offer to any beggars who may congregate in front of his house. John recommends he give them whatever is at hand (such as a little piece of bread,

---

26 Arterbury, *Entertaining Angels*, 119.

some undiluted wine and even some money). These gifts are to be given "without affliction, according to godly fear" (letter 635). Likewise, John also tells another lay questioner to provide his guests with gifts in his hand, quoting "Be content with what you have" (letter 681; see Heb.13:5). The ideal expressed by the holy man is that, when one is required to distribute alms to guests but has nothing or little to hand, there is no expectation that the charitable person will borrow money or provisions from others:

> If one is asked to give something that one does not have, then there is no need to borrow in order to give. For even the Apostle Peter was asked to give alms and responded: "I have no silver or gold"; and he did not borrow any money in order to give some. Indeed, even if one only has the bare necessities, then again there is no need to spend it all, so that he may not later miss it or be afflicted by its absence... For someone who has nothing beyond what is necessary does not have anything to give to another person. He should simply say to the person who is asking: "Forgive me, but I only have what I need myself" (letter 620).

From this passage, it is clear that John wisely suggests a benefactor give what he can but counsels against borrowing in order to give, because such an action causes the giver to be afflicted. He proposes a proper and moderate form of hospitality, which arises from his concern to care for his lay disciples as benefactors themselves, in spiritual terms, as well as to protect their economic status. This response is not surprising, given the attitude of the holy men towards the encouragement of giving gifts to the poor discussed in the previous chapter.

5.2.2 Practising discrimination

Gazan monasticism was closely connected to the neighboring towns, as shown above (see 2.3.3). When monks visited secular towns in Gaza, they often received gifts or money from both ordinary and wealthy inhabitants. In letter 636 we find a layman who contemplates giving his good quality wine and bread to the poor and marginalized, while keeping all of the lower quality bread and wine for himself. However, he hesitates to implement his decision and so asks the Other Old Man for advice. He is particularly troubled by the fact that he feels it necessary to treat his spiritual fathers differently to the poor who seek his charity. These men he serves with the best quality food, and in doing so indicates that he considers them as more worthy than the poor. He questions the Old Man whether or not these acts are proper. John agrees with his approach and also seeks to differentiate between the spiritual fathers and the poor. Consequently, he advises the man to give the poor "what is of less significance to" him, and to show greater respect to his spiritual fathers because they are the servants of God. Such attitude towards voluntary poverty, as expressed by both the supplicant in letter 636 and John's response, is not unique to sixth-century Gaza. Indeed, it is similar to that expressed by many authors from Late Antiquity, who highly value the choice of voluntary poverty in order to aid those less fortunate.[27]

In addition to considerations of the social and religious status of beneficiaries, John of Gaza suggests the application of different levels of hospitality according to the psychological and physical condition of those on the receiving end. According to letter 630, a layman expresses concern about how and to what extent he should distribute his possessions among people in three different situations: those who would unabashedly accept alms in public; those who would be reluctant to receive help publicly because of their nobility of birth (διὰ τὴν εὐγένειαν); and those who are ill. John recommends giving the first group marginally more than they require, while providing the second and third groups with much more than they need (letter 630). Those referred to in the

---

[27] See Allen, Neil and Mayer, *Preaching Poverty in Late Antiquity*, 96-99, 146-47 and 195-96.

second category might well be ruined aristocrats, not ordinary beggars, who commonly begged on the street or at the church door of many Late Roman religious institutions.[28] John's professed attitude towards those who are impoverished and seeking aid appears to work on a sliding scale in proportion to both the psychological conditions and physical circumstances of those on the receiving end of such charity. John appears caught between two ideals. On the one hand, he seems to want to give aid based on the status of the receiver, while on the other, he suggests that those who need more should be the recipients of more aid. However, once again it is noticeable that John pays less attention to the indigent poor.

The practice of a sliding scale of gifts in the *Letters*, which was rooted in both the Hellenistic and Jewish traditions, is also observed in several different Christian discourses from the later Roman Empire.[29] For example, a similar sliding scale can be found in the works of Leo the Great and Gregory the Great.[30] In her study on welcoming strangers in the Mediterranean East during Late Antiquity, Wendy Mayer also comments on the contemporary practice of hospitality:

> In Christianity in particular... different categories of strangers were valued differently. Soldiers and dead

---

28 Daniel Caner, "Charitable Ministrations (Diakoniai), Monasticism, and the Social Aesthetic of Sixth-Century Byzantium," in *Charity and Giving in Monotheistic Religions*, ed. Miriam Frenkel and Yaacov Lev (Berlin: Walter de Gruyter, 2009), 58. On begging in public places by the poor, see Finn, *Almsgiving in the Later Roman Empire*, 99–103; Bronwen Neil, "Models of Gift Giving in the Preaching of Leo the Great," *Journal of Early Christian Studies* 18.2 (2010): 233.

29 On discriminating gifts in the ancient Graeco-Roman world, see Constantelos, "Hellenic Background and Nature of Patristic Philanthropy in the Early Byzantine Era," in *Wealth and Poverty in Early Church and Society*, ed. Susan R. Holman (Grand Rapids: Baker Academic, 2008) 192–93. On the gifts in late-antique Christianity, see Neil, "Models of Gift Giving in the Preaching of Leo the Great," 235–6. On the discrimination of gifts in the early church including the Didascalia and Cyprian, see Rhee, *Loving the Poor, Saving the Rich*, 148–49.

30 Brown, *Poverty and Leadership in the Later Roman Empire*, 60.

saints[31] were received with a degree of enthusiasm. Exiled bishops experienced a mixed reception, as did refugees of status with surviving networks. The indigent refugee and ordinary person without resources or networks of their own were unlikely, on the other hand, to be viewed with much favour.[32]

In this, it is evident that discrimination and discernment with regard to the offering of charity and hospitality towards strangers was not rare in the eastern Mediterranean world and the socio-economic status of the individual recipients was certainly a major factor in exercising such discretion.

As well as providing charitable offerings in entertaining strangers, the Gazan teachers also advised on the provision of accommodation. According to letters 681, 682, 727 and 728, it was not uncommon for the laity to offer hospitality to monks. In letter 681, a layman asks John how he is to receive monks when he sometimes has nothing to offer to them. John responds that he should simply offer all that he has with willingness. Here again we see John recommending that his interlocutor give within his means. Additionally, letter 727 deals with the issue of extending hospitality to a foreign monk (μοναχὸν ξένον) in particular. There is not enough information in the letter to indicate whether the foreign monk is merely a monastic person traveling for a particular reason,[33] or an itinerant monk who would be considered an object of alarm in Late Antiquity.[34] In the letter 727 John first of

---

31 The phrase "dead saints" here means famous dead bishops and ascetics, and their relics.
32 Mayer, "Welcoming the Stranger in the Mediterranean East," 106.
33 For example, a pilgrimage to a sacred place, visit to relatives or eminent saints, trade and so on, see Lucien, *La vie quotidienne des Pères du désert en Egypte au IVe siècle*, 165–75.
34 For more detail on wandering monks in Late Antiquity, see Daniel Caner, *Wandering, Begging Monks: Spiritual Authority and the Promotion of Monasticism in Late Antiquity* (Berkeley: University of California Press, 2002); Dietz, *Wandering Monks, Virgins and Pilgrims*, 88–105.

all suggests the host pray to God and then query the guest about his identity. If the guest is then deemed acceptable, the host is to offer a meal to his guest. Then the advisor recommends sending the visitor away promptly and without additional gifts. From the text, it is recognized that John's response suggests a prudent form of action to protect one of his followers, which reveals much about the concerns of local ascetics over the potential dangers of giving aid and succor to alien monks.

In his homily on Genesis when preaching about Abraham's hospitality to strangers, John Chrysostom, however, suggests a quite different approach to hospitality.

> The loving Lord's intention, you see, was that we should not be indifferent about such friendship nor be too picky about our visitors—hence his words, "Whoever receives one of the least of these in my name receives me". So, don't pay attention to the status of the visitors nor despise the person on the basis of what you can see, but consider that in the visitor you are welcoming your Lord.[35]

Chrysostom advises his congregants not to offer discriminating hospitality to their visitors in proportion to the status or appearance of the guests, reminding them that they can receive Christ in the guise of strangers or the poor. The generous hospitality he suggests depends on his understanding of Christ as guest or stranger. This is quite different from that of the two Gazan anchorites who view such strangers as a potential danger for their followers and their monastic community as a whole.

The correspondence of the Gazan anchorites examined so far, shows them advising their interlocutors to practise hospitality with a moderate and cautious attitude. They also suggest different levels of hospitality to be offered to different sections of soci-

---

35 John Chrysostom, *Homilies on Genesis 41* in *Homilies on Genesis: Saint John Chrysostom*, vol 2:18–45, trans. Robert C. Hill, FC 82 (Washington, DC: Catholic University of America Press, 1988), 408.

ety. Their recommendations indicate some similarities with the traditions of charity and hospitality as demonstrated by ancient Greco-Roman and Jewish societies,[36] but a closer examination indicates differences. The ancient Greeks and Romans, in particular, tended to receive only guests who deserved to be accepted on the basis of their socio-economic status, whereas the authors of the *Letters* welcome visitors whether prominent or insignificant, although providing different levels of hospitality. When we compare the *Letters* to what we know about ancient hospitality, a further difference appears to be a preference for giving provisions and gifts to guests rather than offering accommodation.[37]

5.2.3 Practising discernment

Discernment (διάκρισις) was considered as one of crucial components in the monastic milieu.[38] St. Antony and Evagrius Ponticus understood *diakrisis* as the ability to discern "demonic activity", which tempts desert hermits or monks.[39] On the other hand, John Cassian basically regarded *discretio* as an essential means of protecting a monk from deviating from the monastic life. It enabled a monk not merely to be alert to his thoughts and discern their nature and origin, but also "to distinguish between good

---

36 For the influence of Hellenistic thought on Christian philanthropy (φιλανθρωπία) in the late Roman Empire, see Constantelos, "Hellenic Background and Nature of Patristic Philanthropy in the Early Byzantine Era," 187–208.

37 For the case of Syriac monasticism in the fifth and sixth century, see Mayer "Welcoming the Stranger in the Mediterranean East," 93.

38 On *diakrisis* in late-antique bishops and elite monks, see Kevin Uhalde, *Expectations of Justice in the Age of Augustine* (Philadelphia: University of Pennsylvania Press, 2007); Antony Rich, *Discernment in the Desert Fathers: Diakrisis in the Life and Thought of Early Egyptian Monasticism* (Eugene, OR: Wipf & Stock, 2007); George E. Demacopoulos, *Five Models of Spiritual Direction in the Early Church* (Notre Dame: University of Notre Dame Press, 2007), 8–9, 111–14, 135–36 and 155–56.

39 Demacopoulos, *Five Models of Spiritual Direction in the Early Church*, 113 says that Antony and Evagrius regarded discernment as "the recognition of demonic activity" and "demonic activity to a monk's temptation" respectively. For more detail on *diakrisis* in Evagrius, see Rich, *Discernment in the Desert Fathers*, 39–74.

and bad things, actions and thoughts and to choose how best to respond to them".[40] Moreover, it is for Cassian that discernment was viewed as "an awareness of ignorance".[41] Thus, *discretio* and awareness of one's inner measure are viewed as two sides of the same coin in the monastic *paideia* of Cassian. The inner perception, that is discernment, helps monks to recognise the limits of their knowledge and ability, and motivates them to desire to know more with regard to self-knowledge. Through these processes, they thereby draw closer to perfection.[42] The *Sayings of the Desert Fathers* further understands *diakrisis* as "personal capacity for ascetic life".[43] However, the *Sayings*, unlike Cassian, link the virtue to human wickedness and deficiency, so that discernment enables ascetics to be properly aware of their weakness and sinful nature, unless they fail to recognise such failings in themselves. Simultaneously, it warns that without discernment monks may became arrogant in their achievements, which is a vice which all monks should seek to avoid.[44]

Just as Cassian and the *Sayings* suggest, it is also in the *Letters* that *diakrisis* was a capacity enabling one to check one's own inner condition or capacity. According to a letter of John addressed to an anonymous layperson, discernment (διάκρισις) involves knowing an appropriate level of one's own inner capacity:

> One should always do everything with discernment. To know one's limit is discernment as well as security of thought, in order not to be troubled later. Doing anything beyond one's measure, whether this be almsgiving or anything else, is lack of discernment. For later this brings one to turmoil, despondency, and murmuring (letter 621).

---

40 Rich, *Discernment in the Desert Fathers*, 99.
41 Rich, *Discernment in the Desert Fathers*, 100.
42 Rich, *Discernment in the Desert Fathers*, 100.
43 For more detail on discernment in the *Sayings of the Desert Fathers*, see Rich, *Discernment in the Desert Fathers*, 175–78.
44 Rich, *Discernment in the Desert Fathers*, 177.

Thus, John advises that while all people, rich and poor, need to distribute their possessions at their own level—otherwise they will repent what they have done, according to letter 622. Moreover, John goes on to rebuke the person who fails to spend his belongings carefully, saying: "that person should blame himself for lack of discernment" (letter 624).

Apart from being aware of one's own inner capacity, the nature of discernment, as defined in the *Letters*, is also to be aware of rationale behind the words and deeds of others. In the *Letters*, entertaining the guest with discernment means identifying the background of the person seeking aid and then distributing charity only to the really needy. The sliding scale of almsgiving, discussed above, can be applied to this task, thereby allowing a benefactor to discern between true spiritual fathers and mendicant monks, or between the true poor and unworthy beggars. Both Barsanuphius and John of Gaza recognize the importance of this matter and recommend that their disciples establish the identities and situations of those on the receiving end of charity. In letter 727, John exhorts his interlocutor to check the details of any anonymous foreign monks who come to his house, and only to extend hospitality (albeit truncated hospitality) to those who deserved to be accepted.

John's emphasis on discerning the nature of unidentified guests is echoed in letters addressed to both Dorotheos and Aelianos, as the new abbot of Seridos monastery. When Dorotheos seeks advice on how he should respond to a person who has asked him to share some of his possessions, John strongly recommends that he firstly seek to discern the economic state of the requestor. He also suggests that Dorotheos only disperse his possessions to the poor when he is certain the asker is in fact needy and deserving, and then only in moderation:

> If you learn that the person asking is doing so out of need, then give it joyfully, as if you are doing so on behalf of

God. For that is what joy is about. If you learn, however, that the person does not need it, then do not give it to him, but say: "I have been commanded by the abbot to give nothing to anyone who is not in need" (letter 317).

Further, in letter 587, John responds to Aelianos' query about offering hospitality to visitors who approach his coenobitic community, by suggesting that one should extend hospitality and charity to visitors only within one's own measure. He also warns Aelianos to discreetly make himself aware of the background and reasons behind his visitors' particular situations. Offering a lesson on the worthiness of those who seek charity, he notes that only prudent hospitality prevents beggars from living reckless lives (letter 587).

Here it is clear that when the nature of discernment, as identified and elucidated by John, is compared to his predecessors, the Gazan monk appears to widen the usage of the term. Such discernment is, in John's view, related to checking one's own inner condition, just as Cassian and the *Apophthegmata* suggest, although he extends this ability to also being aware of the inner rationale behind beggars or visitors. Such discernment, in John's view, will protect his followers from the many dangers associated with giving gifts and extending hospitality, and prevent them from wasting their energy and property unnecessarily.

This section has dealt predominantly with advice on the practice of entertaining and caring for guests given to laypeople. However, such hospitality was also essential for monks in the later Roman Empire. Monastic leaders often recommend their disciples entertain and care for strangers.[45] The following section will therefore analyze the hospitality offered by monks in the coenobium of Seridos.

---

45 Hirschfeld, *The Judean Desert Monasteries in the Byzantine Period*, 196; Horn, *Asceticism and Christological Controversy in Fifth-Century Palestine*, 290–91; Vööbus, *History of Asceticism in the Syrian Orient* II, 361–83.

5.3 Monks and entertaining strangers

5.3.1 The xenodocheion (ξενοδοχεῖον) in the monastery of Seridos

A guesthouse or hospice called *xenodocheion* was prevalent across eastern Mediterranean societies in Late Antiquity. Some were erected by monastic and episcopal authorities while others were built by Roman emperors and their families, wealthy aristocrats and sometimes provincial governors.[46] In particular, Christian guest-houses for travelers, the poor and the sick, probably emerged from the mid-fourth century onwards.[47] According to Brown, between the fourth and eighth centuries, approximately forty hospices were established in Constantinople, while forty-five hospitals and twenty-two poor houses were set up outside the great city—and fifty-nine *xenodocheia*.[48] Moreover, some fifth-century Syrian canons record that the philanthropic institutions, which were managed by an overseer appointed by the local bishop, were located in many towns in the Roman province of Osrhoene and its neighboring areas.[49]

Like other cities from the period of the Later Roman Empire,[50] Tabatha, a port city of Gaza, had a *xenodocheion* which was located around the monastery of Seridos, according to the archaeological evidence.[51] Moreover, the charitable facility was built by Seridos outside the Tabatha monastery (letters 570C and 595). The *Practical Teaching on the Christian Life* of Abba Dorotheos also mentions the institution, where he served as a

---

46 See Constantelos, *Byzantine Philanthropy and Social Welfare*, 186–95.
47 Brown thinks that "It is only in the 350s that xenodocheion clearly appear in Christian sources". See Brown, *Poverty and Leadership in the Later Roman Empire*, 34. For the Greek word ξενοδοχεῖον, see Lampe, *A Patristic Greek Lexicon*, 932, s.v. ξενοδοχεῖον.
48 Brown, *Poverty and Leadership in the Later Roman Empire*, 122 n. 114.
49 Vööbus, *History of Asceticism in the Syrian Orient* II, 370–71.
50 See Andrew Crislip, *From Monastery to Hospital: Christian Monasticism and the Transformation of Health Care in Late Antiquity* (Ann Arbor: The University of Michigan Press, 2005), 108–10, 133–34; Finn, *Almsgiving in the Later Roman Empire*, 83.
51 Hirschfeld, "The Monasteries of Gaza: An Archaeological Review," 76.

head of the *xenodocheion* of the Gazan coenobium:

> When I was in the coenobium, the abbot, with approval of the elders, made me the guest-master. At that time, I was recovering from a serious illness. The guests came and I used to spend the whole evening with them, and there would be camel-owners, and I attended to their needs. Very often, when leaving to go to sleep, I would be woken up because of some new need.[52]

Given the location of Gaza and the fact that Dorotheos attended camel-owners, evidently the facility had a role within the pattern of trade between Egypt and the province of Palestine.

However, it is not evident how the *xenodocheion* functioned in Tabatha. Was it for travelers only? The functions of this philanthropic institution must be understood on the basis of the nature of a *xenodocheion* in the late-antique Mediterranean world. Among the various charitable institutions known in the early Byzantine world, the hospice of Sampson is one of the most famous.[53] This hospice is located between the Great Church, also known as Hagia Sophia, and the Eirene Church in Constantinople. Timothy Miller cites various sources which refer to Sampson and his charitable facility, and conjectures that Sampson opened his hospice "for the poor of Constantinople sometime in the late fourth century".[54] According to the work of Procopius of Caesarea which provides more details about the hospice in Constantinople, it was "devoted to those who were at once destitute and suffering from serious illness, those who were, namely, suffering in loss of both property and health".[55] The hospice of

---

52 Dorotheos, *Abba Dorotheos: Practical Teaching on the Christian Life*, lesson 11, 119. On general life of Dorotheos, see Bitton-Ashkelony and Kofsky, *The Monastic School of Gaza*, 42–46.
53 Constantelos, *Byzantine Philanthropy and Social Welfare*, 191.
54 Timothy Miller, *The Birth of the Hospital in the Byzantine Empire* (Baltimore: John Hopkins University Press, 1997), 84. For more detail on the hospital of Sampson, see Miller, *The Birth of the Hospital in the Byzantine Empire*, 80–84.
55 Procopius, *Buildings*, I. II. 14.

Sampson did not merely function as a poorhouse, but as a complex center to care for the poor and the sick.

Hospices in both Judean and Syrian monasteries were similar to that of Sampson. According to Hirschfeld, the philanthropic institutions in the Judean desert not only provided guests with lodging and food free of charge in their hospices, but also cared for the sick and weak.[56] These functions are also confirmed in the fifth-century Syrian canons that mention the duties of the overseer of *xenodocheion*, known as *aksnādākrā*:

> Beds and mattresses and other things which are required for the needs of the sick and needy, shall be made; if, however, the estate (lit. essence) of the house does not suffice, the entire community of the believers shall lay hand on this—everyone according to his strength, and a house of travelling brothers shall be established.[57]

Elsewhere, Procopius of Caesarea highlights the differences between such various philanthropic institutions. According to him, Justinian established two hospices (ξενῶνες) in Jerusalem: one was a temporary dwelling for travelers which was separated from the other, a hospice caring for the sick. According to their main purposes, one was for "the shelter of visiting strangers" and the other "for the poor persons suffering from diseases".[58]

The evidence explored so far, suggests that although there were some hospices in the early Byzantine world which functioned as medical centers or guesthouses only, many more anecdotes indicate the existence of complex centers with both functions. These not only provided travelers or pilgrims with

---

56 Hirschfeld, *The Judean Desert Monasteries in the Byzantine Period*, 199. For more evidence in Late Antiquity, see Constantelos, *Byzantine Philanthropy and Social Welfare*, 186; Miller, *The Birth of the Hospital in the Byzantine Empire*, 27–29; Brown, *Poverty and Leadership in the Later Roman Empire*, 35.
57 Vööbus, *History of Asceticism in the Syrian Orient* II, 371.
58 Procopius, *Buildings*, trans. H. B. Dewing and Glanville Downey, LCL 343 (Cambridge, MA: Harvard University Press, 1940), V. VI. 25–26.

food and lodging, but also offered medical care to sick guests where necessary.[59]

This leads to the conjecture that the hospice in the Gazan coenobium, along with those of other monasteries in the East, was likely to have acted not only as a shelter for travelers, but also as an infirmary. As the *Letters* show, diverse medical activities occurred in the monastery of Seridos, and some monks, including Dorotheos, were employed as medical staffs or orderlies (letter 334). This evidence does not imply the existence of an independent infirmary within the monastic community, but rather suggests that the *xenodocheion* of which Dorotheos of Gaza had charge functioned as one of these more complex centers.

5.3.2 Entertaining ordinary guests

Although many monastic communities in Late Antiquity theoretically sought a life of isolation from secular society, they were often unable to completely separate themselves from the world. Fellow monks and clergymen as well as the members of the laity often visited monasteries for a variety of reasons. There are many references in the *Letters* to travelers coming to the monastery in Tabatha. Some of them come to sell goods (letter 594) or to visit family members (letter 595), while others attend the coenobium seeking medical help from monastic physicians (letters 313 and 548). In addition, the *Letters* indicate that both itinerant monks (letters 588–589) and priests (letter 591) visited the community seeking assistance.

As a result of such visits, monastic leaders in Late Antiquity established a guest-house called *xenodocheion*, and entertained visitors.[60] In addition to building such guesthouses, they also established regulations concerning how to treat guests and supplicants. For example, Pachomius advised his followers, in princi-

---

59   See Miller, *The Birth of the Hospital in the Byzantine Empire*, 27–28.
60   Binns, *Ascetics and Ambassadors of Christ*, 95–96.

ple, to welcome their visitors, both male and female, with greater honour, but to offer different places according to their gender and religious status.[61] The monastic rules of Isaiah of Scetis and St. Benedict also suggested more detailed instructions on welcoming a guest. According to them, monks should receive their guests and then give those people appropriate provisions and lodging to rest, without excessive communication with guests.[62] Among them, Abba Isaiah in particular recommended them to send their guests away clean, well fed and rested, with washed and mended clothes, but displayed, to some extent, a cautious attitude towards wandering monks who can be a potential threat to monastic community.[63]

The *Letters* of Barsanuphius and John, however, present a slightly different face with regard to the practices and nature of monastic hospitality in late antique Gaza. John's attitude towards monastic hospitality is recorded in the letters exchanged between him and Aelianos, abbot of Seridos' coenobium (letters 584 and 590). When the abbot asks John the prophet about the issue of receiving guests, John tells him it is good to receive guests into the guesthouse but that it is necessary to identify the reasons behind their visit before letting them stay in the monastery.

> Practise hospitality and the commandment [for charity] as much as you can; however, balance these also with your patience. Even if you have more than enough in your possession, you should still exercise balance, lest anyone develop a habit of asking continually on the pretext of poverty. Therefore, carefully examine the reasons for which each visitor approaches. If someone happens to be a thief, as the fathers have said, simply give that person a blessing and then ask him to leave. Moreover, since some

---

61   Pachomius, *Precepts*, 51–52. in *Pachomian Koinonia*, vol. 2, 153–54.
62   Abba Isaiah, *Ascetic Discourses*, 3; Benedict, *RB 1980: The Rule of St. Benedict in English*, ed. Timothy Fry (Collegeville, Liturgical Press, 1982), 53.1–24.
63   Abba Isaiah, *Ascetic Discourses*, 3.

of them come here to exploit you, do not allow them any such boldness, for they are trying to exploit you with their greed, since they do not really need anything. And do not give a garment to anyone upon first encounter, unless it is a person who greatly fears God and is embarrassed to ask. So search out the truth, in order to see whether a person is genuinely poor and needy for God's sake rather than a result of a prodigal life; and, afterward, show compassion on that person (letter 587).

With regard to the rules of monastic hospitality outlined by the Gazan anchorite, three important elements are noticed. Firstly, he recommends offering help and hospitality within one's own measure and level, telling his reader to "exercise balance". This is identical to the advice given to lay followers in letters 617 and 620. Secondly, he recommends caution with regard to handing out charity, including clothing, and even goes so far as to note that a monk should only extend welcome to those established to be legitimately in need. While he espouses the Christian virtue of charity, it is nevertheless qualified in order to be only given to those proven worthy recipients. If Dorotheos, as head of the *xenodocheion*, and his assistants followed this recommendation, it is enough to assume they probed the hidden motives of strangers before offering hospitality. For the same reason, mendicant monks (letters 588–589) and unknown guests who were perceived to be potentially dangerous (letter 591) were not permitted to enter into the monastery of Seridos. Finally, John suggests a sliding scale of hospitality and charity depending on the worth of the visitor, giving first to those who are "genuinely poor and needy for God's sake rather than a result of a prodigal life" (letter 587).

Moreover, John can be observed limiting expressions of monastic hospitality to advanced monks, and in this way seeking to protect immature monks from any outside dangers. According to letter 311, Dorotheos asks what Abba Isaiah means when he says "after greeting the guest, ask him how he is, and then be silent, simply there beside him". John's response focuses on the fact that such advice applies to "an elder who was advanced both in age and in [spiritual] measure" only. He then goes on to say that the younger, less experienced monk, who wants to "become a genuine monk will guard himself from such conversations" because "these give rise to disregard, laziness, insubordination, and terrible boldness" (letter 311). Significantly, the teaching of Isaiah is originally addressed to both novices and anchorites in his *Ascetic Discourses,* but John's reinterpretation of the instruction applies the teaching to mature monks only. Here it is evidently that John's intention is to balance monastic responsibility to strangers with practicing one's own ascetic life.

The relationship between charity and ascetic life was indeed a matter of some debate in late-antique monasticism. There were, in general terms, two opposing positions among monastic communities. On the one side was the view that philanthropic activity was an essential component of true Christian asceticism: this view was supported by Pachomius, Basil and Gregory of Nazianzus. Although Basil of Caesarea believed that the ascetic life of a monk was cultivated by contemplation, he did not prohibit their disciples from implementing charity to the socially weak; rather he recommended that "monks could express their active philanthropia" and "established a vast ptochotropheion with its hospital".[64] On the other side of the debate, charity was deemed a danger to such ascetic practices as prayer and contemplation (e.g. Evagrius of Pontus and Neilos of Ankyra). According to Neilos of Ankyra in particular, those who want to attain perfection should flee from "all contact with the world and seek out the desert in the footsteps of Anthony".[65]

---

[64] Miller, *The Birth of the Hospital in the Byzantine Empire,* 119–20. The citation is from 120.
[65] Miller, *The Birth of the Hospital in the Byzantine Empire,* 121–22. The citation is from 122.

The *Letters* of Barsanuphius and John of Gaza, in principle, appear to follow the former ideal. Strictly speaking, they recommend the offering of hospitality with caution because they also recognize the troubles inherent in philanthropic activities. The prudent attitude of the Gazan mentors seemed to make the monastery of Seridos extend its hospitality to strangers and the poor in a somewhat passive way, which eventually prevented the coenobium from becoming an influential patron in sixth-century Gaza.

5.3.3 Entertaining wandering monks

Before welcoming wandering monks in the *Letters*, it is helpful to explore the practice of *xeniteia* (ξενιτεία)[66] in the monastic milieu of the eastern Mediterranean world. The practice of wandering or migration can be found as far back as the early Christian times. The *Didache,* the *Acts of Thomas,* and pseudo-Clément's *Letters to Virgins,* for example, made reference to the the practice of *xeniteia* in the early Church.[67] According to monastic sources in Late Antiquity, there were many tales of monks departing from their homes for diverse reasons. Some of them left their cells or monasteries to make pilgrimage to holy places, to visit families

---

66 On ξενιτεία meaning "wandering", "exile" or "travel in a foreign land", see Geoffrey W. H. Lampe, *A Patristic Greek Lexicon* (Oxford: The Clarendon Press, 1961), 931-32, s.v. ξενιτεία.

67 Kurt Niederwimmer, *The Didache: A Commentary on the Didache,* ed. Harold W. Attridge, trans. Linda M. Maloney, 2nd ed. (Minneapolis: Fortress Press, 1998); Kurt Niederwimmer, "An Examination of the Development of Itinerant Radicalism in the Environment and Tradition of the Didache," in *The Didache in Modern Research* (Leiden: E.J. Brill, 1996), 321–39; Stephen Patterson, "The Legacy of Radical Itinerancy in Early Christianity," in *The Didache in Context: Essay on Its Text, History and Transmission,* ed. Clayton Jefford (Leiden: E.J. Brill, 1995), 313–29; Albertus F. J. Klijn, *The Acts of Thomas: Introduction, Text, and Commentary* (Leiden: E. J. Brill, 1962); pseudo-Clement, "Two Epistles Concerning Virginity," trans. M. B. Riddle in *Ante Nicene Fathers,* vol. III, ed. A. Roberts and J. Donaldson (Grand Rapids: W. B. Eerdmans, 1951). For the itinerancy in the Acts of Thomas and pseudo-Clément's Letters to Virgins, see Caner, *Wandering, Begging Monks,* 50–82; Hyung Guen Choi, "Gaza Monastery and Hospitality during the Sixth Century: The Case of the Letters of Barsanuphius and John of Gaza," *Korea Journal of Christian Studies* 115 (2020): 82-3 [Korean].

or eminent saints, and even to undertake education and trade.[68] Some others were, however, expected to wander without possessions in order to acquire ascetic virtues such as *amerimnia*[69] or closeness to God. In Syriac tradition in particular, the roaming life was also said to imitate Jesus's life.

> In such movement, the monks felt that they imitated fully the life of Him concerning whom they read in the gospel that foxes have their hollows and birds their nests but He has no place where to lay His Head. They also felt that their inner attitude of being strangers and foreigners in the world could find an adequate visible expression in this type of existence. Besides this attitude, they appreciated personal fatigue and toil as a means of mortification of the body. Also, the ideal of poverty could be best served by this manner of life—roaming around, possessing nothing, not even a cave.[70]

Significantly, this passage highlights the rationale which explains why certain Syrian monks followed this lifestyle: that is, they were seeking to imitate Jesus in terms of his wandering, humiliation and voluntary poverty.

Furthermore, physical migration was sometimes seen as a crucial method by which to achieve spiritual growth for non-Chalcedonian monks in fifth-century Palestine in particular. In his *Life of Peter the Iberian* depicting migration of Peter the Iberian and John the Eunuch, Rufus presents the concept of monastic migration with favor because of his understanding of

---

68 See Lucien, *La vie quotidienne des Pères du désert en Egypte au IVe siècle*, 165–75.
69 See Caner, *Wandering, Begging Monks*, 19–49. On *xeniteia* in general, see Antonie Guillaumont, "Le dépaysement comme forme d'ascèse, dans le monachisme ancien," *École Pratique des Hautes Études* 76 (1967): 31–58. See also Graham Gould, "Moving On and Staying Put in the Apophthegmata Patrum," *Studia Patristica* XX (1989): 237.
70 Vööbus, *History of Asceticism in the Syrian Orient* II, 269–71. The quote is from 270. On 'aksēnyā, see Payne Smith, *A Compendious Syriac Dictionary* (Oxford: The Clarendon Press, 1903), 16, s.v. ܐܟܣܢܝܐ.

the nature of *aksēnāyūṯā*[71] as a means of seeking spiritual perfection. In addition to this, he goes on to depict the itinerant life as a method for non-Chalcedonians to keep their faith:

> the day of his departure [from this world] was near. He painstakingly did all these [things] so that he would be perfected in a foreign land ['*aksēnyā*] and also at the end [of his life] weave the crown of a good pilgrimage, loving contempt so much as to be like our Lord and despising glory and honour from men.[72]

Elsewhere, Rufus also tells the story of Stephen, who had been an archdeacon of Jerusalem, and then decided to leave the holy city so as not to have contact with his theological opponents after the council of Chalcedon.[73] Rufus revisits this idea in his report of a conversation between Abba Zeno and Stephen in the *Plerophoriae*. Stephen consults his spiritual father Zeno over a wish to participate in "the virtue of being a traveller" to which Zeno replies that whoever wants to keep the orthodox faith after the issue of the Chalcedon decrees should be resolutely determined to live as a pilgrim and a stranger in a foreign land.[74] Throughout his works, Rufus extols the virtue of wandering and encourages his readers to receive mendicant monks, offering hospitality.[75] On the basis of the work of John Rufus, Horn therefore

---

71 See Smith, *A Compendious Syriac Dictionary*, 16, s.v. ܐܟܣܢܝܘܬܐ meaning 'a stranger or traveler', 'travels', and 'the entertaining of strangers' and 'hospitality'. For more detail on *xeniteia* and ܐܟܣܢܝܘܬܐ, see Guillaumont, "Le dépaysement comme forme d'ascèse, dans le monachisme ancien," *École Pratique des Hautes Études* 76 (1967) : 31–58; Horn, *Asceticism and Christological Controversy in Fifth-Century Palestine*, 257–60.
72 Rufus, *The Life of Peter the Iberian*, 164. The insertion of '*aksēnyā* (ܐܟܣܢܝܐ) in the quotation is mine.
73 Rufus, *The Life of Peter the Iberian*, 176.
74 John Rufus, Plerophories, in *Plérophories, témoignages et révélation*, ed. and trans., F. Nau, PO 8.1 (1911; repr., Turnhout, Belgique: Brepols, 1982), VIII. The quotation is from Horn, *Asceticism and Christological Controversy in Fifth-Century Palestine*, 257 n. 146.
75 See Horn, *Asceticism and Christological Controversy in Fifth-Century Palestine*, 273–99.

argues "that in the long run anti-Chalcedonian ascetic communities in Syria-Palestine developed and benefited significantly from encouraging and cultivating the virtue of hospitality".[76]

Imperial officials and religious authorities, in contrast, viewed monastic migration from a different perspective. For them, this itinerant lifestyle was not a form of pursuit of monastic virtue, but rather a potential threat to the monastic milieu and secular community. They saw the itinerant monk as someone who created serious social problems and posed a threat to both monastic and secular life in urban and rural areas. In terms of an example of the kind of social problem caused, there was often conflict between wandering monks and local residents, which sometimes escalated into violence.[77] For example, there are reports of attacks by monks on Jewish synagogues and Valentinus Chapel at Callinicum in Mesopotamia in 388. This particular episode and further violence by monks acted as a trigger for the commandment of Theodosius I and Valentinian II in 390 that all monks should inhabit deserted places and that they were prohibited to enter into cities or towns.[78]

---

76 Horn, Asceticism and Christological Controversy in Fifth-Century Palestine, 275.
77 For violence between monks and Jews in the fifth century Palestine, see Aryeh Kofsky, "Observation on Christian-Jewish coexistence in Late Antiquity Palestine (Fifth to Seventh Centuries)," Annali: di storia dell' esegesi 23.2 (2006): 439.
78 See André Piganiol, L'empire chrétien (325–395), 2nd ed. (Paris: Presses universitaires de France, 1972), 283–84. On the edict, see CTh 16.3.1. Interestingly the edict was abolished two years later. See CTh 16.3.2. Charles A. Frazee asserts that the significant influence of monks on the imperial leaders was a factor behind the removal of the rule, while Gavin I. Langmuir states that Ambrose, Bishop of Milan, pressured Theodosius to do it. See "Late Roman and Byzantine Legislation on the Monastic Life from the Fourth to the Eighth Centuries," 265–66; Gavin I. Langmui, Toward a Definition of Anti-Semitism (Berkeley: University of California Press; 1990), 70. For more detail with regard to violence by monks in Late Antiquity, see Peter Brown, "Christianization and Religious Conflict," in The Cambridge Ancient History XIII, The Later Empire, A.D. 337-425, ed. Averil Cameron and Peter Garnsey (Cambridge: Cambridge University Press, 1998), 647; Zacharias, "Life of Severos," in Two Early Lives of Severos, trans. Sebastian Brock and Brian Fitzgerald (Liverpool: Liverpool University Press, 2013), 34–43.

In addition, the wandering lifestyle was also seen as a form of disobedience to ecclesiastical or monastic authorities, as well as damage to property and refusal of manual labor.[79] The *Rule of the Master* vividly describes how mendicant monks caused damage to their neighbors including laypeople and other monks.[80] According to the *Rule,* the mendicants compelled their hosts to provide them with hospitality (I.19, 23), at which they overindulged in food and drink (I.20–21). They were also said to mistreat and sometimes kill their donkeys (I. 48–50), to demand new clothing and tunics (I. 46), and often to break the fasting rules of monks (I. 57, 59). Although these descriptions of gyrovagues in the *Rule* seem to be somewhat exaggerated, it is not impossible to suggest that such wanderers indeed offered a level of disruption and harm to contemporary monastic communities and individuals. Actions such as those described above provoked antagonism towards the migration of monks in general. This hostile attitude was expressed through imperial decrees,[81] monastic rules,[82] church councils,[83] and by non-Christian writers.[84]

Taking into consideration contemporary attitudes towards *xeniteia*, it is not surprising that monks in the Mediterranean East also viewed monastic itinerancy in a negative way, at least from the end of the fourth century onwards.[85] Isaiah of Scetis, in the *Sayings of the Desert Fathers*, says: "A beginner who goes from

---

79 See Caner, *Wandering, Begging Monks*, 50-82. For more detail on the gyrovagues, see Dietz, *Wandering Monks, Virgins and Pilgrims*, 88-105.
80 *The Rule of the Master*, trans. Luke Eberle (Kalamazoo: Cistercian Publications, 1977).
81 See Piganiol, *L'empire chretien (325-395)*, 283-84.
82 Rabbula of Edessa restricts the migration of monks in his canons. See Vööbus, *History of Asceticism in the Syrian Orient III: A Contribution to the History of Culture in the Near East*, CSCO 500 (Louvain, 1998), 286; Caner, *Wandering, Begging Monks*, 211 n. 17.
83 For monastic wandering and the Council of Chalcedon, see Peter Hatlie, *The Monks and Monasteries of Constantinople, ca. 350-850* (Cambridge: Cambridge University Press, 2007), 38-41.
84 See Dietz, *Wandering Monks, Virgins and Pilgrims*, 42.
85 Caner, *Wandering, Begging Monks*, 35-38, 81-82.

one monastery to another is like an animal which jumps this way and that, for fear of the halter".[86] In a similar vein, in the *Ascetic Discourses* Isaiah notes that wandering from one place to another makes a monk's soul desolate.[87] The *Letters* also put some emphasis on the virtue of a monk staying in his own cell and not moving from place to place. In response to a monk who asks about traveling to another country in search of salvation, the Great Old Man Barsanuphius says:

> Brother… be assured that wherever you may go, from one side of the earth to the other, you will not benefit as much as you will here. The prayer of the fathers here is to you as an anchor is to a boat… And be carefree of all things; then you will have time for God. Die to all people; for this is exile (letter 259).

The Great Old Man says that true learning can only be found by staying and being anchored to one place.

The *Letters* therefore encourage monastic members tied to particular monasteries to migrate with their abbot's permission, if they have to move. According to letter 356, there was a monk sent to Jerusalem. During his journey, he decided he would like to go down to the Jordan River to pray, but he was not sure whether or not he could go without permission of his abbot. So, he sent a letter to John to consult on this issue. In his reply, John dissuades the monk from going anywhere of his own volition, stressing that it is essential to follow the command of his superior, for that "constitutes prayer and service to God" (letter 356).

Regardless of his own somewhat negative view on the migration of monks, Abba Isaiah advises his readers to extend hospitality not only to ordinary guests, but also to itinerant monks albeit with a note of caution: "If he [a guest] is an itinerant monk, and

---

86   Isaiah 3 in *Sayings of the Desert Fathers*, 59.
87   Isaiah, *Ascetic Discourses*, 7.

there is some of the faithful staying with you, do not show him up before them, but show him mercy in the love of God".[88] However, the *Letters* of Barsanuphius and John of Gaza maintain a differen stance on entertaining the mendicant. In letter 588, John responds to a query from the new abbot of the Tabatha monastery about some *wanderers*[89] who had come to his monastic community. Because of the possibility that they might cause problems, he recommends the abbot give them some provisions and ask them to leave. In the following letter he reiterates that the abbot should not allow them entry despite their demands because excluding them will bring greater benefit to his monastery (letter 589). Here it is certainly recognized that the stance of John of Gaza was much stricter than that of Abba Isaiah. This is lieky to mean that the issue of wandering monks became much more serious in the sixth century.[90]

5.4 Conclusion

In this chapter, it has been seen how ancient views on hospitality and charity towards strangers were interpreted among Christian writers in late antique Gaza. The diverse issues raised in the *Letters* with regard to entertaining strangers suggest that the matter was one of concern for both the secular and monastic sections of Gazan society. Likewise, the Gazan holy men's responses offer us a clear picture of their attitude towards ideals of hospitality as offered to both lay and religious guests.

---

88 Isaiah, *Ascetic Discourses*, 3.
89 On page 134 of her *Disciples of the Desert*, Hevelone-Harper suggests that they might have been monks who brought "unwelcome doctrine." Regarding the contemporary religious climate of fifth and sixth-century Palestine, it is likely that some of the itinerant monks, at least, who approached the monastery of Seridos, were Origenist and non-Chalcedonian monks traveling around Gaza and its neighbouring areas. For discussion of the Origenist and non-Chalcedon monks in early Byzantine Palestine, see section 2.2.3 and chapter 3.
90 Choi, "Gaza Monastery and Hospitality during the Sixth Century: The Case of the Letters of Barsanuphius and John of Gaza," 85.

First of all, John of Gaza demonstrates concern for his lay disciples, as well as consideration for the beneficiaries' mental and physical situations. Simultaneously he also strictly recommends his lay followers extend proper and discriminatory hospitality within their own measure when receiving beggars and spiritual fathers. The rationale behind such discriminaton is primarily related to spiritual and material benefits of a benefator and beneficiary, rather than to social status of those on the receiving end. Here his attitude towards welcoming strangers is likely to be quite different from that of Hellenistic hosts, who extended donor-centered hospitality both as a response to their social responsibility, and in anticipation of potential future reward for philanthropy.

In terms of general monastic hospitality, both Barsanuphius and John hold fairly positive positions, like their predecessors Isaiah of Scetis and Peter the Iberian. However, here again they both sound a note of caution. They suggest that welcoming strangers in a monastic context should nevertheless be done carefully because some guests could pose a threat to a monastic community. They identify potential dangers inherent in hospitality as a result of the negative background of the guest and also in the way some guests could distract monks from their ascetic practices. The Gazan elders differentiate advanced monks from beginners, and strongly urge the former only to carefully extend charity to those in distress, while recommending that the beginner monks keep away from strangers. Such prudent advice by the Gazan anchorites may possibly have limited entertaining and hospitality in the coenobium in Tabatha. In the case of wandering monks, however, their attitude is much more stringent. They recommend prohibiting these monks from entering into the monastic community. In summary, although Barsanuphius and John acknowledge the importance of welcoming the strangers as a monastic responsibility, their primary emphasis is on the spiritual progress of their lay and monastic followers in their care, rather than on offering hospitality to guests themselves. Up to now, it has been argued that Christians in late-antique Gaza were actively involved in helping those in need by extending hospitality to them. The next chapter will therefore focus on the two Gazan anchorites' approach toward their lay and monastic petitioners, exploring their attitudes in caring for the sick in the *Letters*.

Chapter 6
Caring for the Sick in the *Letters*

On opening the pages of *Letters* of Barsanuphius and John, many readers can find here and there that laypeople and monastics in Gaza and its neighboring areas questioned the Gazan mentors with regarding to illness and caring for patients. In this chapter, these issues will be explored. First of all, it considers caring for the sick in the ancient world. Second, it explores causes of illness and diverse medical treatments in the light of the Gazan monastic tradition and, more broadly, of eastern monasticism during Late Antiquity. Third, it investigates Barsanuphius and John's attitude towards lay followers who asked questions about treating their own illness or that of their slaves. The final section deals with the Gazan mentor's positive and negative positions on the treatment of sick monks, and then investigates that to what extent the Gazan mentors offered different medical prescriptions pertaining to dietary regimens, and nursing or medical care according to the questioners' social and religious status.

In seeking to draw out these aspects of caring for sick people as represented in the *Letters*, this chapter will demonstrate that the Gazan Old Men had a positive attitude towards caring for the sick, including slaves, and demonstrate a care and concern for those in their community and surrounds. On the other hand, they also suggest the endurance of bodily suffering in the case of some monks, although there are philanthropic facilities (such as a bathhouse and *xenodocheion*) which monastic patients can use in the monastery of Seridos. There is no doubt that late-antique medicine owed a debt to earlier Greek, Roman and Jewish medical practices.[1] Therefore it starts with an overview of sickness, healing and medical practices in the ancient world.

6.1 Caring for the sick in the ancient world

6.1.1 Caring for the sick in Greco-Roman antiquity

From as early as the fifth century B.C. Greek physicians approached human disease and health within the framework of natural causality. Empedocles (c. 490–430 B.C.) explains that the human body consists of "blood, phlegm, yellow bile and black bile", while Alcmaeon of Croton (c. 500 B.C.) refers to "the dry, the wet, the hot, the cold, the sweet, and bitter".[2] They believed that the human body contained several basic elements called *humours* and its health arose from a harmonious balance of such factors. Likewise, they thought disease or sickness resulted from an imbalance in the humours. The role of doctors was to strive to restore the balance of the fluids through diverse medical treatments such as dietary therapy and pharmacology. This Greek medical tradition, which put emphasis on equilibrium and moderation, was also appropriated by ancient ethical writers. From the fourth century B.C. onwards, ancient philosophers considered the health of the soul was dependant on a balance of the component parts of the soul. They therefore recommended that each individual practise "moderation and self-control" in order to maintain the healthy state of their soul.[3]

The ancient humoral theory was adopted by Hippocrates (c. 460–370 B.C.) who set the foundation for later scientific medicine. According to Owsei Temkin, he used humoral theory

---

[1] For the reception of Greek medicine in the early and late-antique Church, see Gary Ferngren, *Medicine and Health Care in Early Christianity* (Baltimore: John Hopkins University Press, 2009); Miller, *The Birth of the Hospital in the Byzantine Life*, 30–49.
[2] Ferngren, *Medicine and Health Care in Early Christianity*, 18.
[3] Ferngren, *Medicine and Health Care in Early Christianity*, 29.

in combination with dietary regimes and drugs to adjust any imbalances in a patient's health; for example, a cold and moist condition was to be cured by implementing "a regime (or drug therapy) that was warming and drying".[4] In addition, Hippocratic doctors believed not only that the body and soul were closely interwoven, but also that the bodily condition affected a person's mental state and vice versa.[5] This understanding of the link between body and mind caused them to treat their patients as a whole. Thus, Hippocrates advises his followers to not only often visit their patients, but also to give them positive encouragement, seeing the relationship between physician and patient as important in the healing process.[6] He also urges his followers to "treat patients and their families respectfully and ethically" as far as they could.[7]

The medical practices of Hippocrates and his ancestors took a major step forward in the medical schools of the Mediterranean world during the Hellenistic period, under the auspices of a number of different theoretical positions: Dogmatism (also called Rationalism), Empiricism and Methodism.[8] The first theoretical position, with exponents such as Herophilus (335–280 B.C.) and Erasistratus of Cos (304–250 B.C.), posited that all diseases had their causes; for the dogmatists, a duty of a physician was to find a cause, or multiple causes, of their patients' illness on the basis of knowledge of internal organs and anatomical

---

4　Owsei Temkin, *Hippocrates in a World of Pagans and Christians* (Baltimore: John Hopkins University Press, 1991), 12–13. For Hippocrates' life, see Robert E. Adler, *Medical Firsts: From Hippocrates to the Human Genome* (New Jersey: John Wiley & Sons, 2004), 7–12.
5　Temkin, *Hippocrates in a World of Pagans and Christians*, 13.
6　Adler, *Medical Firsts*, 10.
7　Adler, *Medical Firsts*. 10.
8　On the three medical sects in the ancient world, see R. J. Hankinson, ed., *Galen on the Therapeutic Method: Book I and II* (Oxford: Clarendon Press, 1991), xxvi–xxxiii. Vivian Nutton, "The Rise of Medicine," in *The Cambridge of History of Medicine*, ed. Roy Porter (Cambridge: Cambridge University Press, 2006), 52–53; Ferngren, *Medicine and Health Care in Early Christianity*, 19–20.

structures of the body, as well as applying the theory of the humor.[9] Proper medical treatment was to be directed towards first finding and then curing the hidden causes of individual diseases.[10] In contrast, the Empiricists, as the name indicates, rejected the anatomical investigation and physiological theory of the Dogmatists and stressed the importance of prior clinical experience.[11] The last group, the Methodists, believed all diseases came from "the fluid, the costive, and the mixed" and that all bodies exhibited symptoms of individual illnesses. Their physicians first checked the symptoms of a disease and gave medical treatment according to the source of the symptoms.[12]

Both the Dogmatists and Empiricists exerted enormous influence on the second-century great physician Galen (AD 129–c. 210/216),[13] who stressed both the need to observe the inner parts of the body and its physiological function, as well as the importance of gaining anatomical knowledge through dissecting animals.[14] In addition, Galen also inherited the humors theory (blood, phlegm, yellow bile, and black bile) from Hippocrates, believing that all structures of the body were composed of these four fluids and that the composition rates of the humors were different according to their different parts. Like Hippocrates, he believed that diseases and sickness came from imbalance of the four humors.[15] He also viewed medicine as a means by which to practise philanthropy because "regardless of whether or not *philanthropia* provided the motives for any particular physician, the art itself, when practiced by a competent physician, relieved

9 Hankinson, *Galen on the Therapeutic Method*, xxvii.
10 Hankinson, *Galen on the Therapeutic Method*, xxvii.
11 Nutton, "The Rise of Medicine," 53.
12 Hankinson, *Galen on the Therapeutic Method*, xxxi.
13 For Galen's life, see Hankinson, *Galen on the Therapeutic Method*, xix–xxv.
14 Hankinson, *Galen on the Therapeutic Method*, xxxii–xxxiii.
15 Johnston, *Galen on diseases and symptoms*, rev. ed. (Cambridge: Cambridge University Press, 2011), 19–20.

humankind's sufferings".[16]

According to ancient Greek and Roman sources, some physicians including Xenotimos at Cos (c. 3 B.C.) used their diverse medical skills (for example, drug treatments, dietary regimens and surgical operations, etc.) to care for sick citizens, while some others as public doctors did their best to look after both citizen patients and non-citizens in the cities.[17] In particular, Damiadas, a Greek physician of Gytheion in the first century B.C., "provided the due treatment, skillfully serving those in need, showing unlimited energy and devotion [*philotimia*] in serving fairly all alike, whether poor or rich, slave or free or foreigners".[18]

As well as physicians, the Classical world also offered a variety of health care institutions: *valetudinaria* (charitable institutions) for slaves and Roman soldiers, medical centers attached to temples dedicated to Asclepius, the Greek god of medicine (*asklepieia*), individual offices or surgeries of physicians (*iateria*), and public physicians (*demosieuontes iatroi*).[19] Among these, the *valetudinaria* and the *asklepieia* disappeared from the Roman Empire after the Christianization of the Empire, while both the *iateria* and public *demosieuontes iateroi* continued to contribute towards shaping Christian hospitals in Late Antiquity and Byzantium.[20]

Rodney Stark discusses a number of these health-care institutions and the importance of nursing care in his intriguing work *The Rise of Christianity*.[21] According to him, many people in the Greco-Roman world were afflicted with infectious diseases arising from the insanitary conditions within their dwellings as well as the natural disasters that fell upon various ancient cities.[22]

16   Ferngren, *Medicine and Health Care in Early Christianity*, 93.
17   Hands, *Charities and Social Aid in Greece and Rome*, 202–9.
18   Hands, *Charities and Social Aid in Greece and Rome*, 205.
19   For the institutional facilities in the ancient world, see Miller, *The Birth of the Hospital in the Byzantine Empire*, 37–49.
20   Miller, *The Birth of the Hospital in the Byzantine Empire*, 49.
21   Rodney Stark, *The Rise of Christianity* (New York: Harper Collins, 1997).
22   Stark, *The Rise of Christianity*, 147–62.

Ancient doctors, however, were not very effective in terms of medical care for infection and epidemic disease, nor were they particularly knowledgeable about the immune system in the body.[23]

It is here that nursing care provides medical personnel with the opportunity to save the lives of their patients. Some patients were able to naturally fight off infection but then were often too weak to feed themselves and keep themselves clean. Thus, they were often inflicted by another infection, which could potentially kill them, or they starved to death as a result of being too weak to care for their nutritional needs. The availability of nursing care, particularly the provision of food and water to patients, nourishing them and keeping them clean and warm, meant a lot more recovered from illness that would have otherwise taken them.[24] The early Christians provided nursing care to the poor and sick in their communities as an expression of love and charity. This care for the sick was socially beneficial. It also helped Christianity to grow by giving it an advantage in terms of the way non-Christian communities dealt with infectious disease.[25]

The medical treatments and institutions regarding medical and nursing care in the ancient world must have, to some extent, contributed to the improvement of public health in Classical cities. However, the poor and those marginalized by society (e.g. foreigners and slaves) seemed not able to access appropriate medical and nursing practice because contemporary philanthropic activity, including medical attention in ancient cities, had been primarily limited to citizens and their friends or relatives.[26]

Such an attitude towards the poor and marginalized was, Gary Ferngren argues, linked to the ancients' interpretation of human worth. The ancients did not primarily think about "inher-

---

23 Stark, *The Rise of Christianity*, 88.
24 Stark, *The Rise of Christianity*, 88.
25 Stark, *The Rise of Christianity*, 91–93.
26 Ferngren, *Medicine and Health Care in Early Christianity*, 95–97; Constantelos, *Byzantine Philanthropy and Social Welfare*, 11.

ent human rights" (i.e. the biblical teaching that all individuals are born with intrinsic rights), but rather believed that rights were defined only on the basis of "membership in a society (a family, kinship group, or state) that granted them".[27] This social determination of a person's worth and rights naturally leads to little sympathy for those outside the civil group (e.g. slaves or the indigent).

Furthermore, the apathy towards the sick poor in the Classical world appears to be, to some extent, related to the doctrine of Stoicism. Stoic philosophy places some emphasis on love and kindness for all human beings including enemies, as well as "humane treatment of every person, civilized or barbarian, slave or free".[28] On the other hand, it also fostered a level of apathy towards suffering and sickness because it also taught that physical pain was *adiaphoros* (ἀδιάφορος) which meant neither good nor bad, and must be endured without complaint.[29] According to the *Eclogae* of Stobaeus, which contains extensive extracts taken from many Stoic writers,

> Zeno says that those things exist which participate in being. And of the things which exist some are good, some bad, some indifferent. Good are the following sorts of item: wisdom, moderation, justice, courage, and all that is virtue or participates in virtue. Bad are the following sorts of item: folly, intemperance, injustice, cowardice, and all that is vice or participates in vice. *Indifferent are the following sorts of item: life death, reputation illrepute, pleasure exertion, wealth poverty, health sickness, and things like these.*[30] (Emphasis added)

---

27 Ferngren, *Medicine and Health Care in Early Christianity*, 95.
28 Ferngren, *Medicine and Health Care in Early Christianity*, 92, 96. The quotation is from 96. For introduction to Stoicism, see David Sedley, "The School, from Zeno to Arius Didymus," in *The Cambridge Companion to the Stoics*, ed. Brad Inwood (Cambridge: Cambridge University Press, 2003), 7.
29 Ferngren, *Medicine and Health Care in Early Christianity*, 96-97. For the term ἀδιάφορος, see Lampe, *A Patristic Greek Lexicon*, 35, s.v. ἀδιάφορος.
30 Stobaeus, *Eclogae*, II 57.18-58.4, quoted in Malcolm Schofield, "Stoic Ethics," *The Cambridge Companion to the Stoics* (Cambridge University Press, 2006), 239. doi:10.1017/CCOL052177005X.010.

Ferngren notes, in connection with writings like the above, that one may find "a kind of hardness in Stoic teaching that has little place for the gentle virtues".[31]

6.1.2 Caring for the sick in early Jewish and Christian tradition

The Bible also makes direct and indirect references to regulations and anecdotes regarding diseases and health care.[32] In some passages of the Old Testament, human illness was interpreted as evidence of God's punishment for betrayal of him and/or his words (Exod. 15:26; Num. 12:9–12; Deut. 28:15; 2 Chr. 21:6–19). Because illness was therefore sometimes interpreted "as the result of sin", the sick were often considered "ritually unclean and in a state of unholiness".[33] In others, sickness however was understood to be part of the pedagogical method of God (Job 5:17–18), or alternatively as the works of evil spirits under the hand of God (Judg. 9:23; 1 Sam. 16:14). Still others maintained a silence about the actual causes of human disease (2 Kgs. 5:1–14; 20:1), and showed thereapeutic compassion to those seeking a cure directly from God or via the mediation of a prophet on God's behalf (1 Kgs. 17:17–23; 2 Kgs. 20:1–11). Overall, the ancient Israelites believed that illness and health were at the whim and control of God and God was the ultimate physician.

Nevertheless, a closer inspection of the Bible reveals other medical practices including (a) magical healing which was strictly prohibited by the Scripture (Exod. 22:17; Lev. 20:27; Deut. 18:

---

31 Ferngren, *Medicine and Health Care in Early Christianity*, 97.
32 See Joshua O. Leibowitz, ed., *Proceedings of the third International Symposium on Medicine in Bible and Talmud* (Jerusalem: The Division of the History of Medicine, the Hebrew University-Hadassah Medical School, 1988); Nigel Allan, "The Physician in Ancient Israel: His Status and Function," *Medical History* 45 (2001): 377–94; Ferngren, *Medicine and Health Care in Early Christianity*, 23–24.
33 Allan, "The Physician in Ancient Israel: His Status and Function," 378.

9–15)[34], (b) healing by priests or prophets through ritual procedure (Lev. 14:1–9; 2 Kgs. 5:1–14), and (c) healing at the hands of professional physicians (2 Chr. 16:12; Tob. 2:10; Sir. 38:1–15).

In contrast to the ancient Greeks and Romans who, as discussed above, often overlooked the poor and sick in their societies, the Hebrew Bible required its people to show deep compassion for the poor and patients regardless of their social class. According to Ferngren, this was as a result of the concept of *imago Dei* whereby all humans are made in the image of God (Gen. 1:26–27).[35] This concept provided not only ancient Jews but also early Christians with a religious foundation for a new understanding of humanity. For example, in his fourth homily on Ecclesiastes in particular, Gregory of Nyssa discusses slavery in the context of the framework of the doctrine of *imago Dei* as observed in the Old Testament. According to him, God does not allow anyone created in the image of God to enslave others likewise created in the image of God.[36] Moreover, Gregory states that both slaves and their owners come from the same ancestors and therefore neither can rule over the other.[37] Thus only God is allowed to rule over humanity. The doctrine of *imago Dei* set a solid foundation for the belief that every person had intrinsic value as a result of bearing God's image, which translated into a necessity to care for the sick regardless of social status and wealth.[38]

In addition to the Hebrew Bible, there are also many anecdotes regarding sickness and healing in the New Testament.

---

34 This could reflect an ambivalent attitude towards magical practices in ancient Hebrew communities, but is outside the scope of this book. See Allan, "The Physician in Ancient Israel," 386.
35 For more detail on the implications of the *imago Dei*, see Ferngren, *Medicine and Health Care in Early Christianity*, 97–104.
36 Gregory of Nyssa, *Homilies on Ecclesiastes: An English Version with Supporting Studies*, trans. Stuart G. Hall and Rachel Moriarty (Berlin: de Gruyter, 1993), 336.6.
37 Gregory of Nyssa, *Homilies on Ecclesiastes*, 337.13.
38 Ferngren, *Medicine and Health Care in Early Christianity*, 98.

The Gospels in particular include tales of miraculous healings performed by Jesus.[39] In terms of the range of people, he is reported to have cured people from a variety of social strata (Mark 2:1–12; Matt. 8:15–13; John 4:46–54; John 11; Luke 7:11–17). In all of these accounts, the writers of the Gospels portray Jesus as an ideal physician who unselfishly restores the sick to health. This image of Christ the physician (*Christus medicus*) in the New Testament was later adopted by many early Church writers such as Tertullian, Origen, Athanasius, Ambrose, Augustine, Evagrius, Basil of Caesarea, and Barsanuphius and John.[40]

The book of Acts of the Apostles also has references to miraculous cures performed by the Apostles (Acts 3:1–10; 5:12–16; 20:7–12). Among them, it is necessary to pay heed to Peter's healing at a gate known as the Beautiful Gate (Acts 3:1–10) in order to understand the meaning of his healing. In his speech to the assembled people after curing the disabled person, Peter spoke "of the healing as a sign that salvation has come" and entreated his audience to repent, or rather to be healed of their bodily sickness.[41] This implies not merely that Peter's miraculous healing performed in the name of Jesus represented the power of Christ, but also that the Apostles themselves understood healing as a part of the salvific work of Christ.[42] This has implications for the monastics who later take on a healing role as part of their dedication to God.

As has been discussed above, different approaches to caring for the sick in the ancient world varied depending on the contemporary understanding of sickness and healing. The ancient

---

39 For more detail on Jesus's miraculous healing, see Ferngren, *Medicine and Health Care in Early Christianity*, 178 n. 9.
40 Lee M. Jefferson, *Christ the Miracle Worker in Early Christian Art* (Minneapolis: Fortress Press, 2014), 55–86; Evagrius, *On Thoughts*, 3; Basil, *The Letter*, XLVI, 306-7. For a more detailed discussion of this image of Christ on the *Letters*, see section 6.2.
41 Ferngren, *Medicine and Health Care in Early Christianity*, 66.
42 Ferngren, *Medicine and Health Care in Early Christianity*, 66.

Greeks and Romans believed that human illness was a matter for doctors to solve through investigation of the nature of the illness, the symptoms and an understanding of anatomy. Some cared for the sick with nursing practice. Disease was viewed as caused by an imbalance in the four humors comprising the human body. They also perceived a mental element to physical ailments and saw that a healthy body was a requirement for a healthy soul.

In the Scriptures, however, sickness was sometimes viewed as what was allowed by God for the sake of spiritual benefits and therefore to be endured rather than avoided. Their attitude towards healing was also somewhat dependent on their perception of humanity in terms of the *imago Dei*. Finally, in the New Testament, healing comes to be seen as part of the work of Christ, a fact which is important in the development of care for the poor and sick as an element of the monastic life.

6.2 Sickness and healing as portrayed in the *Letters*

Early Christians, who inherited the biblical teachings with regard to illness and health, also adopted Greek and Roman medical practices. These practices permeated through society in diverse ways.[43] Many early Church Fathers (including Origen, Athenagoras of Athens, Basil the Great, Gregory of Nyssa and Nemesius of Emesa) sought medical cures themselves from physicians while also displaying a familiarity with ancient medicine, revealing a clear understanding of various theories of disease and

---

43 See Schenkewitz, *Dorotheos of Gaza and the Discourse of Healing in Gazan Monasticism*, 31–43; Wendy Mayer, "Medicine in Transition: Christian Adaption in the Late Fourth-Century East," in *Shifting Genres in Late Antiquity*, ed. G. Greatrex, H. Elton and L. McMahon (Farnham: Ashgate, 2015), 11–26. For discussion of the late antique Church's reception of paganism, see Ramsay MacMullen, *Christianity and Paganism in the Fourth to Eighth centuries* (New Haven: Yale University Press, 1997).

medical practices.[44]

Basil of Caesarea, in particular, thought of medicine as a crucial gift granted to humanity by God in order to heal body and soul:

> Each of the [medical] arts is bestowed on us by God to supply for the infirmity of nature... the medical art is permitted us by God who orders our whole life, as a pattern for the healing of the soul, that we may be advised to remove what is in excess or to make up what is lacking.[45]

A similar idea is evident in Gregory of Nyssa's *The Life of St. Macrina*.[46] According to Basil the Great's concept of disease, as expressed in his *Longer Rules* 55, Adam and Eve started to suffer from physical disease after their expulsion from Eden as a result of their sin.[47] However, they were not left in pain alone, but rather provided with natural remedies from God which have "properties beneficial to the body".[48] On first glance, it appears that Basil interprets healing via medicinal arts as a sign of God's grace for fallen humanity and therefore he sees no reason for sick people, including monks, to be denied medical aid.[49]

Some lines later in the same Rules, Basil the Great comments on the different causes of human illness such as improper life-

---

44 Ferngren, *Medicine and Health Care in Early Christianity*, 25–29; Susan Holman, *The Hungry Are Dying* (Oxford: Oxford University Press, 2001), 155–60; Georgios Panteleakos, Effie Poulakou-Rebelakou, Michael Koutsilieris, "Anatomy and Physiology in the Work of Nemesius of Emesa 'On the Nature of Man'," *Acta Medico-Historica Adriatica* 11.2 (2013): 319–28.
45 Basil, *Longer Rules*, 55.1. For more detail on medical treatment in Basil, see Basil of Caesarea, The Asketikon of St Basil the Great (Oxford: Oxford University Press, 2005), 264 n. 459. For the influence of Galen on St. Basil, see Schenkewitz, *Dorotheos of Gaza and the Discourse of Healing in Gazan Monasticism*, 31–43.
46 Gregory of Nyssa, *The Life of St. Macrina*, 185.
47 Basil, *Longer Rules*, 55. 1.
48 Basil, *Longer Rules*, 55. 2.
49 See Crislip, *From Monastery to Hospital*, 30.

style, other bodily diseases, sin or the influence of Satan.[50] He recommends that while we can benefit from medical remedies to cure some ills, the sickness which comes as punishment from God in order to correct and edify needs to be endured. There appears to be no one complete panacea for all sickness, except for the glory of God and the benefit of the soul:

> Therefore we must neither avoid the art completely nor place all our hopes in it...whether we use the precepts of the medical art or decline them in accordance with one of the principles set out above, let us preserve the goal of being well pleasing to God and arrange all things for the soul's benefit, fulfilling the commandment of the Apostle who said: *Whether you eat or drink, or whatever you do, do it all to the glory of God* (1 Corinthians 10:31). (Emphasis added)[51]

Basil's views on sickness and healing are reflected among the various medical discourses found in the *Letters* of Barsanuphius and John of Gaza. The *Letters* primarily adhere to the teachings of the biblical tradition and early Christian writers like Basil. In letter 525, John notes that both health and sickness originate from God.

> Both health and illness come from God, who said: "I will kill and I will make alive; I will wound and I will heal..." Therefore, whenever God wills, he dispenses health from a doctor or, if he wants, through a mere word. As for prolonging or abbreviating an illness, this belongs to God's foresight. Thus, those who submit themselves entirely to God are carefree, and he does with them as he wills and as is best (letters 525).

According to John, God can work through a doctor or directly. He recommends submission to God's will as a necessity, although

---

50 Basil, *Longer Rules*, 55. 4.
51 Basil, *Longer Rules*, 55. 5.

he does not suggest that mere submission is enough to cure all ills.

He reiterates this viewpoint in a later response to a layman who is concerned about his state of health and the medical care he has received (letter 770). In this, John recommends that the sufferer keep in mind that no one is able to cure anything without God's assistance, and that God can, whenever he wants, act directly to confer health on those suffering from bodily diseases. John of Gaza takes this interpretation of illness and medical care one step further and emphasizes that no one can even die without God's permission. He states that a person cannot die although they may have been "bitten by tens of thousands of serpents" (letter 781). It is clear that John's perception of illness and healing is that it is all in the control of God. Like the ideas expressed in the Hebrew Bible, John's belief leads him to attempt to persuade his interlocutors to entrust both their illness and its cure to God (letters 532 and 770).

Such understanding of illness and healing in the letters of the Gazan anchorites is passed on to their disciple Dorotheos. His work, too, indicates that both human illness and heath are at God's disposal. He tells the story of a sick elder who lives with his brother.[52] According to the story, the old man usually ate his food seasoned with honey. One day, his disciple mistakenly put harmful linseed oil in his mentor's food instead of the honey. Although he recognized the mistake, nevertheless the holy old man still ate his meal in silence. The brother belatedly realized his mistake, including the potential danger to his elder and was upset. To which the older monk replied "if God wanted me to eat honey, [you] would have put honey on". Dorotheos interprets this story as a lesson that the holy elder spoke correctly, noting that God could have transformed the harmful oil into honey if he had so wanted.

---

52 Dorotheos, *Abba Dorotheos: Practical Teaching on the Christian Life*, lesson 7. 87.

In addition, the Gazan ascetics also acknowledge that some diseases are attributable to demonic activities (letters 88 and 519). Monastic leaders therefore sought ways to distinguish legitimate illness from sickness caused by demons and counterfeit sickness.[53] The main criterion which John suggests to achieve this purpose is to check whether or not the sick person continues to eat regularly and well:

> The matter of illness is quite clear. For if the body cannot tolerate regular food, it is evident that it is unwell and one should relax one's ministry. If, however, the body accepts the customary food and does not rise for liturgy, it is evident that this comes from the demons (letter 519).

John associates lethargy with demonic influence. He determines that those who are truly sick often exhibit lack of appetite as a symptom, while those afflicted by demon-induced lethargy and laziness are usually not put off their food.

In addition to identifying the causes of sickness where possible, the *Letters* also indicate that the monastery of Seridos had a generally positive attitude towards medical treatments including the application of holy water (letter 753) and baths (letters 770 and 771).[54] However, magical spells were absolutely prohibited by John because they destroyed "the soul through transgressing God's decree" (letter 753). In the same vein, Augustine and other early Church Fathers expressed the belief that magical powers were all to be attributed to demonic forces and therefore avoided.[55]

Finally, no discussion of representations of health in the *Letters* would be complete without raising the issues of the metaphor of *Christus medicus*, Christ the Physician. The correspon-

---

53 For the case of canon of Shenoute, see Bentley Layton, introduction to *The Canons of Our Fathers*, 56.
54 See 6.3 "Laypeople and caring for the sick in the *Letters*"; Di Segni, "Monastery, City and Village in Byzantine Gaza," 45 notes that sick people appeared to receive various different types of medical help such as medication and advice.
55 Ferngren, *Medicine and Health Care in Early Christianity*, 79 n. 124.

dence of both Barsanuphius and John of Gaza often portrays Christ as a great physician, healing both souls and bodily illnesses (letters 59, 61, 107, 109, 199, 212, 532 and 553).[56] In letter 199 in particular, Barsanuphius says to an anonymous hermit: "Jesus is the Physician of souls and bodies. If you have a wound, I shall lead you toward him and pray to him to heal you in both, that is, if you also desire this". In letters 109 and 553, he takes this image further and refers to Christ as a healer who is able to even cure passions and evil thoughts including anger, irritation and envy. All of these were certainly very important for a monastic community.

The idea of freedom from bodily and spiritual diseases through the agency of Christ as a physician is also present in the writings of Dorotheos. He notes that although a doctor occasionally may make a wrong diagnosis or prescribe the wrong medicine, Jesus Christ, as a true and good physician who knows everything about the souls of his patients, will always provide an appropriate prescription.[57]

Isaiah of Scetis, predecessor of Barsanuphius and John, also depicts Christ as a spiritual physician able to heal all human problems.[58] In his *Ascetic Discourse* 25 in particular, he compares Christ to the bronze serpent in the Old Testament (Numbers 21) and speaks of him as healing all people poisoned due to "the bites of the invisible serpent". However, the *Christus medicus* of Isaiah of Scetis is, interestingly, slightly different to that of Barsanuphius and John. The healing that Christ offers is "not the salvific healing of the cross but the restoration to individuals those particular

---

56 For more detail on the image of Christ the Physician in the *Letters*, see Schenkewitz, *Dorotheos of Gaza and the Discourse of Healing in Gazan Monasticism*, 47–50.
57 Dorotheos, *Abba Dorotheos: Practical Teaching on the Christian Life*, lesson 11, 113. For more detail on Christ as a physician in the work of Dorotheos, see Schenkewitz, *Dorotheos of Gaza and the Discourse of Healing in Gazan Monasticism*, 56–57.
58 Isaiah, *Ascetic Discourses*, 25. The same image is also in *Ascetic Discourse* 8;

functions they lacked".⁵⁹ This is based on his theory of health and illness. According to Isaiah, Adam whom God created in the beginning was a healthy person in accordance with nature, although his heathy state was seriously distorted "toward that which is contrary to nature" when he "listened to the one who deceived him" in Paradise.⁶⁰ The Creator then had pity on his people because of his great love, and the Logos with God himself became a complete human "in every way like us except without sin" in order to transform the distorted nature back into a healthy state according to nature.⁶¹ Through Christ, human beings can come to "enjoy healing from Adam's sin. This healing was a return to one's created nature".⁶²

6.3 Laypeople and caring for the sick

Some of the *Letters* indicate that the holy Gazan advisers recommended medical cures to lay petitioners who were unwell. One of these medical treatments was bathing and we know that there were certainly public baths in Gaza.⁶³ According to letter 770, when an anonymous layman who had been prescribed bathing as a cure by his doctor hesitates to bathe, John reassures him saying that bathing is not forbidden for laypeople. He goes on to note that medical remedies such as those offered by physicians are appropriate for those who are not "perfect" as long as that person also recognises that only God can truly heal:

> As for showing yourself to the doctor, it belongs to the more perfect to leave everything to God, even if this is a difficult thing to do; it is the weaker person who shows

---

59   Schenkewitz, *Dorotheos of Gaza and the Discourse of Healing in Gazan Monasticism*, 43.
60   Isaiah, *Ascetic Discourses*, 2.
61   Isaiah, *Ascetic Discourses*, 2.
62   Schenkewitz, *Dorotheos of Gaza and the Discourse of Healing in Gazan Monasticism*, 44.
63   Champion, *Explaining the Cosmos*, 32.

himself to the doctor. Indeed, not only is this not sinful, but it is even humble; for being weaker, one needed to visit the doctor. One should, however, remember that, without God, not even a doctor can do anything. Rather, it is God who bestow health to the ill, whenever he so desires (letter 770).

In the passage, God is primarily portrayed as the ultimate medical authority, although John admits that such access to God is not always within the reach of ordinary "weaker" people. In this case, medical personnel are an acceptable alternative.

In the following letter, John responds to another lay questioner who was also reluctant to bathe for fear of offending those who expected him to refuse a bath due to his piety. John gives a stern but mild reprimand:

> For you are a secular man; and, as we have said, a bath is not forbidden for a layperson, at least whenever necessary... Bathing self-indulgently and unnecessarily is sinful and truly scandalous. On the other hand, bathing only when necessary is not a scandal; so the one who is scandalized bears the judgement. If you are embarrassed about this, then this is vainglory from the devil (letter 771).

From these two letters, three important things about John's understanding of baths as medical prescription are identified. First of all, John strongly urges lay persons to bathe for bodily healing when necessary without being ashamed of their actions. This advice was not surprising because bathing as a medical cure was often used in late-antique Christianity.[64]

Here a question arises regarding a bath discovered in the monastery of Seridos:[65] Who used the medical facility? With

---

64 Yegül, *Baths and Bathing in Classical Antiquity*, 315–17.
65 Hirschfeld, "The Monasticism of Gaza: An Archaeological Review," 76. For other baths in early Byzantine Palestine, see Binns, *Ascetics and Ambassadors of Christ*, 129, 169.

regard to the bathing facility, Bitton-Ashkelony and Kofsky argue that they are not sure that the baths "served the monastic community at large or only guests and sick people".[66] Archaeological and literary sources providing information about the baths is scarce. Nonetheless, monastic sources from Egypt and other places in Palestine can offer a context on who might have used this monastic facility. There were a variety of views about bathing in late-antique monasticism. These ranged from strict restrictions on bathing (Pachomius and Shenoute) to the allowance of bathing for the sake of health, and to even further use of public baths in order to maintain personal and public hygiene (Augustine).[67]

Among them, the Egyptian monks' negative stance on bathing might be rooted in the contemporary practice of being unwashed—*alousia* (ἀλουσία)—which was prevalent in the East.[68] To ascetics of the eastern Mediterranean world, the avoidance of washing was seen as a means of rejecting worldly luxury and pleasure. This was a way by which they could obtain "grace and godliness" and "the spirit's triumph over the body".[69] The account of Abba John, a solitary of the lavra of St. Sabas in the *Lives of the Monks of Palestine* of Cyril, reflects a contemporary ascetic stance on washing. The Abba still, although he had been appointed as a bishop of Colina, followed monastic life.

> In particular he abstained from washing, carefully avoiding not only being seen by another but also seeing himself naked; thinking of the nakedness of Adam and what is written in that passage [Gen 3:7–11], he judged abstaining from washing one of the greatest virtues.[70]

---

66 Bitton-Ashkelony and Kofsky, *The Monastic School of Gaza*, 193.
67 Crislip, *From Monastery to Hospital*, 30.
68 Yegül, *Baths and Bathing in Classical Antiquity*, 318; Binns, *Ascetics and Ambassadors of Christ*, 169 n. 91.
69 Yegül, *Baths and Bathing in Classical Antiquity*, 318.
70 Cyril of Scythopolis, *The Lives of the Monks of Palestine*, 202.16–203.

This monastic ethos in the East, which valued the *alousia* rather than hygiene and cleanliness, makes it unlikely to assume that monks were regularly allowed to bathe in the monasteries, including the coenobium of Seridos.[71] In addition, many monastic leaders in Late Antiquity allow their monastics to be permitted to bathe their body only for the sake of curing physical illness.[72] Therefore it seems likely that the bath-house in the Gazan monastery was primarily created and administrated for the sake of the lay community of Gaza and travelers, and sometimes for the sake of sick monks within the community if necessary.

The second thing to notice about letters 770 and 771 is that the advisor classifies patients into two categories—those who are weak in faith and those who are perfect—and then gives different kinds of guidance in proportion to the condition of the patient. That is, he recommends the former group to consult a physician, while the latter is to entrust everything to God. Such advice which John offers is, as shown in previous chapters, not different from the advice given by the Gazan holy men towards those who give alms and who entertain hospitality. The strong, or advanced in faith, are to act as they should and the weak are to take the easier path, each according to their abilities.

This style of guidance on medical care can be also found in the writings of the third-century theologian Origen. According to him, all Christians were divided into two categories: those who wanted to live in an ordinary way, and those who chose to live in a more superior fashion. In his work, *Contra Celsum* which deals with medicine for healing the body, Origen states: "A man ought to use medical means to heal his body if he aims to live in the simple and ordinary way. If he wishes to live in a way

---

71 For archaeological evidence, see Hirschfeld, "The Monasticism of Gaza: An Archaeological Review," 76; Bitton-Ashkelony and Kofsky, *The Monastic School of Gaza*, 193.
72 Crislip, *From Monastery to Hospital*, 30; Benedict, *RB 1980: The Rule of St. Benedict in English*, 36.1–10.

superior to that of the multitude, he should do this by devotion to the supreme God and by praying to Him".[73] The instruction of both Origen and the sixth-century Gazan holy men therefore appears to be based primarily on the assumption that individual patients have different inner needs that can be measured in different ways. They should thus choose proper medical treatment depending on their individual inner states.

Lastly, it is known from the letters pertaining to a bath as medical treatment that medical care is not set in opposition to God's healing: rather the two elements cooperate with each other. As Barsanuphius says to Dorotheos: "do not forget that without God there can be no healing. One who applies oneself to medicine should do so in the name of God, and God will come to one's assistance" (letter 327). Further, in letter 508 he suggests that when a sick monk receives help from a doctor, he is allowing God's will to be demonstrated.

In addition to giving permission for bathing as medical therapy to laypeople, the *Letters* suggest that Barsanuphius sometimes helps sick people with miraculous healings of their illnesses through prayer. In letter 643, there is unnamed layman who has fallen ill and is suffering from fever. He urges Barsanuphius to pray for him and sends him some water which the Great Old Man agrees to bless. Following the prayers of Barsanuphius, the patient is immediately healed and excitedly starts to tell everyone of his recovery. When he suffers a relapse into fever on the next day, he again asks Barsanuphius to pray for him and the respected mentor replies that "this happened to you in order that you may not be a chatterbox" before agreeing to pray for him. Following this subsequent instruction and prayer, the layman recovers completely. Another example is found in letter 784. According to it, some friends of a very pious and generous layman, who was nearly dead

---

73 Origen, *Contra Celsum*, 6. 80. For medicine in Origen, see Ferngren, *Medicine and Health Care in Early Christianity*, 27.

from some illness, ask the Other Old Man whether the man will die or not. Although the Gazan prophet advises them to prepare the man's death, he nevertheless asks Barsanuphius to pray for his "additional life for the sake of his good work of hospitality". Soon after, the patient miraculously recovers from his sickness.

As demonstrated above, when lay Christians consult the Old Men about their own sickness or their relatives' ill health, they are encouraged to seek appropriate medical therapies. In addition, sometimes Barsanuphius cures his audience directly by means of a miraculous power. This is quite different to the treatment and advice offered to monastic petitioners.

Nevertheless, some letters indicate that John occasionally avoided a direct reply when responding to questions of illness or cure among the laity (letters 637, 778A and 778B). According to letter 637, John responds to a sick layman who asks whether he will live or die:

> If I tell you that you will die, then your salvation will be the result of the fact that you are constrained by circumstance. For if you see that you are at the jaws of death, and then you will necessarily abandon everything that you have. If, however, you expect to live many years, and your thought tells you that you must be saved, you will apply your thought to that which is good. Then, even if you happen to die immediately, your salvation will be result of free will and not constraint (letter 637).

His refusal to give a direct answer to the addressee is related to a hope that the patient will be saved through a free and voluntary choice, not "the constraint of the fear of death".[74] His obscure response demonstrates not only his concern for the soul of the interlocutor but also his educative role. Here we see how he teaches the questioner about the correct way to seek salvation.

---

74 Hevelone-Harper, *Disciples of the Desert*, 87.

In other letters, by contrast, his vague answers may be better ascribed to a desire not to impede the will of God. Letters 778A and 778B are a clear example of this issue. According to letter 778A, there was a teacher of philosophy who had two sons. When one of them became ill he applied to John for advice. John replied to the pious man that his son would live, and the son recovered as prophesied. Later his other son falls sick and he returns for advice. This time John responds: "We shall pray; however, it is up to God to have mercy on him. Therefore, cut off your will and give thanks to him in all circumstance" (letter 778A). The philosopher interprets this to mean that the other boy will also live. However, the second son dies. This throws the philosopher into confusion, and once again he goes to the spiritual advisor to enquire why John has not revealed the coming death of his son. John replies:

> As for not speaking to you clearly, you should understand this from your own experience. Behold, you are a teacher of worldly wisdom and you have students. Now, if you order one of them to write a letter, would your student write what you want, or would you let him write whatever he wants? Surely, he would write whatever you dictate and not whatever he happened to want. The same applies to the saints. They do not speak of their own accord, but it is God who speaks through them as he desires, sometimes in the form of a shadow and at other times with clarity. In fact, in order that you may be assured that this is so, the Lord himself said to his disciples: "It is not you who speak, but the Spirit of your Father is speaking through you". Therefore, God speaks as he wills, not as they will (letter 778B).

In saying that saints can repeat only what God wants them to reveal because they are "a channel for the voice of God", John of Gaza also implies that his prophecy regarding the health of the patient is from God's own will, and not his own. John's words are not the reason that the person is saved or not: he is merely a conduit for the will of God.

6.3.1 Caring for a sick slave

Lay Christians in Gaza and its surrounding areas sometimes asked the respected saints how to manage their sick slaves. In ancient Greece and Rome, were slaves regarded as possessions.[75] A slave-master therefore had the right to decide all things related to a slave's life such as food, clothing, work, sale and education. There is evidence to suggest some slaveholders willingly abandoned servants who were the victims of serious diseases,[76] while others sold slaves at markets when they were sick,[77] and yet more sent injured slaves to hospices called *valetudinaria*. These institutions offered nursing and medical care to slaves and soldiers from the end of the Roman Republic onwards, because their economic or military profit resulted from recovering military and labour power.[78]

The characteristics of slavery in the ancient world lasted well into the time of the late Roman Empire, although there is some evidence of an amelioration of conditions.[79] Kyle Harper encapsulates the crucial features of slavery in Late Antiquity as follows:

---

75 For slavery in Greece and Rome, See Jean Andreau and Raymond Descat, *The Slave in Greece and Rome*, trans. Marion Leopold (Madison: University of Wisconsin Press, 2011); Peter Garnsey, *Ideas of Slavery from Aristotle to Augustine* (Cambridge: Cambridge University Press, 1996), 105-52.
76 Sandra Joshel, *Slavery in the Roman World* (Cambridge: Cambridge University Press, 2010), 71
77 Catherine Hezser, *Jewish Slavery in Antiquity* (2005; repr., Oxford: Oxford University Press, 2009), 262.
78 For more information on slave hospitals, see Peregrine Horden, "Christian Hospitality in Late Antiquity: Break or Bridge?" in *Gesundheit-Krankheit Kulturtransfer medizinischen Wissens von der Spätantike bis in die Frühe Neuzeit*, ed. Florian Steger and Kay Peter Jankrift (Weimar; Vienna: Böhlau, 2004), 89-90.
79 On slavery in the late Roman Empire, See Kyle Harper, *Slavery in the Late Roman World, AD 275-425* (Cambridge: Cambridge University Press, 2011); Ramsay MacMullen, "Late Roman Slavery," *Historia* 36 (1987): 359-82; Roger Bagnall, *Egypt in Late Antiquity* (Princeton: Princeton University Press, 1993), 208-14. Harper claims that, unlike agricultural slavery, household slavery in the eastern Mediterranean society not only remained prevalent well up to the sixth and seventh centuries, but also functioned as a bridge "between late Roman slavery and the establishment of Islam". See Harper, *Slavery in the Late Roman World*, 504-6.

> The essential characteristic of slavery, distinguishing it from all other human relationships, is the commodification of the human being, the reduction of the human body to a piece of property. In late antiquity the experience of slavery was diverse, because circumstances and masters and slavers were diverse. But the essential core of the slave experience, shared by slaves of all stripes, was the fact that a slave was human property.[80]

In the Late Roman world slaves still remained, to a greater or lesser degree, marginal beings primarily regarded as "human property". Therefore, the law of Justinian did not prohibit slaveholders from throwing away male and female slaves when they were sick.[81]

Like other Christian authors in the late Roman World,[82] John the Prophet fundamentally has no antipathy to the slavery system, so he willingly encourages one layperson to acquire household slaves (οἰκέτας) in the name of the Lord (letter 649).[83] However, he also advises his petitioner who wants to discipline his house-slave to instruct the domestic slave out of his loving heart so as to reduce his sins (letter 656). He goes on to reinforce the idea that the master should discipline his slave not with anger, but rather with care and godly fear (letters 656–657). While John seems to have no desire to end slavery, the Gazan anchorite clearly seeks to urge the interlocutors to handle their slaves humanely, unlike other secular slave-owners who sometimes employed physical violence toward their male and female slavers

---

80 Harper, *Slavery in the Late Roman World*, 35.
81 In his law, Justinian ordered that sick slaves abandoned by their owners were free if they recovered. See James A. S. Evans, *The Age of Justinian: The Circumstances of Imperial Power* (London & New York: Routledge, 1996, repr., London: Tayor & Francis, 2000), 208.
82 Harper, *Slavery in the Late Roman World*, 506-8. For the attitude of John Chrysostom towards slavery, see Jaclyn Maxwell, *Christianisation and Communication in Late Antiquity: John Chrysostom and His Congregation in Antioch* (Cambridge: Cambridge University Press, 2006), 78.
83 For the term οἰκέτης, see Harper, *Slavery in The Late Roman World*, 513-18.

to compel them to submission.[84]

This humane treatment also applies to sick slaves as depicted in the *Letters*. In response to a query from a wealthy Christian with a maimed slave (οἰκέτης), who consults John on whether he should keep his injured servant, John recommends that he not keep the slave in his house. Although he notes that it is pious to live with such a slave, if the wealthy man and his family members can do so, he also advises the man to send his servant to a poorhouse (πτωχοτροφεῖον) with sufficient meals, garments and a bed (letter 765). In the next letter, the same person again enquires about his slave, because the slave wants to take his daily subsistence from his owner as well as other donors at the poorhouse. John replies that the owner should, in principle, not allow his servant to receive offerings from both sides. But allowing this to happen might make the slave liable to grumbling at his master. So John advises the addressee to permit his slave to do whatever he wants (letter 766). What is particularly interesting here is that John thought it permissible for the slave to be cared for in a poorhouse (πτωχοτροφεῖον) when injured.

This advice with regard to the treatment of a sick or injured slave is quite different to that espoused by those masters in the Roman world who abandoned their sick slaves on the island of Aesculapius, or who only offered medical treatment to slaves in order to maintain military and labor power or to seek economic benefit. However, it does not imply that the most significant reason why John might have suggested such humane treatment for the sick *doulos* was, as the evidence seems to suggest, the illness of the slave per se. Rather John just urges the slave-owner to treat his servant humanely.

However, some other letters reveal a different picture. In them, John appears to offer advice to the slave master that is

---

84 For the use of violence against slavers in late-antique society, see Harper, *Slavery in The Late Roman World*, 227-36.

tailored to offer spiritual comfort to the owner and not for the benefit of the slave. This attitude is confirmed in the dialogues between John and another slaveholder. According to letters 779 to 781, a Christ-loving person owned a slave who was bitten by a dog. The slaveholder sent John a letter asking whether or not his slave was likely to survive, to which John replied with reassurance and the citation of the following biblical passage: "Not a sparrow falls into a trap apart from your Father who is in heaven" (letter 779). The man believed this meant his slave would live, but the servant, unexpectedly, died two days later (letter 780). The questioner, shocked, again sought advice, asking "Why did you say that there was nothing wrong with him?" To which John responds:

> Since you suspected that he would certainly die from the dog's bite, I indicated to you that this was not the case and told you that there was nothing wrong with him. For there is nothing wrong with death that comes from God... it is not possible for anyone to die without God's decree (letter 781).

This response indicates not only John's understanding that God controls all human life and death, including the life and death of a slave, but also his intention to give such advice to his petitioner as would reassure him.

On the issue of managing his runaway slaves (letters 653 and 654), John again demonstrates a desire to offer comfort to the master rather than any support for the slave. According to letter 653, a devout layman has a slave (δοῦλος) who has returned to his master after running away. The master regrets taking him back and asks John if he should release the slave or not. John instructs the owner to keep his slave for a while, testing both himself and the slave. If the slave corrects his behavior, then he should be kept. On the other hand, unless he changes his nature, the slaveholder should send the slave away for his own sake. Interestingly,

John notes that if the master wants to keep the slave although his behaviors and attitudes remain unchanged, he will "receive the reward of patience" from God.

This advice is quite extraordinary, given the treatment of runaway slaves in the late-antique context. In ancient times, a runaway of a slave was considered as the loss of valuable property for a slave-holder and, perhaps more importantly, as a potential increase in danger to the contemporary social community and municipal authorities.[85] Therefore slave-owners and other officers, as some late-antique sources attest, demonstrate an unfavorable attitude towards runaway slaves. They not only hired agents to arrest such slaves, but also retained the authority to beat, accuse or detain runaway slaves if necessary.[86]

In the light of this historical context, it is reasonable to conclude that John's advice about the generous treatment of slaves was in reality aimed at psychological and spiritual advantages that might in some cases be gained by the slave-owner.

6.4 Monks and caring for the sick

6.4.1 Positive attitudes towards caring for a fellow monk

Monasteries in the late-antique period, as many modern scholars point out, became important shelters for the poor and the sick.[87] Particularly, the fourth and fifth century monastic rules and hagiographies often indicate how contemporary monasteries cared for their sick fellows, although we do not know how much they reflected the reality.

Firstly, monasteries primarily provided sick monks with nursing care, giving special diets and clothes to them. St. Shenoute's

---

85 William Westermann, *The Slave Systems of Greek and Roman Antiquity* (Philadelphia: The American Philosophical Society, 1955), 107.
86 Bagnall, *Egypt in Late Antiquity*, 209–10.
87 See Crislip, *From Monastery to Hospital*; Miller, *The Birth of the Hospital in the Byzantine Empire*; Ferngren, *Medicine and Health Care in Early Christianity*, 109.

canons allowed such monks to have two meals per day[88] while ordinary monks have only one meal in the refectory.[89] According to the *Lives* of Pachomius, special food such as "soup, fish and perhaps even meat" were also offered to the sick in a Pachomian monastery.[90] The Desert Fathers, furthermore, entertained their visitors with cordial hospitality, and mitigated strict dietary rules for patients.[91] Secondly, monks are allowed to stay "in the infirmary as long as necessary", and were provided with special provisions and items to improve their health, albeit all within the purview of the monastic canons.[92] Such consideration for sick monks climaxed under the guidance of the fourth- century bishop and monastic leader Augustine. He exhorted monastic leaders to consider their sick monks by providing them with exceptional food and clothes in order to recover their health quickly.[93] Elsewhere, Augustine also preached that the sick monks should be allowed to receive nourishment from pious laypeople outside their monastic community.[94]

In addition to a good diet and special items, ill or injured monks were also expected to be exempt from monastic obligations, including those which were regarded as pivotal parts of monastic life: manual labor, fasting, communal meals, worship and prayer.[95]

As discussed above, the ascetic leaders appear to have cared very much about the various patients in their communities.

---

88 Shenoute, *The Canons of Our Fathers*, 175, 176.
89 Shenoute, *The Canons of Our Fathers*, 195. Regnault, *La vie quotidienne des Pères du désert en Egypte au IVe siècle*, 78 says that it was before end of the fourth century that eating one meal a day was common in the tradition of Desert fathers.
90 Philip Rousseau, *Pachomius: The Making of a Community in Fourth-Century Egypt* (Berkeley: University of California Press, 1985), 84 n. 43.
91 Regnault, *La vie quotidienne des Pères du désert en Egypte au IVe siècle*, 85–87.
92 See Layton, introduction to *The Canons of Our Fathers*, 57.
93 Augustine, *Praeceptum*, 3.3–5.
94 Augustine, *Sermon*, 356. 13.
95 Layton, *The Canons of Our Fathers*, 57; Crislip, *From Monastery to Hospital*, 70–74.

Nevertheless, certain monks expressed opposition against sick monastics who were suspected of malingering, or who were disliked by their brethren for other reasons.[96] Some monks were known to mock their sick brethren, considering them "as less worthy members of the community" and being jealous of "the special foods afforded to the sick".[97] Because of this, sick brothers occasionally became even more stressed and unwell. We know this from the response of various monastic leaders, including Theodore and Shenoute, who tried to relieve such psychological pressure by forbidding other monks from attributing the illness of others to sin and from scorning their sick fellows.[98]

Generally speaking, although there were some monks who complained about the generous treatment for monastic patients, the monasteries of the Mediterranean East tended to treat their sick fellows well, supplying material comfort and maintaining their dignity. This is certainly true of the coenobitic community of Seridos. In particular, both nursing and medical care were certainly applied in terms of care and concern for sick monks. For example, sick brothers in the monastery were excused regular fasting (letter 77). They were also provided with more meals per day (letter 78).[99] Furthermore, as archaeological and literary evidence indicates, the coenobium maintained such philanthropic institutions as a bathhouse and *xenodocheion*.[100] Dorotheos of Gaza served in the *xenodocheion* of the monastery with the assistance of other brothers from the monastery (letter 334).

---

96   Crislip, *From Monastery to Hospital*, 86–89.
97   Crislip, *From Monastery to Hospital*, 89–90; see also Shenoute, *The Canons of Our Fathers*, 127.
98   Crislip, *From Monastery to Hospital*, 77.
99   See Bitton-Ashkelony and Kofsky, *The Monastic School of Gaza*, 186 n. 26. For more detail on communal meals in the monastery of Seridos, see pages 185–88. For evidence of a monk's diet in the Judean desert, see Hirschfeld, *The Judean Desert Monasteries in the Byzantine Period*, 82–91.
100 See letters 313, 316, 323, 327, 330, 333, 334 and 336; See also Hirschfeld, "The Monasticism of Gaza: An Archaeological Review," 76; Bitton-Ashkelony and Kofsky, *The Monastic School of Gaza*, 192.

According to Crislip, some monks healed the sick as monastic doctors on the basis of "the full breadth of medical skill, ranging from dietary therapy and hygiene, to the application of pharmaceuticals, to complicated surgery"; others functioned as attendant nurses, not only "providing pillows, mattresses, special clothing" and adequate nourishment, but also performing "hygienic duties such as bathing the sick and emptying chamber pots".[101] In addition to direct medical care for the sick, others assisted in indirect ways by supporting hospices or infirmaries with financial or administrative help.[102]

Both Barsanuphius and John of Gaza encouraged their monastic addressees to consult not only physicians, but also their spiritual fathers. For example, Barsanuphius reassures a monk worried about eye disease that God is surely with him. He then suggests the monk meet with a skilled doctor to deal with the issue, mentioning that this is not a sin, but rather "a cause for your humility" (letter 225). Elsewhere, John advises a monk requiring surgery to consult his spiritual father before meeting physicians:

> It is certainly necessary, child, for anyone who has any illness to ask one of the fathers about this and to do everything in accordance with his opinion. For there are times when the elder will have the gift of healing and may secretly work this healing; so it is not always necessary to seek doctors of the body (letter 534).

Here is it clear that, if their patients really needed medical cure, the two Gazan elders indeed sent them to get medical care. Their commitment to the maintenance of monastic virtue and spirituality, clearly understood the requirement to relieve bodily suffer-

---

101 Crislip, *From Monastery to Hospital*, 14–17.
102 Crislip, *From Monastery to Hospital*, 17; Miller, *The Birth of the Hospital in the Byzantine Empire*, 118–40; Constantelos, *Byzantine Philanthropy and Social Welfare*, 152–221.

ing among their followers.

John is also known to have encouraged monastic physicians to care for and cure the sick who attended the medical facility of the Gazan monastery. When Dorotheos of Gaza hesitated to consult patients because he believed the medical works would disturb him from keeping his monastic silence, John advised him to do his hospital work as much as he could within his own measure, saying that the hospital work provided him with the opportunity to have mercy on others (letters 313 and 314).

6.4.2 Negative attitudes towards caring for a fellow monk

The two Great Old Men were also known to persuade their monastic disciples to endure bodily suffering, although the community of Seridos had medical institutions and philanthropic regulations regarding sick monks. In letter 532, John advises an unnamed brother, who is worried about bodily illness, to endure his physical illness, mentioning that believing in God is more beneficial than consulting a doctor or taking medicine. Some lines later, John mentions that he does not allow himself to travel to cities and towns in order to seek medical care from doctors, since he fears that he will be condemned on the Day of Judgement for doing just that (letter 532).

This attitude is also found in letters of Barsanuphius. When Andrew confesses his mistakes to Barsanuphius and asks him about bodily sickness, the Great Old Man replies that if Andrew were to entrust his every care and concern to God, God would deal with all his affairs at his own disposal. Barsanuphius later urges Andrew to "surrender oneself to him unto death and with the whole heart" because the Lord knows well what is "good for our soul and body", and lightens the burden of sin (letter 72). Furthermore, in letter 78, Barsanuphius further elucidates his perspective. When Andrew, suffering from rheumatism in his hands and feet, is obliged to be exempt from regular fasting in order to relieve his weakness, this exemption causes him greater psychological stress. Barsanuphius responds to his anguished query by stressing that he should not be anxious about his arthritis.

> As for fasting, do not grieve. For as I have already told you, God does not require of us anything beyond our strength. What else is fasting but discipline of the body, in order to enslave a healthy body and weaken it on account of the passions? For he says: "Whenever I am weak, then I am strong". Illness, however, is greater than mere discipline, being reckoned as a substitute for the regular [ascetic] way; and it is even of greater value [than asceticism] for the person who endures it with patience and gives thanks to God. That person reaps the fruit of salvation from such patience (letter 78).

Here Barsanuphius lays the emphasis on the illness, regarding it as an ascetic practice which is greater than other spiritual disciplines.[103] He advises Andrew to endure bodily suffering with willingness because such patience leads him to participation in the salvation of God, and not to concern himself about the things his body cannot handle.

This understanding of sickness is similar to that expressed by other ascetics, including the hagiographies of Palladius and John Moschos. Both of these men considered illness as a means to discipline one's ascetic practices.[104] To endure sickness "without treatment while carrying on with one's daily activities was to deny the physical for the spiritual, to declare one's commitment to the

---

103 Schenkewitz, *Dorotheos of Gaza and the Discourse of Healing in Gazan Monasticism*, 48, says that "Barsanuphius utilized the metaphor of medical healing to offer spiritual advice". For more detail on illness and healing in the *Letters*, see Andrew Crislip, *Thorns in the Flesh: Illness and Sanctity in Late Ancienth Christianity* (Philadelphia: University of Pennsylvania Press, 2012), 138–65.
104 Susan Ashbrook Harvey, "Physicians and Ascetics in John of Ephesus: An Expedient Alliance," *Dumbarton Oaks Paper* 38 (1984): 89.

divine by divorcing oneself from the temporal real".[105] In short, the promotion of suffering as part of sickness meant the Gazan holy men were necessarily sometimes reluctant to suggest medical care to their monastic followers.

Likewise, endurance of illness or hardship was also a crucial means for monks to inherit the kingdom of God. In the correspondence of Barsanuphius sent to John of Beersheba, who suffered from various afflictions including bodily diseases, he says that the patience of long-suffering helps an ascetic "enter the harbour of his rest and afterward live silently and entirely carefree" with his soul replying on the Lord in everything (letter 2). Barsanuphius thus encourages John of Beersheba to give thanks in every circumstance, including hardship and weakness.[106]

This understanding of endurance accords with Isaiah of Scetis. In his *Ascetic Discourses*, he instructs his ascetic readers to endure bodily illness:

> Should you be taken ill while silent in your cell, do not be discouraged but give thanks to the Lord. If you see your soul disturbed, say to it, "Is not this illness better for you than the Hell that you will go to?", and you will again find inner peace.[107]

For him, an ascetic who suffered bodily diseases was in fact imitating Christ's suffering on the cross.[108] For the non-Chalcedonians (including Abba Isaiah and Philoxenus of Mabbugh), ascetics were primarily treated as "a living embodiment of Christ on his way to the Cross" because they often "suffered hardship,

---

105 Harvey, "Physicians and Ascetics in John of Ephesus: An Expedient Alliance," 89.
106 For more detail on the promotion of endurance as a virtue in the *Letters*, see Mezynski, "The Effects of the Origenist Controversy on the Pastoral Theology of Barsanuphius and John," 123–45.
107 Isaiah, *Ascetic Discourses*, 4.
108 Schenkewitz, *Dorotheos of Gaza and the Discourse of Healing in Gazan Monasticism*, 43–46.

exile, and persecution" due to their religious belief.[109] Isaiah therefore recommends the endurance of physical illness as a way to cultivate *hesychia* (ἡσυχία) and to gain *imitatio Christi*, the ideal to which all monks were supposed to aspire.

Both the positive and negative attitudes towards medical care and healing demonstrated in the *Letters* give rise to an important question: Why did the Gazan ascetics offer inconsistent advice to the petitioners who sought answers on the need for medical help? Schenkewitz argues that their ambiguity towards medical care might "issue from the individual basis and intimacy with their interlocutors, something not clearly discerned from the preserved letters".[110] However, there is support for a different interpretation. This alternative approach takes into account the Gazan ascetics' practice of differentiating between their questioners on the basis of their inner and outer measure (see section 6.3.1 above). Such inconsistency appears to be related to differing levels of prescription that are in proportion to the perceived specific spiritual condition or capacity of the receiver. Here, once again, we can clearly see how the Gazan holy men consider individual circumstances in their patterns of spiritual guidance.

6.5 Conclusion

On the basis of the evidence mentioned above, it is evident that Barsanuphius and John of Gaza both adopted elements of the biblical as well as the Greek and Roman traditions of medicine, although the scriptural tradition appears to have been essential to their understanding of the cause of sickness and the nature of medical treatment. The Gazan elders usually suggest that lay patients seek medical therapies (including baths and medication)

---

109 Horn, *Asceticism and Christological Controversy in Fifth-Century Palestine*, 341.
110 Schenkewitz, *Dorotheos of Gaza and the Discourse of Healing in Gazan Monasticism*, 50.

to relieve their bodily suffering, without shame. According to the *Letters,* they also appear to require slave-owners to treat their sick slaves with humanity, and to provide all that is necessary. It must be qualified that this advice appears to arise more from a concern for the slave-owners' psychological and spiritual benefit.

In terms of caring for sick monks, the coenobium of Seridos generally provided sick fellow monks with nursing care to help them recover. In addition, the two Gazan elders permitted some of their sick monks to seek direct medical therapy. Yet, at the same time, they also express a contradictory position. They strongly urge some of the sick monks to endure bodily suffering without medical cure in order to advance their monastic virtues and spiritualty. This apparently ambiguous attitude towards monastic patients actually reflects their practices elsewhere, demonstrating the importance they placed on spiritual care and concern for their monastic disciples. Thus, their medical advice can be interpreted as a means by which they sought to help, correct and lead both their lay and monastic disciples. The holy men clearly express a desire to spiritually enhance their followers rather than to merely contribute to the improvement of their bodily health.

Chapter 7
Concluding Remarks

Because of its geographical position and socio-economic prosperity in the late Roman Empire, late antique Gaza emerged as one of a key traffic, commercial and intellectual hubs in the eastern Mediterranean world. The city of Gaza, as a heart of material and cultural interchange in the East, was crowded with diverse people coming from near and far during this period. It naturally prompted Gazan residents to encounter outsider cultures. The open and dynamic atmosphere and the position of Gaza enabled Gazan citizens to easily adopt and consult with diverse cultures from neighboring cities and areas including Alexandria, Antioch and Cappadocia. In this, Christians in Gaza might actually encounter many Christian documents in the late antique period which were circulated across the roads of Roman Empire in the East.[1]

During the fifth and sixth-century in particular, the monastic movement in Byzantine Palestine flourished, which was in parallel with the growth of Christianity. The monastery of Seridos in Gaza was established at that moment and then well managed by Abba Seridos under the influence of his spiritual mentors Barsanuphius and John of Gaza. Contemporary lay and monastic Christians as well as even episcopal leaders often sent letters to Seridos and Dorotheos via messengers to ask the Gazan mentors about diverse issues including charity. The mentors then answered the questions in a variety of different ways. This book

---

1   For example, the Scriptures and the *Apophthegmata Patrum*, as well as writings of John Chrysostom in Antioch, of Basil the Great in Asia Minor, and of Origen, Didymus the Blind and Evagrius of Pontus in Egypt.

has so far investigated such philanthropic activities as represented in the *Letters* of Barsanuphius and John of Gaza. The advice they provided relating to diverse philanthropic issues has, in particular, been analyzed in the context of monasticism in the Mediterranean East during Late Antiquity.

A central claim of this book is that Barsanuphius and John, popularly called holy men, not only performed their roles as patrons and guardians of the poor and other social inferiors, as ecclesiastical leaders routinely did, but also acted as *defenders (or protectors) of benefactors*. The primary concern of the two Gazan elders was in *implementing* charitable activities rather than in the beneficiaries themselves or in abstract discussions of charity. This was demonstrated in the discourses on giving gifts to the poor (chapter four), on entertaining the strangers (chapter five), and on caring for the sick (chapter six).

In the chapter four, which discussed the relationship between almsgiving and the *Letters*, we saw that the practice of giving alms to the poor was regarded as one of pivotal virtues in the *Letters*, in the same vein as the early Jewish and Christian writings. In their spiritual guidance offered to their disciples with regard to the gift-giving, the two Gazan elders regarded the poor as Christ in disguise and as spiritual donors who give spiritual gifts to their benefactors, as the New Testament had already mentioned. Taking it one step further, they offered practical and realistic advice on giving alms. They showed a marked preference for indirect giving, although both direct and indirect almsgiving was mentioned in their compiled letters. Indirect almsgiving was portrayed as providing the giver with greater spiritual benefits. In simple terms, this meant the avoidance of the vainglory and secular anxiety often associated with public almsgiving.

In addition, Barsanuphius and John suggested further practical acts which were undertaken in consideration of the personal circumstances of people and their community. For instance, the holy men of Gaza in the *Letters* promoted monastic almsgiving as a matter of spiritual benefit, whereas they imposed some significant limitations and restrictions. John of Gaza in particular did not permit all monks to take part in eleemosynary activities. Instead, he differentiated between advanced and beginner monks, making sure only the former were in charge of distributing monastic alms to the needy. In terms of other restrictions, John advised one donor, who had sought to give his money to a monk to distribute, not to burden the monastic. While this might seem to go against the previous exhortations of John and Barsanuphius with regard to giving alms, it should be interpreted as indicative of the concern of the Gazan elder to protect his own monastic followers. His emphasis appeared to be on the need for them to concentrate on their ascetic life, rather than to practice philanthropic activities. In other words, monks in the *Letters* were often encouraged to give alms and do charitable works to a degree which did not distract them from conducting their essential ascetic duties.

Lastly, the *Letters* did not give any direct evidence regarding the nature of episcopal almsgiving as it was practiced in early Byzantine Palestine and in Gaza in particular. However, from the correspondence between the holy men of Gaza and other church authorities, some understanding was able to be gained of the role of episcopacy in terms of charity, and of caring for the poor and marginalized. For example, Barsanuphius strongly urged a certain bishop, as God's steward, to protect the poor from municipal officials who sought to take church revenue (letter 830). In the following letter, the same ascetic urged the bishop and other civil authorities to protect their citizens from outside military officials. In terms of protection of the poor as an essential element of charitable life, the holy men thus expected their Christian bishops to perform their roles as guardians and protectors of the weak and marginalized.

The attitude of the respected Gazan ascetics toward the poor and their followers as benefactors is more obvious in the discourses on entertaining the stranger in the *Letters*. As seen in chapter 5, the *Letters* primarily stressed the importance of moderate charity, by espousing different levels of welcome and care, on the basis of the concept of *diakrisis*, or discerning the motives behind those seeking charitable hospitality in conjunction with an understanding of one's own inner measure (letters 620, 635 and 681). In addition, John the Prophet also suggested a sliding scale of charity which offered different levels of care and sustenance to visitors in accordance with their individual religious status and physical condition (letters 630 and 636). Here his primary concern was for those who have voluntarily renounced their property for the sake of God, as well as the psychologically and physically weak, rather than the beggar only. Notwithstanding, this was different from the position outlined by ancient pagan hosts in the Greek and Roman traditions, which put an emphasis on extending charity to their fellow-citizens or relatives, and on giving in anticipation of future socio-economic recompense.

In addition to lay Christians, the philanthropic welcome was also an important monastic virtue in the correspondence between John and his monastic followers, which had been already promoted by his monastic predecessors (e.g. Basil of Caesarea, Gregory of Nazianzus and Pachomius). However, John did not permit all monks to participate in welcoming strangers, especially the poor and needy. On the grounds that the exercise of charity, in terms of entertaining strangers, potentially hindered monastics from implementing their proper ascetic practices unless they were very careful, he recommended younger monastics not to participate in such activities. This was reconfirmed in his advice towards Aelianos, abbot of the Gazan monastery, in which he suggested offering monastic almsgiving and hospitality to the needy only so far as in proportion to one's abilities and possessions. With regard to itinerant monks, John the Prophet recommended providing them with provisions and possibly other necessary items, but not allowing them to enter, in case that they caused problems. The advice was somewhat different from that of his predecessors Abba Isaiah and Peter the Iberian. This reflected his negative view on them and his effort to prevent fellow monks from suffering ill effects as the result of any of the dangers associated with charitable actions. Here, it is reasonable to conclude that the limited and cautious approach of John towards monastic hospitality seemed to be focused on the promotion of ascetic practices such as prayer and isolation, and that he appeared to have the salvation of the souls of their followers as a primary concern.

Chapter six, which dealt with caring for the sick in the context of the eastern Mediterranean world during Late Antiquity, showed more diverse aspects relating to the attitude of the Gazan anchorites toward social inferiors. It was identified from the *Letters* that although the Gazan anchorites adopted elements of the Scriptures and of Greco-Roman traditions regarding medicine, the scriptural tradition exerted much more influence on their understanding of the cause of illness and medical treatment. The letters of Barsanuphius and John suggested that curing physical sickness, particularly among the sick laity in general, was not a sin, and was therefore actually to be encouraged. They could even be seen advising their interlocutors to cure bodily disease using contemporary medical practices. Nevertheless, the holy men still interpreted proper medical care as connected to, and cooperating with, divine healing, because God might work through medicine and medical practitioners, and in the end, God could decide if someone is to regain health or not.

As part of this discussion of the treatment of the sick, John of Gaza also touched on the role of slave-owners in terms of their treatment of their slaves. He told the owners to handle their servants with humanity, particularly those slaves who were perhaps ill or wounded. While John's attitude towards sick slaves appeared quite generous, there was nevertheless no implication that he offered any challenge to the maintenance of slavery in the later Roman Empire. Perhaps somewhat ironically, his concern for the treatment of slaves, particularly sick slaves, appeared to be based more on an intention to care for spiritual benefits of the slave owners.

Unlike the medical treatment of normal patients in the secular world, the *Letters* of John of Gaza and Barsanuphius expressed a somewhat ambivalent attitude in terms of the treatment of sick monks. Like other monasteries in the Mediterranean East during the late-antique period, the monastery of Seridos provided sick monastics with medical facilities (such as a bath and a hospice) and nursing care. Moreover, the Gazan advisors permitted some of their monastic questioners to consult with physicians in order to obtain medical treatment. Simultaneously, they also advised other sick monks to put up with their bodily suffering, in order to gain spiritual benefit and ascetic profit. This rejection of medical care seemed, as we saw above, to be tied to Barsanuphius and John's understanding of sickness and healing, particularly the role of God in the healing process, and the concept of the *Christus medicus*.

Upon consideration of all these facts, this study has identified four major features in relation to spiritual guidance Barsanuphius and John employed in letters related to charity. First, the Gazan elders could be clearly observed offering ideal answers as well as practical suggestions to their lay and monastic interlocutors with regard to merciful works. They consistently recommended their readers implement only what they felt capable of in proportion to their individual psychological, financial, physical and religious circumstances. Such a moderate compromise between ideals and reality was likely to relieve the spiritual burden of their questioners, enabling them to clarify their idealistic aims with regard to eleemosynary activities. On the other hand, such spiritual guidance with regard to charity might also have had the negative effect of causing an inner tension between the moral and divine obligation of charity and the realistic issues for pious lay donors and monks.

Second, the spiritual directions given by the Gazan mentors towards the laity were sometimes quite different from those given to monastic Christians. Lay Christians were usually encouraged to take part in aiding the poor within their own measure and ability, either by giving gifts to a monastery or church and by showing hospitality to those in need. In contrast, only the more mature monks were encouraged to help travelers and the poor, especially at the gatehouse and *xenodocheion* of the Tabatha monastery. A similar divide was evidenced in the advice Barsanuphius and John directed towards lay and monastic patients. While they urged the laity to seek appropriate medical treatment, and reminded them that curing bodily illness was not shameful, they had a tendency to view illness among monks as an opportunity to mature. Illness and suffering for monks was presented as offering spiritual benefits, making them turn their eyes to God, and follow the right path to salvation. Such proper flexibility and consideration for others presented in the two holy men seemed to attractive to Christians in the monastery of Seridos as well as others beyond that in the Mediterranean East.

The correspondence between the two anchorites and their petitioners in relation to philanthropic activities, also clearly demonstrated that the Gazan holy men had a holistic approach to the merciful practice because it was a crucial, but complex issue for all Christians. While it was a means for the indigent to relieve their pressing necessities (a beneficiary), it was also opportunity to offer diverse spiritual or material benefits for a donor (a benefactor) and charitable agents (a third party). Furthermore, the merciful practice helped monastic and lay individuals to balance contemplation and action, which led to a well-balanced Christian life. Such an understanding of charity led both John and Barsanuphius to perceive the connections among the various aspects that constitute charity. This helped them to advise their followers with holistic perspectives, and it finally affected the spiritual life of their lay and monastic Christians.

The last feature is that the Gazan elders, as shown above, tended to prioritize the tangible and intangible benefits for lay and monastic benefactors before the benefits of mercy to the needy. Such kinds of guidance identified in the letters of Barsanuphius and John of Gaza were, to a considerable extent, not irrelevant to their concerns for their lay and ascetic followers. It meant that their primary focus was on the importance of protecting their believers and keeping them from any internal or external perils which could potentially befall a benefactor during almsgiving, entertaining strangers and/or caring for the sick.

Moreover, the evidence presented in the study on wealth and philanthropy in the *Letters* suggests the image of the holy man as a defender (or a protector) of a benefactor as well as beneficiary. This consequently enables us to extend our understanding of holy men in the late antique world. As mentioned above, the holy man in Late Antiquity was usually understood as a spiritual father and meditator as well as an intercessor. In addition, he was not only an exemplar to his local and sometimes even to a wider community, but also an educator and, in some sense, a healer in late-antique society. However, this investigation of the letters of Barsanuphius and John of Gaza also revealed that these holy men not only maintained all of the roles listed above, but also acted as protectors in Gaza and its neighboring areas.

The findings of this research also provide valuable insights for the debate on the shift from the Greco-Roman perspectives on the poor and charity to the Christian view in late antique period, and for the relation between an ideal charity and its reality in poverty and wealth discourses. Based on rhetorical strategies on charity and on bishops or monks' activities, not a few scholars argued that a great influence of Greco-Roman euergetism still existed on late antique Christianity, and Neil in particular assumed the shift occurred sometime in the sixth century.[2] In this situation, the evidence from this study has confirmed Suh's study which asserted that the transition already took place in Gaza in early sixth century at least.[3] This is supported by the fact that the Gazan holy men in the *Letters* primarily offered realistic advice to their questioners in accordance with their own socio-economic and spiritual circumstances, with keeping in their biblical perspectives on the poor and charity.

Finally, as already identified above, the document of two elders has been considered as a unique source to give a picture of diverse spiritual guidance of the Gazan elders regarding charity matters as well as social-economic, theological and spirituality-related issues which many questioners asked about. It is recognized from the letters that both Barsanuphius and John used and adopted profusely the Scriptures to respond to a variety of questions of their disciples in the context of spiritual direction. So further research is needed to better understand how the Gazan anchorites read, memorized, cited, and used Scriptures in their letters addressed to their disciples. The study on the Bible and its related issues in the two elders' letters leads not only to deep understanding of the Gazan holy men, and their letters and spiritual direction, but also to a broader historical picture of the Scriptures in monastic movements in the Mediterranean East during Late Antiquity.

---

2   See section 1.1. Previous research.
3   For the study of Suh, section 1.1. Previous research

Bibliography

Primary sources

Abba Isaiah. *Abba Isaiah of Scetis: Ascetic Discourses*. Translated by John Chryssavgis and Pachomios Penkett. Kalamazoo: Cistercian Publications, 2002.

———. *Les cinq recensions de l'Ascéticon syriaque d'Abba Isaïe*. Corpus Scriptorum Christianorum Orientalium 289–290, 293–294, Syr. 120–123. Louvain: Secrétariat du CorpusSCO, 1968.

Acts of the Council of Chalcedon. Translated by Richard Price and Michael Gaddis. Translated Texts for Historians Volume 45. Liverpool: Liverpool Press, 2005.

Ambrose. Epistola 66. In vol. 16 of Patrologia Latina. Edited by J-P. Migne. 217 vols. Paris, 1844–1864.

Athanasius. *The Life of Saint Antony*. Translated by Robert T. Meyer. New York: Newman Press, 1978.

Augustine. *Praeceptum*. In A. Zumkeller. *Augustine's Ideal of the Religious Life*. Translated by Edmund Colledge. New York: Fordham University Press, 1986.

———. *Sermon 356*. In *Sermons 341–400*. The Works of St. Augustine III/10. Translated by Edmund Hill. New York: New City Press, 1995.

Barsanuphius and John of Gaza. *Biblos Barsanouphiou kai Ioannou*. Edited by Nikodemos Hagiorita. Venice, 1816.

———. *Biblos Psychophelestate*. Edited by Soterios Schoinas. Volos, 1960.

———. *Barsanuphe et Jean de Gaza: Correspondance*. Edited and translated by François Neyt, Paula de Angelis-Noah, and Lucien Regnault. Sources Chrétiennes, 426, 427, 450, 451, 468. Paris: Éditions du Cerf, 1997–2002.

———. *Barsanuphius and John: Questions and Responses*. Translated by John Chryssavgis. 2 vols. Washington. D.C: Catholic University of America Press, 2006–2007.

Basil of Caesarea. *Longer Rules / Short Rules*. In *The Asketikon of St Basil the Great*. Translated by Anna Silvas. Oxford: Oxford University Press, 2005.

———. *Letters, Volume I: Letters 1–58*. Translated by Roy J. Deferrari. Loeb Classical Library 190. Cambridge, MA: Harvard University Press, 1926.

Benedict. *RB 1980: The Rule of St. Benedict in English*. Edited by Timothy Fry. Collegeville: Liturgical Press, 1982.

Choricius of Gaza. *First Encomium to Marcian Bishop of Gaza*. In "Choricius of Gaza: An Approach to His work". Translated by Fotios K. Litsas. Ph.D., University of Chicago, 1980.

———. *The Second Encomium to Marcian Bishop of Gaza*. In "Choricius of Gaza: An Approach to His work". Translated by Fotios K. Litsas. Ph.D., University of Chicago, 1980.

Cyril of Scythopolis. *The Lives of the Monks of Palestine*. Translated by Richard M. Price. Kalamazoo: Cistercian Publications, 1991.

Demetrius. *De Elocutione* 228. Pages 16–19 in *Ancient Epistolary Theorists*. Edited and translated by Abraham Malherbe. Atlanta: Scholars Press, 1988.

Didascalia Apostolorum in Syriac. Translated by Arthur Vööbus. Corpus Scriptorum Christianorum Orientalium 402. Louvain: Secrétariat du CorpusSCO, 1979.

Dorotheos of Gaza. *Abba Dorotheos: Practical Teaching on the Christian Life*. Translated by Constantine Scouteris. Athens: University of Athens, 2000.

———. *Instructions*. In *Dorothée de Gaza: Oeuvres spirituelles*. Sources Chrétiennes 92. Edited and translated by L. Regunault and J. de Préville. Paris: Éditions du Cerf, 1963.

———. *Dorotheos of Gaza: Discourses and Sayings*. Translated by E.P. Wheeler. Kalamazoo: Cistercian Publications, 1977.

———. *Vie De Saint Dosithée*. In *Dorothée de Gaza: Oeuvres spirituelles*. Sources Chrétiennes 92. Edited and translated by Lucien Regnault and J. de Preville. Paris: Éditions du Cerf, 1963.

Eusebius of Caesarea. *The Proof of the Gospel*. Translated by W. J. Ferrar. London: S.P.C.K, 1920.

———. *Ecclesiastical History. Volume II: Books 6–10*. Translated by J. E. L. Oulton. Loeb Classical Library 265. Cambridge, MA: Harvard University Press, 1932.

Evagrius. *Evagrius of Pontus: The Greek Ascetic Corpus*. Translated by Robert E. Sinkewicz. Oxford: Oxford University Press, 2006.

Galen. *Galen on Diseases and Symptoms*. Translated by Ian Johnston. Cambridge: Cambridge University Press, 2006.

———. *Galen on the Therapeutic Method: Book I and II*. Translated by R. J. Hankinson. Oxford: Clarendon Press, 1991.

———. *On the Constitution of the Art of Medicine; The Art of Medicine; A Method of Medicine to Glaucon*. Edited and translated by Ian Johnston. Loeb Classical Library 523. Cambridge, MA: Harvard University Press, 2016.

Gregory of Nazianzus. *Epistula* 51. Pages 58–61 in *Ancient Epistolary Theorists*. Edited and translated by Abraham Malherbe. Atlanta: Scholars Press, 1988.

Gregory of Nyssa. *Homilies on Ecclesiastes: An English Version with Supporting Studies*. Translated by Stuart G. Hall and Rachel Moriarty. Berlin: de Gruyter, 1993.

———. *The Life of St. Macrina*. In *Saint Gregory of Nyssa: Ascetical Works*. Translated by Virginia Woods Callahan. Fathers of the Church 58. Washington, DC: Catholic University Press, 1967.

Gregory of the Great. *The Letters of Gregory of the Great*. Edited and translated by John R. C. Martyn. Ontario: Pontifical Institute of Mediaeval Studies, 2004.

Homer. *Odyssey, Volume I: Books 1–12*. Translated by A. T. Murray. Revised by George E. Dimock. Loeb Classical Library 104. Cambridge, MA: Harvard University Press, 1919.

———. *Odyssey, Volume II: Books 13–24*. Translated by A. T. Murray. Revised by George E. Dimock. Loeb Classical Library 105. Cambridge, MA: Harvard University Press, 1919.

Jerome. *Life of Hilarion*. In *Early Christian Lives*. Edited and translated by Carolinne White. Penguin Books, 1998.

John Cassian. *The Institutes*. Translated by Boniface Ramsey. New York: Newman Press, 2000.

John Chrysostom. *The Homilies on First Corinthians*. In vol. 12 of *The Nicene and Post-Nicene Fathers*, Series 1. Edited by Philip Schaff. 1886–1889. 14 vols. Repr., Peabody, MA: Hendrickson, 1994.

———. *The Homilies on the Gospel of St. John*. In vol. 14 of *The Nicene and Post-Nicene Fathers*, Series 1. Edited by Philip Schaff. 1886–1889. 14 vols. Repr., Peabody, MA: Hendrickson, 1994.

———. *Homilies on Genesis 41* in *Homilies on Genesis: Saint John Chrysostom*. Translated by Robert C. Hill. Washington, DC: Catholic University of America Press, 1988.

John Moschos. *The Spiritual Meadow of John of Moschos*. Translated by John Wortley. Kalamazoo: Cistercian Publications, 1992.

John of Ephesus. *Historia Ecclesiastica*. Translated by R. Payne Smith. Oxford: Oxford University Press, 1860.

John Rufus. Plerophories. In *Plérophories, témoignages et révélation*. Edited and translated by F. Nau, Patrologia Orientalis 8.1. 1911. Reprinted, Turnhout: Brepols, 1982.

———. *The Life of Peter the Iberian*. In *John Rufus: The Lives of Peter the Iberian, Theodosius of Jerusalem, and the Monk Romanus*. Translated by Cornelia Horn and Robert Phenix Jr. Leiden: Brill, 2008.

Julius Victor. *Ars Rhetorica* 27. Pages 63–67 in *Ancient Epistolary Theorists*. Edited and translated by Abraham Malherbe. Atlanta: Scholars Press, 1988.

Leo the Great. *Sermons*. Translated by Jane Patricia Freeland and Agnes Josephine Conway. Fathers of the Church 93. Washington, DC: Catholic University of America Press, 1996.

Mark the Deacon. *The Life of Porphyry, Bishop of Gaza*. Oxford: Clarendon Press, 1913.

Maximus of Turin. *The Sermons of St. Maximus of Turin*. Translated by Boniface Ramsey. New York: Newman Press, 1989.

Origen. *Contra Celsum*. Translated by Henry Chadwick. Cambridge: Cambridge University Press, 1965.

Pachomius. *Pachomian Koinonia*. 3 vols. Translated by Arman Veilleux. Kalamazoo: Cistercian, 1980–82.

Piacenza Pilgrim. *Travels* 33. In *Jerusalem Pilgrims before the Crusades*. Edited and translated by John Wilkinson. Warminster, England: Aris & Phillips, 2002.

Procopius of Caesarea. *Buildings*. Translated by H. B. Dewing and Glanville Downey. Loeb Classical Library 343. Cambridge, MA: Harvard University Press, 1940.

Pseudo Libanius. Ἐπιστολιμαῖοι χαρακτῆρες 50. Pages 68–81 in *Ancient Epistolary Theorists*. Edited and translated by Abraham Malherbe. Atlanta: Scholars Press, 1988.

Pseudo-Clement. *Two Epistles Concerning Virginity*. In vol. 8 of *Ante Nicene Fathers*. Edited by A. Roberts and J. Donaldson. 1885-1887. 10 vols. Repr., Grand Rapids: Eerdmans, 1951.

Pseudo-Zachariah Rhetor. *The Chronicle of Pseudo-Zachariah Rhetor*. Translated by Robert Phenix and Cornelia Horn. Translated Texts for Historians Volume 55. Liverpool: Liverpool University Press, 2011.

Rule of the Master. Translated by Luke Eberle. Kalamazoo: Cistercian Publications, 1977.

Sayings of the Desert Fathers: The Alphabetical Collection. Translated by Benedicta Ward. London: Mowbrays, 1975.

Shenoute. *The Canons of Our Fathers*: *Monastic Rules of Shenoute*. Translated by Bentley Layton. Oxford: Oxford University Press, 2014.

Sidonius. *Letters: Books 3–9*. Translated by W. B. Anderson. Loeb Classical Library 420. Cambridge, MA: Harvard University Press, 1965.

Sozomen. *Ecclesiastical History*. In vol. 2 of *The Nicene and Post-Nicene Fathers*, Series 2. Edited by Philip Schaff. 14 vols. Repr., Peabody, MA: Hendrickson, 1995.

Theophanes the Confessor. *The Chronicle of Theophanes Confessor: Byzantine and Near Eastern History, AD 284–813*. Translated by Cyril Manco and Roger Scott. Oxford: Clarendon Press, 1997.

Zachariah Rhetor. *Vita Isaiae Monachi*. Edited and Translated by E. W. Brook. Corpus Scriptorum Christianorum Orientalium 7–8. Paris: E typographeo reipublicae 1907. Reprinted, Peeters, 1960.

Zacharias. *'Life' of Severos*. In *Two Early Lives of Severos*. Translated by Sebastian Brock and Brian Fitzgerald. Liverpool: Liverpool University Press, 2013.

Secondary sources

Adler, Robert E. *Medical Firsts: From Hippocrates to the Human Genome*. New Jersey: John Wiley & Sons, 2004.

Allan, Nigel. "The Physician in Ancient Israel: His Status and Function." *Medical History* 45 (2001): 377–94.

Allen, Pauline, and Bronwen Neil. *Crisis Management in Late Antiquity (410–590 CE): A Survey of the Evidence from Episcopal Letters*. Leiden: Brill, 2013.

Allen, Pauline, Bronwen Neil and Wendy Mayer. *Preaching Poverty in Late Antiquity: Perceptions and Realities*. Leipzig: Evangelische Verlagsanstalt, 2009.

Allen, Pauline. "Challenges in Approaching Patristic Texts from the Perspective of Contemporary Catholic Social Teaching." Pages 30–44 in *Reading Patristic Texts on Social Ethics: Issues and Challenges for Twenty-First Century Christian Social Thought*. Edited by John Leemans, Brian J. Matz and Johan Verstraeten. Washington, DC: Catholic University of America Press, 2011.

———. "How to Study Episcopal Letter-Writing in Late Antiquity: An Overview of Published Work on the Fifth and Sixth Centuries." Pages 130–42 in *Patrologia Pacifica: Selected Papers Presented to the Asia Pacific Early Christian Studies Society*. Edited by Vladimir Baranov, Kazuhiko Demura and Basil Lourié. Piscataway, NJ: Gorgias Press, 2010.

———. "It's in the Post: Techniques and Difficulties of Letter-Writing in Antiquity with Regard to Augustine of Hippo." Australian Academy of the Humanities, A.D. Trendall Annual Memorial Lecture, September 2005, *The Australian Academy of the Humanities Proceedings 2005*. Canberra: The Australian Academy of the Humanities, 2006.

Andreau, Jean, and Raymond Descat. *The Slave in Greece and Rome*. Translated by Marion Leopold. Madison: University of Wisconsin Press, 2011.

Arterbury, Andrew. *Entertaining Angels: Early Christian Hospitality in Its Mediterranean Setting*. Sheffield: Sheffield Phoenix Press, 2005.

Ashkenazi, Yakov. "Sophists and Priests in Late Antique Gaza: According to Choricius the Rhetor." Pages 195–208 in *Christian Gaza in Late Antiquity*. Edited by Bitton-Ashkelony and A. Kofsky. Leiden: Brill, 2004.

Avi-Yohan, M. "The Economics of Byzantine Palestine." *Israel Exploration Journal* 8.1 (1958): 39–51.

Bagnall, Roger, and Raffaella Cribiore. *Women's Letters from Ancient Egypt: 300 BC–AD 800*. Ann Arbor: University of Michigan Press, 2006.

Bagnall, Roger. "Monk and Property: Rhetoric, Law, and Patronage in *the Apophthegmata Patrum* and the Papyri." *Greek, Roman, and Byzantium Studies* 42 (2001): 7–24.

———. *Egypt in Late Antiquity*. New Jersey: Princeton University Press, 1993.

Bar, Doron. "Rural Monasticism as a Key Element in the Christianization of Byzantine Palestine." *Harvard Theological Review* 98.1 (2005): 49–65.

Baynes, Norman. "The Thought-World of East Rome." Pages 24–46 in *Byzantine Studies and Other Essays*. 1955. Repr., Westport: Greenwood Press, 1974.

Becker, Adam H. "Anti-Judaism and Care for the Poor in Aphrahat's Demonstration 20." *Journal of Early Christian Studies* 10.3 (2002): 305–27.

Belayche, Nicole. "Pagan Festivals in Fourth-Century Gaza." Pages 5–22 in *Christian Gaza in Late Antiquity*. Edited by Bitton-Ashkelony and A. Kofsky. Leiden: Brill, 2004.

Binns, John. *Ascetics and Ambassadors of Christ: The Monasteries of Palestine 314–631*. Oxford: Clarendon Press, 1996.

Bitton-Ashkelony, Brouria, and Aryeh Kofsky. "Gazan Monasticism in the Fourth-Sixth Centuries: From Anchoritic to Cenobitic." *Proche-Orient Chrétien* 50:2 (2000): 14–62.

_____. *The Monastic School of Gaza*. Leiden: Brill: 2006.

Bitton-Ashkelony, Brouria. *Encountering the Sacred: The Debate on Christian Pilgrimage in Late Antiquity*. Berkeley: University of California Press, 2005.

Blumell, Lincoln H. "The Message and the Medium: Some Observations on Epistolary Communication in Late Antiquity." *Journal of Graeco-Roman Christianity and Judaism* 10 (2014): 24–67.

_____. *Lettered Christians: Christians, Letters and Late Antique Oxyrhynchus*. Leiden: Brill, 2012.

Bobertz, Charles A. "Cyprian of Carthage as Patron: A Social Historical Study of the Role of Bishop in the Ancient Christian Community of North Africa." PhD diss., Yale University, 1988.

Brakke, David. "Care for the Poor, Fear of Poverty, and Love of Money: Evagrius Ponticus on the Monk's Economic Vulnerability." Pages 76–87 in *Wealth and Poverty in Early Church and Society*. Edited by Susan R. Holman. Grand Rapids: Baker Academic, 2008.

Bregman, Jay. *Synesius of Cyrene, Philosopher-Bishop*. Berkeley: University of California Press, 1982.

Brock, Sebastian, and Susan Ashbrook Harvey. *Holy Women of the Syrian Orient*. Berkeley: University of California Press, 1987.

Brock, Sebastian. *A Brief Outline of Syriac Literature*. Rev. ed. Kottayam: St Ephrem Ecumenical Research Institute, 2009.

_____. *Introduction to Syrian Studies*. Piscataway: Gorgias Press, 2006.

———. *Spirituality in the Syriac Tradition*. 2nd ed. Kottayam: St Ephrem Ecumenical Research Institute, 2005.

Broshi, Magen. "The Population of Western Palestine in the Roman-Byzantine Period." *Bulletin of the American Schools of Orientals Research* 236 (1979): 1–10.

Brown, Peter. *Treasure in Heaven: The Holy Poor in Early Christianity*. Charlottesville & London: University of Virginia Press, 2016.

———. "Arbiters of the Holy: The Christian Holy Man in Late Antiquity." Pages 57–78 in *Authority and the Sacred: Aspects of the Christianisation of the Roman World*. Cambridge: Cambridge University Press, 1995.

———. "Christianization and Religious Conflict." Pages 632–64 in *The Cambridge Ancient History XIII, The Later Empire, A.D. 337–425*. Edited by Averil Cameron and Peter Garnsey. Cambridge: Cambridge University Press, 1998.

———. "The Rise and Function of the Holy Man in Late Antiquity." *The Journal of Roman Studies* 61 (1971): 80–101.

———. "The Saint as Exemplar in Late Antiquity." *Representations* 2 (1983): 1–25.

———. *Poverty and Leadership in the Late Roman Empire*. London: University Press of New England, 2002.

———. *The Cults of the Saints: Its Rise and Function in Latin Christianity*. Chicago: University of Chicago Press, 1981.

———. *Through the Eye of a Needle: Wealth, the Fall of Rome, and the Making of Christianity in the West, 350–550 A.D.* New Jersey: Princeton University Press, 2014.

Burton-Christie, Douglas. *The Word in the Desert*. Oxford: Oxford University Press, 1993.

Cameron, Averil. *The Mediterranean World in Late Antiquity: AD 395–700*. 2nd ed. London: Routledge, 2012.

Caner, Daniel. "Charitable Ministrations (*Diakoniai*), Monasticism, and the Social Aesthetic of Sixth-Century Byzantium." Pages 45–73 in *Charity and Giving in Monotheistic Religions*. Edited by Miriam Frenkel and Yaacov Lev. Berlin: Walter de Gruyter, 2009.

———. "Wealth, Stewardship, and Charitable 'Blessings' in Early Byzantine Monasticism." Pages 221–42 in *Wealth and Poverty in Early Church and Society*. Edited by Susan R. Holman. Grand Rapids: Baker Academic, 2008.

———. *Wandering, Begging Monks: Spiritual Authority and the Promotion of Monasticism in Late Antiquity*. Berkeley: University of California Press, 2002.

Casson, Lionel. *Travel in the Ancient World*. London: Allen & Unwin, 1974.

Chadwick, Henry. "The Role of the Christian Bishop in Ancient Society." Pages 1–14 in *The Role of the Christian Bishop in Ancient Society: Protocol of the 35th Colloquy, 25 February 1979*. Edited by H. C. Hobbs and W. Wuellner. Berkeley: The Center for Hermeneutical Studies in Hellenistic and Modern Culture, 1980.

Champion, Michael W. *Explaining the Cosmos: Creation and Cultural Interaction in Late-Antique Gaza*. Oxford: Oxford University Press, 2014.

Chitty, Derwas. "Abba Isaiah." *Journal of Theological Studies* 22.1 (1971): 47–72.

Choat, Malcolm. "The Epistolary Culture of Monasticism between Literature and Papyri." *Cistercian Studies Quarterly* 48.2 (2013): 227–37.

———. "Epistolary Formulae in Early Coptic Letters." *Orientalia Lovaniensia Analecta* 163 (2007): 667–77.

———. "Monastic letter collections in Late Antique Egypt: Structure, Purpose, and Transmission." Pages 73–90 in *Cultures in Contact: Transfer of Knowledge in the Mediterranean Context*. Edited by Sofía Torallas Tovar and Juan Pedro Monferrer-Sala. Cordoba: CNERU (Cordoba Near Eastern Research Unit) — Beirut: CEDRAC (Centre de Documentation et de Recherches Arabes Chrétiennes) — Oriens Academic, 2013.

Choi, Hyung Guen. "Gaza Monastery and Hospitality during the Sixth Century: The Case of the Letters of Barsanuphius and John of Gaza." *Korea Journal of Christian Studies* 115 (2020): 67–90 [Korean].

Chryssavgis, John. "The Identity and Integrity of the Old Men of Gaza." *Studia Patristica* 39 (2006): 307–14.

———. "The Road from Egypt to Palestine. The Sayings of the Desert Fathers: Destination and Destiny." *Aram Periodical* 15 (2003): 97–108.

Clark, Elizabeth. *The Origenist Controversy: The Cultural Construction of an Early Christian Debate*. New Jersey: Princeton University Press, 1992.

Connolly, R. Hugh. *Didascalia Apostolorum: The Syriac Version Translated and Accompanied by the Verona Latin Fragments*. Eugene, Oregon: Wipf & Stock, 2009.

Constable, G. *Letters and Letter-Collections*. Turnhout: Brepols, 1976.

Constable, Olivia Remie. *Housing the Stranger in the Mediterranean World: Lodging, Trade and Travel in Late Antiquity and the Middle Ages*. Cambridge: Cambridge University Press, 2003.

Constantelos, Demetrios. "Hellenic Background and Nature of Patristic Philanthropy in the Early Byzantine Era." Pages 187–208 in *Wealth and Poverty in Early Church and Society*. Edited by Susan R. Holman. Grand Rapids: Baker Academic, 2008.

———. *Byzantine Philanthropy and Social Welfare*. New Jersey: Rutgers University Press, 1968.

Constas, Nicholas. "Death and Dying in Byzantium." Pages 124–45 in *Byzantine Christianity*. Edited by Derek Krueger. Minneapolis: Fortress Press, 2010.

Cororan, Simon. "State Correspondence in the Roman Empire: Imperial Communication from Augustus to Justinian." Pages 172–209 in *State Correspondence in the Ancient World: From New Kingdom Egypt to the Roman Empire*. Edited Karen Radner. Oxford: Oxford University Press, 2014.

Costa, C. D. N., ed. *Greek Fictional Letters*. Oxford: Oxford University Press, 2001.

Countryman, Louis. *The Rich Christian in the Church of the Early Empire*. New York: Edwin Mellen Press, 1980.

Crislip, Andrew. *From Monastery to Hospital: Christian Monasticism and the Transformation of Health Care in Late Antiquity*. Ann Arbor: University of Michigan Press, 2005.

———, *Thorns in the Flesh: Illness and Sanctity in Late Ancienth Christianity*. Philadelphia: University of Pennsylvania Press, 2012.

Demacopoulos, George. *Five Models of Spiritual Direction in the Early Church*. Notre Dame: University of Notre Dame Press, 2007.

DeVinne, Michael. "The Advocacy of Empty Bellies: Episcopal Representation of the Poor in the Late Roman Empire." PhD diss., Stanford University, 1995.

Dey, Hendrik. "*Diaconiae, Xenodochia, Hospitalia* and Monasteries: 'Social Security' and the Meaning of Monasticism in Early Medieval Rome." *Early Medieval Europe* 16.4 (2008): 398–422.

Di Segni, Leah, and Yoram Tsafrir. "The Ethnic Composition of Jerusalem's Population in the Byzantine Period (312–638 CE)." *Liber Annuus* 62 (2012): 405–54.

Di Segni, Leah. "Late-antique Gaza: Hirarion, Choricius, Giraffes, Mimes and Ecphrasis." Review of *Gaza Dans L'Antiqué Tardive. Archéologie, Rhétorique et Historie. Actes du Colloque International de Poiters (6–7 mai 2004)*. Edited by Chatherine Saliou. *Journal of Roman Archaeology* 20 (2007): 643–55. doi:10.1017/S1047759400006085.

———. "Monastery, City and Village in Byzantine Gaza." *Proche-Orient Chrétien* 55 (2005): 24–51.

Dietz, Mariel. *Wandering Monks, Virgins and Pilgrims: Ascetic Travel in the Mediterranean World, A.D. 300–800*. University Park: Pennsylvania State University Press, 2005.

Doty, William. "The Classification of Epistolary Literature." *The Catholic Biblical Quarterly* 31.2 (1969): 183–99.

Downey, Glanville. "The Christian Schools of Palestine: A Chapter in Literary History." *Harvard Library Bulletin* (1958): 297–319.

Ekonomou, Andrew. *Byzantine Rome and the Greek Popes*. Lanham: Lexington Books, 2009.

Elm, Susanna. *Virgins of God: The Making of Asceticism in Late Antiquity*. Oxford: Oxford University Press, 1994.

Evans, James A. S. *The Age of Justinian: The Circumstances of Imperial Power*. London & New York: Routledge, 1996. Repr., London: Tayor & Francis, 2000.

Ferngren, Gary. *Medicine and Health Care in Early Christianity*. Baltimore: John Hopkins University Press, 2009.

Finn, Richard. *Almsgiving in the Later Roman Empire*. Oxford: Oxford University Press, 2006.

Fowler, Alastair. *Kinds of Literature: An Introduction to the Theory of Genres and Models*. Oxford: Clarendon Press, 1982.

Frazee, Charles. "Late Roman and Byzantine Legislation on the Monastic Life from the Fourth to the Eighth Centuries." *Church History* 51.3 (1982): 263–79.

Garnsey, Peter. *Ideas of Slavery from Aristotle to Augustine*. Cambridge: Cambridge University Press, 1996.

Garrison, Roman. *Redemptive Almsgiving in Early Christianity*. Journal for the Study of the New Testament Supplement Series 77. Sheffield: Sheffield Academic Press, 1993.

Gillett, Andrew. "Communication in Late Antiquity: Use and Reuse." Pages 815–47 in *Oxford Handbook of Late Antiquity*, Edited by Scott Fitzgerald Johnson. Oxford: Oxford University Press, 2012. doi: 10.1093/oxfordhb/9780195336931.013.0025.

Glucker, Carol. *The City of Gaza in the Roman and Byzantine Periods*. BAR International Series 325. British Archaeological Reports, 1987.

Goehring, James. *Ascetics, Society and the Desert: Studies in Early Egyptian Monasticism*. Harrisburg: Trinity Press International, 1999.

———. *The Letter of Ammon and Pachomian Monasticism*. Berlin & New York: De Gruyter, 1985.

Gould, Graham. *The Desert Fathers on Monastic Community*. Oxford: Clarendon Press, 1993.

———. "Lay Christians, Bishops and Clergy in the *Apophthegmata Patrum*." *Studia Patristica* 25 (1993): 396–404.

———. "Moving On and Staying Put in the *Apophthegmata Patrum*." *Studia Patristica* 20 (1989): 231–37.

Gregory, Timothy. "The Survival of Paganism in Christian Greece: A Critical Essay." *The American Journal of Philology* 107.2 (1986): 229–42.

Guillaumont, Antoine. "Le dépaysement comme forme d'ascèse, dans le monachisme ancien." *École pratique des hautes études*. Section des sciences religieuses. Annuaire 1968–1969. 76 (1967): 31–58. doi: 10.3406/ephe.1967.16468

Hands, Arthur R. *Charities and Social Aid in Greece and Rome*. London: Thames & Hudson, 1968.

Harnack, Adolf. *The Mission and Expansion of Christianity in the First Three Centuries*. Edited and translated by James Moffatt. 2nd rev. and enl. ed. New York: G. P. Putnam's Sons, 1908.

Harper, Kyle. *Slavery in the Late Roman World, AD 275–425*. Cambridge: Cambridge University Press, 2011.

Harvey, Susan Ashbrook. "Physicians and Ascetics in John of Ephesus: An Expedient Alliance." *Dumbarton Oaks Paper* 38 (1984): 87–93.

Hatlie, Peter. *The Monks and Monasteries of Constantinople, ca. 350–850*. Cambridge: Cambridge University Press, 2007.

Hevelone-Harper, Jennifer. "Disciples of the Desert: Monks, Laity, and Spiritual Authority in Sixth-Century Gaza." PhD diss., Princeton University, 2000.

———. *Disciples of the Desert: Monks, Laity and Spiritual Authority in Sixth-Century Gaza*. Baltimore: John Hopkins University Press, 2005.

———. "The Letter Collection of Barsanuphius and John." Pages 418–32 in *Late Antique Letter Collection: A Critical Introduction and Reference Guide*. Edited by Christiana Sogno, Dradley Storin and Edward Watts. California: University of California Press, 2017.

Hezser, Catherine. *Jewish Slavery in Antiquity*. Oxford: Oxford University Press, 2009.

Hirschfeld, Yizhar. "The Monasticism of Gaza: An Archaeological Review." Pages 61–88 in *Christian Gaza in Late Antiquity*. Edited by Brouria Bitton-Ashkelony and Aryeh Kofsky. Leiden: Brill, 2004.

———. *The Judean Desert Monasteries in the Byzantine Period*. New Haven: Yale University Press, 1992.

Holman, Susan. *The Hungry Are Dying*. Oxford: Oxford University Press, 2001.

Hombergen, Daniël. "Barsanuphius and John of Gaza and the Origenist Controversy." Pages 173–82 in *Christian Gaza in Late Antiquity*. Edited by Bitton-Ashkelony and A. Kofsky. Leiden: Brill, 2004.

Horden, Peregrine. "Christian Hospitality in Late Antiquity: Break or Bridge?" Pages 77–100 in *Gesundheit – Krankheit Kulturtransfer medizinischen Wissens von der Spätantike bis in die Frühe Neuzeit*. Edited by Florian Steger and Kay Peter Jankrift. Weimar & Vienna: Böhlau, 2004.

Horn, Cornelia. *Asceticism and Christological Controversy in Fifth-Century Palestine: The Career of Peter the Iberian*. Oxford: Oxford University Press, 2006.

Hunt, Edward. *Holy Land Pilgrimage in the Later Roman Empire AD 312–460*. Oxford: Clarendon Press, 1982.

Jefferson, Lee. *Christ the Miracle Worker in Early Christian Art*. Minneapolis: Fortress Press, 2014.

Jones, A. H. M. *The Later Roman Empire 284–602*. 2 vols. Baltimore: Johns Hopkins University Press, 1986.

———. *The Decline of the Ancient World*. New York: Routledge, 2014.

Joshel, Sandra. *Slavery in the Roman World*. Cambridge: Cambridge University Press, 2010.

Kasher, Aryeh. "Gaza During the Graeco-Roman Era." *The Jerusalem Cathedra* 2 (1982): 63–78.

Kingsley, Sean A. "The Economic Impact of the Palestinian Wine Trade in Late Antiquity." Pages 44–68 in *Economy and Exchange in the East Mediterranean during Late Antiquity*. Edited by Sean A. Kingsley and Michael Decker. Oxford: Oxbow Books, 2001.

Klauck, Hans-Josef. *Ancient Letters and the New Testament: A Guide to Context and Exegesis*. Waco: Baylor University Press, 2006.

Klijn, Albertus F. J. *The Acts of Thomas: Introduction, Text, and Commentary*. Leiden: Brill, 1962.

Kofsky, Aryeh. "Observation on Christian-Jewish Coexistence in Late Antiquity Palestine (Fifth to Seventh Centuries)." *Annali di storia dell' esegesi* 23.2 (2006): 433–46.

———. "Peter the Iberian: Pilgrimage, Monasticism and Ecclesiastical Politics in Byzantine Palestine." *Liber Annuus* 47 (1997): 209–22.

Krueger, Derek. "Christian Piety and Practice in the Sixth Century." Pages 291–315 in *The Cambridge Companion to the Age of Justinian*. Edited by Michael Maas. Cambridge: Cambridge University Press, 2005. doi:10.1017/CCOL0521817463.012.

———, ed. *Byzantine Christianity*. Minneapolis: Fortress Press, 2010.

Laiou, Angeliki, and Cécile Morrisson. *The Byzantine Economy*. Cambridge: Cambridge University Press, 2007.

Lamoreaux, John. "Episcopal Courts in Late Antiquity." *Journal of Early Christian Studies* 3.2 (1995): 143–67.

Lampe, Geoffrey W. H. *A Patristic Greek Lexicon*. Oxford: Clarendon Press, 1961.

Langmui, Gavin I. *Toward a Definition of Anti-Semitism*. Berkeley: University of California Press, 1990.

Laniado, Avshalom. "The Early Byzantine State and the Christian Ideal of Voluntary Poverty." Pages 15–43 in *Charity and Giving in Monotheistic Religion*. Edited by Miriam Frenkel and Yaacov Lev. Berlin: Walter de Gruyter, 2009.

Lavan, Luke. "Religious Space in Late Antiquity." Pages 159–202 in *Objects in Context, Objects in Use: Material Spatiality in Late Antiquity*. Edited by Luke Lavan, Ellen Swift and Toon Putzeys. Leiden: Brill, 2008.

Lee, A. D. *Pagans and Christians in Late Antiquity: A Sourcebook*. London: Routledge, 2000.

Leibowitz, Joshua, ed. *Proceedings of the third International Symposium on Medicine in Bible and Talmud*. Jerusalem: The Division of the History of Medicine, the Hebrew University-Hadassah Medical School, 1988.

Liebeschuetz, J. H. W. G. *Decline and Fall of the Roman City*. Oxford: Oxford University Press, 2001.

Litsas, Fotios. "Choricius of Gaza: An Approach to His work." PhD diss., University of Chicago, 1980.

Loewenberg, Frank M. "On the Development of Philanthropic Institutions in Ancient Judaism: Provisions for Poor Travelers." *Nonprofit and Volunteer Sector Quarterly* 23:3 (1994): 193–207.

López, Ariel G. *Shenoute of Atripe and the Uses of Poverty: Rural Patronage, Religious Conflict, and Monasticism in Late Antique Egypt*. Berkeley: University of California Press, 2013.

Lucien, Regnault. *La vie quotidienne des Pères du désert en Egypte au IVe siècle*. Paris: Hachette, 1990.

Luiselli, Raffaele. "Greek Letters on Papyrus: First to Eighth Centuries: A Survey." Pages 677-737 in *Documentary Letters from the Middle East: The Evidence in Greek, Coptic, South Arabian, Pehlevi, and Arabic (1st–15th c CE)*. Edited by Andreas Kaplony and Eva Mira Grob. Bern: Peter Lang, 2008.

MacGinnis, John. *State Correspondence in the Ancient World: From New Kingdom Egypt to the Roman Empire*. Edited by Karen Radner. Oxford: Oxford University Press, 2014.

MacMullen, Ramsay. "Late Roman Slavery." *Historia* 36 (1987): 359–82.

_____. *Christianity and Paganism in the Fourth to Eighth Centuries*. New Haven: Yale University Press, 1997.

Malherbe, Abraham. *Ancient Epistolary Theorists*. Atlanta: Scholars Press, 1988.

Marinides, Nicholas. "Lay Piety in Byzantium, ca. 600–730." PhD diss., Princeton University, 2014.

Marrou, Henry I. *A History of Education in Antiquity*. Translated by George Lamb. London: Sheed and Ward, 1956.

Mathieson, Erica. *Christian Women in the Greek Papyri of Egypt to 400 CE*. Turnhout: Brepols, 2014.

Maxwell, Jaclyn. "Lay Piety in the Sermons of John Chrysostom." Pages 19–38 in *Byzantine Christianity*. Edited by Derek Krueger. Minneapolis: Fortress Press, 2010.

_____. *Christianisation and Communication in Late Antiquity: John Chrysostom and His Congregation in Antioch*. Cambridge: Cambridge University Press, 2006.

Mayer, Wendy. "Medicine in Transition: Christian Adaption in the Late Fourth-Century East." Pages 11–26 in *Shifting Genres in Late Antiquity*. Edited by G. Greatrex, H. Elton and L. McMahon. Farnham: Ashgate, 2015.

———. "Welcoming the Stranger in the Mediterranean East: Syrian and Constantinople." *Journal of Australian Early Medieval Association* 5 (2009): 89–106.

Mayerson, Philip. "The Wine and Vineyards of Gaza in the Byzantine Period." *Bulletin of the American Schools of Oriental Research* 257 (1985): 75–80.

McNary-Zak, Bernadette. *Letters and Asceticism in Fourth-Century Egypt*. Lanham, MD & Oxford: University Press of America, 2000.

Meeks, Wayne. *The Origins of Christian Morality: The First Two Centuries*. New Haven: Yale University Press, 1993.

Mezynski, David. "The Effects of the Origenist Controversy on the Pastoral Theology of Barsanuphius and John." PhD diss., Fordham University, 2012.

Millar, Fergus. *The Emperor in the Roman World: 31 BC–AD 337*. London: Duckworth, 1977.

Miller, Timothy. *The Birth of the Hospital in the Byzantine Empire*. Baltimore: John Hopkins University Press, 1997.

Morello, Ruth and A. D. Morrison, eds. *Ancient Letters: Classical and Late Antique Epistolography*. Oxford: Oxford University Press, 2007.

Morrisson, Cécile, and Jean-Pierre Sodini. "The Sixth-Century Economy." Pages 171–220 in vol.1 of *The Economic History of Byzantium: From the Seventh through the Fifteenth Century*. Edited by Angeliki Laiou. Washington, DC: Dumbarton Oaks Research Library and Collection, 2002.

Nam, Sung-Hyun. "The Poor Euergetes in the Hagiographic Literature." *Journal for the Promotion of Classical Studies* 25 (2009): 301–37 [Korean].

Neil, Bronwen. "Models of Gift Giving in the Preaching of Leo the Great." *Journal of Early Christian Studies* 18.2 (2010): 225–59.

Newsom, Carol. "Spying Out the Land: A Report from Genealogy." Pages 19–30 in *Bakhtin and Genre Theory in Biblical Studies*. Edited by Roland Boer. Atlanta: Society Biblical Literature, 2007.

Niederwimmer, Kurt. "An Examination of the Development of Itinerant Radicalism in the Environment and Tradition of the Didache." Pages 321–39 in *The Didache in Modern Research*. Edited by Jonathan A. Draper. Leiden: Brill, 1996.

———. *The Didache: A Commentary on the Didache*. Edited by Harold W. Attridge. Translated by Linda M. Maloney. 2nd ed. Minneapolis: Fortress Press, 1998.

Nobbs, Alanna. "Formulas of Belief in Greek Papyrus Letters of the Third and Fourth Centuries." Pages 233–37 in vol. 1 of *Ancient History in a Modern University: Early Christianity, Late Antiquity, and Beyond*. Edited by Tom Hillard, R. A. Kearsley, C. E. V. Nixon and A. M. Nobbs. Grand Rapids: William B. Eerdmans, 1988.

Nutton, Vivian. "From Galen to Alexander, Aspects of Medicine and Medical Practice in Late Antiquity." *Dumbarton Oaks Papers* 38 (1984): 1–14.

———. "The Rise of Medicine." Pages 46–70 in *The Cambridge of History of Medicine*. Edited by Roy Porter. Cambridge: Cambridge University Press, 2006.

O'Brien, Mary. *Title of Address in Christian Latin Epistolography to 543 A.D.* Washington, DC: Catholic University of America, 1930.

Oden, Amy, ed. *And You Welcomed Me*. Nashville: Abingdon Press, 2001.

Panteleakos, Georgios, Effie Poulakou-Rebelakou, and Michael Koutsilieris. "Anatomy and Physiology in the Work of Nemesius of Emesa 'On the Nature of Man.'" *Acta Medico-Historica Adriatica* 11.2 (2013): 319–28.

Parrinello, Rosa Maria. "The Justinianean Legislation regarding Wives of the Monks and Its Context: The Letters of Barsanuphius and John of Gaza." Pages 193–204 in *Männlich und weiblich schuf Er sie: Studien zur Genderkonstruktion und zum Eherecht in den Mittelmeerreligionen*. Edited by Christian Bourdignon, Matthias Morgenstern and Christiane Tietz. Göttingen: Vandenhoeck & Ruprecht, 2011.

Patlagean, Evelyn. "The Poor." Pages 15–42 in *The Byzantines*. Edited by Guglielmo Cavallo. Translated by Thomas Dunlap, Teresa Lavender Fagan and Charles Lambert. Chicago: University of Chicago Press, 1997.

Patrich, Joseph. *Sabas, Leader of Palestinian Monasticism: A Comparative Study in Eastern Monasticism, Fourth to Seventh*. Washington, DC: Dumbarton Oaks Research Library and Collection Centuries, 1995.

Patterson, Stephen. "The Legacy of Radical Itinerancy in Early Christianity." Pages 313–29 in *The Didache in Context: Essay on Its Text, History and Transmission*. Edited by Clayton Jefford. Leiden: Brill, 1995.

Perrone, Lorenzo. "'Trembling at the Thought of Shipwreck': The Anxious Self in the Letters of Barsanuphius and John of Gaza." Pages 9–36 in *Between Personal and Institutional Religion: Self, Doctrine, and Practice in Late Antique Eastern Christianity*. Edited by Brouria Bitton-Ashkelony and Lorenzo Perrone. Turnhout: Brepols, 2013. doi:10.1484/M.CELAMA-EB.1.100739.

———. "Palestinian Monasticism, the Bible, and Theology in the Wake of the Second Origenist Controversy." Pages 245–59 in *The Sabaite Heritage in the Orthodox Church from the Fifth Century to the Present*. Edited by Joseph Patrich. Leuven: Peeters, 2002.

———. "Scripture for a Life of Perfection. The Bible in Late Antique Monasticism: The Case of Palestine." Pages 393–418 in *The Reception and Interpretation of the Bible in Late Antiquity*. Edited by Lorenzo DiTommaso and Lucian Turcescu. Leiden: Brill, 2008.

Piganiol, André. *L'empire chrétien (325–395)*. 2nd ed. Paris: Presses universitaires de France, 1972.

Platte, Elizabeth L. "Monks and Matrons: The Economy of Charity in the Late Antique Mediterranean." PhD diss., University of Michigan, 2013.

Poster, Carol. "A Conversation Halved: Epistolary Theory in Graeco-Roman Antiquity." Pages 21–51 in *Letter-Writing Manuals and Instruction from Antiquity to the Present: Historical and Bibliographic Studies*. Edited by Linda Mitchell. Columbia: University of South Carolina Press, 2007.

Ramsey, Boniface. "Almsgiving in the Latin Church: The Late Fourth and Fifth Centuries." *Theological Studies* 43.2 (1982), 226–59.

Rapp, Claudia. "'For next to God, you are my salvation': Reflection on the Rise of the Holy Men in Late Antiquity." Pages 63–81 in *The Cult of Saints in Late Antiquity and the Middle Ages*. Edited by James Howard-Johnston and Paul Antony Hayward. Oxford: Oxford University Press, 1999.

———. *Holy Bishops in Late Antiquity*. Berkeley: University of California Press, 2005.

Rebillard, Éric. "The Church, the Living, and the Dead." Pages 220–30 in *A Companion to Late Antiquity*. Edited by Philip Rousseau. Malden, MA: Wiley-Blackwell, 2009.

———. *Care of the Dead in Late Antiquity*. Ithaca: Cornell University Press, 2009.

René, Elter, and Hassoune Ayman. "Le monastère de Saint-Hilarion à Umm-el-'Amr." *Comptes rendus des séances de l'Académie des Inscriptions et Belles-Lettres* 148.1 (2004): 359–82.

Rhee, Helen. *Loving the Poor, Saving the Rich*. Grand Rapids: Baker Academic, 2012.

Rich, Antony. *Discernment in the Desert Fathers: Diakrisis in the Life and Thought of Early Egyptian Monasticism*. Eugene, OR: Wipf & Stock, 2007.

Richards, Ernest Randolph. *The Secretary in the Letters of Paul*, WUNT 2.42. Tübingen: Mohr Siebeck, 1991.

———. *Paul and First-Century Letter Writing: Secretaries, Composition and Collection*. Downer Grove, IL: InterVarsity Press, 2004.

Richter, Tonio Sebastian. "Coptic Letters." Pages 739-70 in *Documentary Letters from the Middle East: The Evidence in Greek, Coptic, South Arabian, Pehlevi, and Arabic (1st - 15th c CE)*. Edited by Andreas Kaplony and Eva Mira Grob. Bern: Peter Lang, 2008.

Romeny, Bas Ter Haar. "Procopius of Gaza and His Library." Pages 173–90 in *From Rome to Constantinople: Studies in Honour of Averil Cameron*. Edited by Hagit Amirav and Bas Ter Haar Romeny. Leuven: Peeters, 2007.

Rosenmeyer, Patricia. *Ancient Epistolary Fictions: The Letter in Greek Literature*. Cambridge: Cambridge University Press, 2001.

_____. *Ancient Greek Literary Letters: Selections in Translation*. London: Routledge, 2006.

Rousseau, Philip. *Pachomius: The Making of a Community in Fourth-Century Egypt*. Berkeley: University of California Press, 1985.

Rubenson, Samuel. "The Egyptian Relation of Early Palestine Monastic." Pages 35–46 in *The Christian Heritage in the Holy Land*, Edited by Anthony O'Mahony, Goran Gunner and Kevork Hintlian. London: Scorpion Cavendish, 1995.

_____. "Asceticism and Monasticism, I: Eastern." Pages 637–68 in *The Cambridge History of Christianity*, II: *Constantine to c. 600*. Edited by Augustine Casiday and Frederick W. Norris. Cambridge: Cambridge University Press, 2007.

_____. *The Letters of St. Antony: Monasticism and the Making of Saint*. Minneapolis: Fortress Press, 1995.

Rutgers, Leonard Victor. "Archaeological Evidence for the Interaction of Jews and Non-Jews in Late Antiquity." *American Journal of Archaeology* 96.1 (1992): 101–18.

Schenkewitz, Kyle. *Dorotheos of Gaza and the Discourse of Healing in Gazan Monasticism*. New York: Peter Lang, 2016.

Sedley, David. "The School, from Zeno to Arius Didymus." Pages 7–32 in *The Cambridge Companion to the Stoics*. Edited by Brad Inwood. Cambridge: Cambridge University Press, 2003. doi:10.1017/CCOL052177005X.002

Sheldon-William, I. P. "The Reaction against Proclus." Pages 473–91 in *Cambridge History of Later Greek and Early Medieval Philosophy*. Edited by Arthur H. Armstrong. Cambridge: Cambridge University Press. doi:10.1017/CHOL9780521040549.032.

Sinkewicz, Robert. *Evagrius of Pontus: The Greek Ascetic Corpus*. Oxford: Oxford University Press, 2006.

Smith, Payne. *A Compendious Syriac Dictionary*. Oxford: Clarendon Press, 1903.

Stander, Hennie. "Chrysostom on Letters and Letter-Writing." Pages 49–62 in *Patrologia Pacifica: Selected Papers Presented to the Asia Pacific Early Christian Studies Society*. Edited by Vladimir Baranov, Kazuhiko Demura and Basil Lourié. Piscataway, NJ: Gorgias Press, 2010.

Stark, Rodney, *The Rise of Christianity*. New York: HarperCollins, 1997.

Stemberger, Gunter. *Juden und Christen im 'Heiligen Land'*. München: C. H. Beck Verlag, 1987.

Steppa, Jan-Eric. *John Rufus and the World Vision of Anti-Chalcedonian Culture.* 2nd ed. Piscataway, NJ: Gorgias Press, 2005.
Sterk, Andreas. *Renouncing the World Yet Leading the Church: The Monk-Bishops in Late Antiquity.* Cambridge, MA: Harvard University Press, 2004.
Stowers, Stanley Kent. *Letter Writing in Graeco-Roman Antiquity.* Philadelphia: Westminster Press. 1986.
Suh, Wonmo "A Study of 'Poverty Discourses' in Sixth-Century Gaza." *Korea Journal of Christian Studies* 82 (2012): 203–30 [Korean].
Talbot, Alice-Mary. "The Devotional Life of Laywomen." Pages 201–20 in *Byzantine Christianity.* Edited by Derek Krueger. Minneapolis: Fortress Press, 2010.
———. "A Monastic World." Pages 257–78 in *A Social History of Byzantium.* Edited by John Haldon. Malden: Wiley-Blackwell, 2008.
Temkin, Owsei. *Hippocrates in a World of Pagans and Christians.* Baltimore: John Hopkins University Press, 1991.
Toda, Satoshi. "Pachomian Monasticism and Poverty." Pages 191–200 in *Prayer and Spirituality in the Early Church Volume 5: Poverty and Riches.* Edited by Geoffrey Dunn, David Luckensmeyer and Lawrence Cross. Strathfield: St Paul's Publications, 2009.
Torrance, Alexis. "Barsanuphius, John, and Dorotheos on Scripture: Voice from the Desert in Sixth-Century Gaza." Pages 67–82 in *What Is the Bible? The Patristic Doctrine of Scripture.* Edited by Matthew Baker and Mark Mourachian. Minneapolis: Fortress Press, 2016.
———. "Standing in the Breach: The Significance and Function of the Saint in the Letters of Barsanuphius and John of Gaza." *Journal of Early Christian Studies* 17.3 (2009): 459–73.
Trapp, Michael, ed. *Greek and Latin Letters: An Anthology with Translation.* Cambridge: Cambridge University Press, 2003.
Uhalde, Kevin. *Expectations of Justice in the Age of Augustine.* Philadelphia: University of Pennsylvania Press, 2007.
Veyne, Paul. *Bread and Circuses: Historical Sociology and Political Pluralism.* Translated by Brain Pearce. London: Allen Lane, 1990.
Vööbus, Arthur. *History of Asceticism in the Syrian Orient* II. Corpus Scriptorum Christianorum Orientalium 197. Louvain: Peeters, 1960.
———. *History of Asceticism in the Syrian Orient* III. Corpus Scriptorum Christianorum Orientalium 500. Louvain: Peeters, 1998.
Wells, Charles Bradford. *Royal Correspondence in the Hellenistic Period: A Study in Greek Epigraphy.* 1934. Repr., Roma: L'Erma di Bretschneider, 1966.
Westermann, William. *The Slave Systems of Greek and Roman Antiquity.* Philadelphia: The American Philosophical Society, 1955.
Wilkinson, John, ed. *Jerusalem Pilgrims Before the Crusades.* 2nd ed. Warminster, England: Aris & Phillips, 2002.

Wittgenstein, Ludwig. *Philosophical Investigations*. Translated by G. E. M. Anscombe, P. M. S. Hacker and Joachim Schulte. 4th ed. Oxford: Willey Blackwell, 2009.

Yegül, Fikret. *Baths and Bathing in Classical Antiquity*. Cambridge, MA: MIT Press, 1995.

Zecher, Jonathan. *The Role of Death in the Ladder of Divine Ascent and the Greek Ascetic Tradition*. Oxford: Oxford University Press, 2015.

Zuiderhoek, Arjan. *The Politics of Munificence in the Roman Empire*. Cambridge: Cambridge University Press, 2009.

www.ingramcontent.com/pod-product-compliance
Lightning Source LLC
Chambersburg PA
CBHW071728080526
44588CB00013B/1944